Early praise for *iOS 8 SDK Development*

Not many books cover both programming interfaces and deeper software engineering topics. It's refreshing to see both covered, expertly, in one book. Chris and Janie are masters at making technical content approachable. It's like having two of your best friends teaching you iOS.

➤ **Mark Dalrymple**
    Author of *Advanced Mac OS X Programming: The Big Nerd Ranch Guide* and co-founder of CocoaHeads, the international Mac and iOS programming community

iOS 8 SDK Development is a fantastic resource for learning how to make a modern iOS app. Whether you're new to iOS in general or just new to Swift, you will leave the book with a fully functional, modern iOS app with all of the most important features covered. This book is my new go-to recommendation for those looking to get started on the platform.

➤ **Jeff Kelley**
    iOS developer at Detroit Labs and author of *Learn Cocoa Touch for iOS*

This is a really good book. The app you will create while you learn Swift and iOS development is even quite usable when you are done. Learning Swift is essential now in the Apple development world, and this book does a great job teaching it. The authors have put a lot of thought and craft into it, and you will benefit. I highly recommend it.

➤ **Eric Knapp**
    Program Director, Mobile Applications Development, Madison College

Whether you're new to iOS programming or just need some help getting up to speed on iOS 8 and Swift, this is the perfect book for you. Chris and Janie take you on a well-thought-out and fun journey into iOS SDK development.

➤ **Dave Klein**
Founder of CocoaConf and author of *Grails: A Quick-Start Guide*

iOS 8 SDK Development is an excellent book for experienced developers hoping to develop iOS applications professionally. It is a guided tour of the Swift language, an extended SDK tutorial using a variety of modern iOS APIs, and a showcase of effective techniques for organizing and editing projects in the latest version of Xcode.

➤ **Steven Huwig**

A new programming language and new APIs. Whether you are a seasoned developer or a beginner, there's a lot to learn in the new iOS 8 SDK. Chris and Janie take your hand and walk you through Swift and the new APIs, providing great insights and detailed explanations while building a real application.

➤ **Cesare Rocchi**
Studio Magnolia

iOS 8 SDK Development

Creating iPhone and iPad Apps with Swift

Chris Adamson

Janie Clayton

The Pragmatic Bookshelf

Dallas, Texas • Raleigh, North Carolina

Many of the designations used by manufacturers and sellers to distinguish their products are claimed as trademarks. Where those designations appear in this book, and The Pragmatic Programmers, LLC was aware of a trademark claim, the designations have been printed in initial capital letters or in all capitals. The Pragmatic Starter Kit, The Pragmatic Programmer, Pragmatic Programming, Pragmatic Bookshelf, PragProg and the linking *g* device are trademarks of The Pragmatic Programmers, LLC.

Every precaution was taken in the preparation of this book. However, the publisher assumes no responsibility for errors or omissions, or for damages that may result from the use of information (including program listings) contained herein.

Our Pragmatic courses, workshops, and other products can help you and your team create better software and have more fun. For more information, as well as the latest Pragmatic titles, please visit us at *https://pragprog.com*.

The team that produced this book includes:

Rebecca Gulick (editor)
Potomac Indexing, LLC (indexer)
Liz Welch (copyeditor)
Dave Thomas (typesetter)
Janet Furlow (producer)
Ellie Callahan (support)

For international rights, please contact *rights@pragprog.com*.

Printed in the United States of America.
ISBN-13: 978-1-941222-64-5
Printed on acid-free paper.
Book version: P1.0—March 2015

Contents

Acknowledgments

We've said in the past that keeping up with the breakneck pace of iOS technology developments is a challenge, but Apple really outdid itself this year by giving us a whole new programming language to work with. What was once going to be a touch-up of an old edition became a full-on rewrite of the whole thing. And we wouldn't have gotten it done without a lot of help.

At Pragmatic Programmers, Susannah Pfalzer reached out to get a new introductory iOS book back on track, once it was clear the old title had gotten too dusty. Our editor, Rebecca Gulick, made time to meet with us across three time zones, and consistently had good feedback to keep us on track and deliver the best book possible for our readers. The Prags' book-writing system continues to be a great way to build a technical book, based as it is on Agile principles, source code management, and *no Microsoft Word*, so thanks to Dave and Andy for keeping the show rolling. We're also just vain enough to always get a kick out of seeing our names attached to upcoming speaking appearances in the Prags' weekly newsletter.

Speaking of conferences, this pairing of authors wouldn't have happened without CocoaConf, so thanks to the Klein family for taking that show on the road to cities near and far. Speakers and attendees at that conference have been generous with their time and insights to us, and we always come away from it with more to think and write about. Well, except maybe for CocoaConf Boston 2014, where we basically had to hole up in a room for the weekend and bang out the Photos chapter and fix all the Xcode 6.1 breakage.

We're very grateful to all the people who've submitted errata on the early betas—hundreds so far, and more surely to come—as well as participants on the book's forum, who sometimes help each other before we have time to get a word in edgewise. We're also grateful to our tech reviewers, who took the time to read the whole thing and help us make it better: Jeff Holland, Steven Huwig, Jeff Kelley, Eric Knapp, Cesare Rocchi, and Kim Shrier.

From Chris Adamson

It wasn't easy losing a coauthor on this title, as evidenced by the fact that I tried to go it alone without Bill Dudney after he returned to Apple, and I wasn't able to get it done for iOS 7. So, thanks to Bill for the two books that we were able to do together. I also consider myself lucky that Rebecca Gulick and Susannah Pfalzer planted the idea in my head to seek out a coauthor, as that led me to working with Janie.

It's been really fun working with someone who sees the material without a lot of legacy bias, who sees the ideas of Cocoa and Swift for what they are, and how to make them easy and *fun* to grasp. I find that I've been trying to adapt my writing style to be more like Janie's as we've worked on this book: more analogies and big picture, less grind-it-out. So, thanks, Janie, for helping me be a better author and refine my voice even after five books.

We had some crunch times, and I appreciate my family giving me a little latitude to get things done when I needed to. I keep thinking the next one will go more smoothly, but they never do. At some point, maybe I'll get used to it.

Obligatory end-of-book music check: This time it was Kate Nash, Kalafina, M83, King Crimson, the "Kagerou Project" song cycle, and various of the Key/Visual Art's anime and visual novel soundtracks that were released on iTunes in 2014. Current stats at http://www.last.fm/user/invalidname.

From Janie Clayton

I know that both Chris and I earlier thanked Eric Knapp for tech reviewing the book, but I want to give a more comprehensive shout-out to my first programming teacher. When I was starting out in school for programming Eric was my first teacher, and he was the only one I had who really cared about whether or not I understood the material. His patience in explaining the fundamentals as many times as I needed and never making me feel stupid really helped me get over the initial hump in learning programming. He is also responsible for getting me to my first CocoaConf and connecting me to a lot of the people who made a difference in my life. Thanks a lot, man; keep doing what you do!

I would like to thank my boss and mentor, Brad Larson. When he brought me on board I thought the book would be done in a month, tops. Three months and one last-minute impromptu trip to Boston later, the book is finally finished. I want to thank him for his patience with this project and for his generosity with his time to help me be a better programmer. I also want to thank him for his belief in me that I can do things I didn't think were possible, which pushes me to do more than I thought I could.

I would like to thank my high school physics teacher, Kevin Mirus. "Doc" Mirus is among the smartest people I have ever met, but he could explain some of the most complicated scientific concepts very simply and clearly. Learning from him taught me that if you understand something really well you can explain it to anyone. This lesson has stayed with me my entire adult life. I am sorry I didn't go to college for plasma physics, but I eventually got a job working with robots, so I didn't completely let you down.

In the spirit of self-congratulatory acknowledgments, I would like to thank my coauthor, Chris Adamson. I always wanted to write a book, and being able to work with someone who has already been to the rodeo before was a tremendous gift. I think if I had had to write the book by myself it would never have gotten done. I have no idea how you are able to do all the things you do. Doing half of what you do has burned me out. I want to thank you for bringing me on to this project and giving me a chance to fulfill a dream.

Lastly, I would like to thank my husband, Ehren Hasz. When I would get burned out and start wandering around the house, rambling incoherently, he would gently pry my laptop out of my hands, send me to take a bath, and bring me wine. I know that the time working on the book was hard, and I appreciate him taking care of me.

Introduction

Sometimes it starts with an idea: *"I'm going to write an app to organize my music," "I'm going to write a kick-ass game," "I'm going to start a website, and I'd better have a native app too."* Other times, it's more of an inkling: *"I bet I could figure out iOS apps," "I wonder how different that is," "If I have to write another freaking login web page, I'm going to scream."* And sometimes, like Everest, it's worth conquering just because it's there.

Whatever your reason for wanting to learn iOS development, it's a good one. The platform is well established as the leader of the smartphone and tablet revolution, and its thoughtful and comprehensive tools and frameworks empower us to make great applications for iPhone, iPad, and iPod touch users.

It's also an exciting time to get into iOS development, or even to come back if you dipped a toe in the water a while back but didn't take the plunge. With Apple's announcements at WWDC 2014, development for the platform just got a *lot* more interesting, thanks to a much greater level of interaction between apps, between iOS and other devices, and even between developers thanks to new testing and collaboration tools. To top it off, Apple introduced an entirely new programming language, Swift, which it intends as a safer, simpler, and faster alternative to Objective-C, which has served iOS and Mac OS X well throughout their entire lifetimes.

About This Edition

This is our third time around with an introductory iOS book for Pragmatic Programmers. *iPhone SDK Development* came out in 2009 and covered iPhone OS 3, then was replaced by a 100% rewrite, *iOS SDK Development* in 2012, covering iOS 6. The book you're reading started out as an update to that, but with all the changes in iOS 7 and 8 (including a change of programming language), it is overwhelmingly new material. If you do catch a bogus copy-and-paste from old material—a reference to an .h or .m file would be a dead give-away—we hope you'll let us know on the errata page.

In preparing this edition, we looked for a balance of topics appropriate to our intended audience: developers already comfortable with object-oriented programming, who are new to the iOS platform. We always look for a mix of the new and the fundamental, the shiny and the solid. We're also interested in spending time on things we've learned from our own experience, both good and bad. You'll see we spend a lot of time on "soft" topics like refactoring, debugging, project organization, and testing, and less time on just touring our favorite frameworks (sorry, AV Foundation). We think it's important to think of iOS development not just as a grab-bag of APIs, but as a process for turning time and enthusiasm into apps that work well, that can be maintained, and that delight and enlighten.

New hotness sometimes means clearing out the old and busted. In the previous edition, we bet pretty heavily on document-based apps and the ability to store them in iCloud. Two years later, we're not seeing much interest in document-driven apps on the App Store, and as for iCloud, as a certain Dark Lord of the Sith said, "you have failed me for the last time." In their place, we hope you'll enjoy some of the neat new features of iOS 8, including the ability to expose your app's functionality to other apps with extensions, and a variety of tools for making apps look good and work well on both iPhone and iPad. On this latter point, our previous edition's sample projects were iPhone-only, but this time, we are all-in on Universal apps that support the iPhone and iPad form-factors, as well as the extra screen space afforded by the iPhone 6 models.

You may also notice a major change on the cover from the previous edition. The aforementioned books were written by Chris Adamson and Bill Dudney, the second coming after Bill did a two-year stint at Apple as a developer evangelist. In 2013, Bill returned to Apple to work on UIKit, so he's unable to contribute to this title, because of corporate policy and because he's really busy bringing us the very software this book is all about. So for this edition, please welcome new coauthor Janie Clayton. Janie is an iOS developer and self-described "human vertex shader" from Madison, Wisconsin, who's previously served as a technical reviewer for other Pragmatic Programmer iOS titles, and is a speaker at iOS conferences like CocoaConf and 360iDev. She also has uncanny nerd compatibility with Chris, the first person at CocoaConf Chicago to correctly identify the etymology of her youngest pug's name.[1] The first in-person editorial meeting for this book took place at Anime Central in Chicago, probably marking the first time a Prags book has kicked off in cos-

---

1. Janie's dog is named "Delia Derbyshire," after the unjustly uncredited co-composer of the *Doctor Who* theme music.

play...although considering *Build iOS Games with Sprite Kit* authors Jonathan Penn and Josh Smith, we can't be 100% sure of that.

So Here's the Plan

Our goal for this book is to get readers fully grounded in the essentials of iOS development, comfortable with the tools, the techniques, and the conventions they'll use to make iOS apps whether by themselves or as part of a team. We don't try to cover everything in the iOS SDK in part because doing so made for a 600-page book in 2009, and would be well into the thousands today. Instead, this book should serve as a prerequisite to all the other topic-specific iOS books published by Pragmatic Programmers, as well as those from other publishers.

In this edition, we have chosen to develop a single sample app through the course of the entire book. The advantages of this approach include less time spent starting projects and wiring up user interfaces, and a greater sense of how to manage an app as it evolves and adds features. This gives us a more reality-based approach to app development than we could get with a series of trivial projects, and more naturally leads to the payoff in the last chapter of submitting an app to the App Store and managing its ongoing development life cycle.

Speaking of payoff, here's the course we're going to take through the book:

Expectations and Technical Requirements

The technical requirements for iOS development are pretty simple: the latest version of Xcode, and a Mac OS X computer that can run it. As of our publication in late 2014, that means Xcode 6.1.1, and a Mac running either OS X 10.9 ("Mavericks") or 10.10 ("Yosemite").

All code in this book uses the Swift programming language, which is new in Xcode 6, making this book one of the first to offer a thorough guide to using Swift with the iOS frameworks. Since there are no experts on Swift today other than the people who created it, we expect it will be as new to you as it was to us over the summer while we wrote the book (compounded by the fact that we had to reset when each beta of Xcode 6 changed the language). Fortunately, it's a neat language that cleans out a lot of cruft from C and Objective-C, and we think you'll be able to pick it up quickly, provided you're a proficient programmer in at least one object-oriented language. That can be one of the many curly-brace descendants of C (C++, C#, or Java), or an OO scripting language like Ruby or Python.

Online Resources

This book isn't just about static words on a page or screen. It comes with a web page, http://www.pragprog.com/titles/adios2, where you can learn more and access useful resources:

- Download the complete source code for all the code examples in the book as ready-to-build Xcode projects.

- Participate in a discussion forum with other readers, fellow developers, and the authors.

- Help improve the book by reporting errata, such as content suggestions and typos.

If you're reading the ebook, you can also access the source file for any code listing by clicking on the gray-green rectangle before the listing.

As we build our sample projects in this book, we will often write simple code, only to rewrite it with more ambitious code later as our knowledge increases.

All the different versions would be hard to put in one source file. So in the downloadable book code, we often have multiple copies of each project, each representing a different stage of its development. The different stages use numbered folders, like PragmaticTweets-1-1, PragmaticTweets-2-1, and so on, with the first number representing the chapter number and the second being a revision within that chapter. These folder names also appear in the captions for each code example in the text. You can either code along for the entire book from scratch, or copy over one of these "stages" and pick up from there.

And So It Begins

So, new platform, new programming language, new opportunities for new ideas and new apps. We can't wait to see what you come up with. Let's get started.

Swift is a moving target

The Swift programming language is in a period of rapid development and improvement, and that puts early adopters like us on the proverbial "bleeding edge." And we've done a little bleeding already: Changes to the language have broken the code in this book several times during its development, forcing us to issue quick updates.

We expect this is going to continue for a while: Swift language changes we've seen in the Xcode 6.3 betas will break the code we wrote for Xcode 6.1. It's not major—when you open our older code, Xcode's tooltips usually offer to make the needed change for you—but it's still something to watch for.

For the time being, we will "lock" each release of the book and its sample code to one version of Xcode. For example, this release works with Xcode 6.1: The code won't build in Xcode 6.0, nor do we expect it to build for 6.3. When the next version of Xcode comes out with code-breaking changes, we will update the book's contents and sample code for that version of Swift. If you bought this as an ebook from pragprog.com, come back to the book's home page at http://www.pragprog.com/titles/adios2 to generate an update, or set up your pragprog.com account to automatically send updates to your Dropbox. For store-bought paper copies, come to the home page for updated sample code and, if you like, a discount on adding the ebook version.

CHAPTER 1

Playing Around with Xcode

If we're going to create iOS apps, we need the right tools for the job. In this chapter, we're going to get properly equipped for the journey and play around a little with the tools that Apple provides us.

To develop iOS 8 apps, we use Xcode 6. Although "Xcode" generally refers to the *integrated development environment* (IDE), in which we develop code and user interfaces and run a build process to generate the actual apps, it can also mean the entire collection of material we'll need to build iOS applications. When we download Xcode, we get not only the Xcode app itself but also the software development kits (SDKs) for iOS and Mac OS X, which contain documentation, frameworks, helper applications, sample code, and more. These all live inside the Xcode application itself, so we don't have a bunch of fiddly little files to manage.

Xcode is available for free via the Mac App Store, so download it now if you haven't already done so. Xcode typically supports the current version of OS X and one back, so for Xcode 6, you'll need to be on Mac OS X 10.9.3 ("Mavericks") or newer (currently Mac OS X 10.10 "Yosemite"). The Mac App Store will put Xcode in the /Applications directory. It's a good idea to drag it from there to the Dock so you'll have a shortcut always handy.

Before we commit to building a full-blown app, let's play around with Xcode a little.

Xcode Playgrounds

When we first launch Xcode, it may need to do some one-time-only setup work, such as asking permission to install components like the Mobile Device framework. When Xcode finally comes up, we get a greeting window (like the one below) that shows a few quick-start buttons on the left, along with a list of most recent items we've opened on the right. We'll be starting a project here shortly, but to warm up, we're going to play in a *playground*. This is a new feature in Xcode 6 that lets us interact with Swift code, to try out ideas by just writing code and seeing the results immediately, without an entire build-and-deploy cycle.

The greeting window offers a button to "Get started with a playground." This will bring up a sheet asking if we want to create an iOS or OS X playground, as seen below. Give it a name (or accept the default MyPlayground), make sure the type is iOS, and click the Next button. In the file dialog that appears, choose a name and location for the .playground file that will be created; for this example, keep the default name MyPlayground.playground.

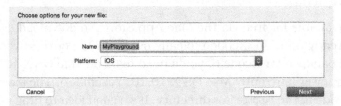

The playground opens as a window with two panes: some source code on the left, and a strip on the right that shows the result of evaluating each line of code. The initial code looks like this:

```
// Playground - noun: a place where people can play

import UIKit

var str = "Hello, playground"
```

This is our first look at Swift, and it looks a lot like other C-based programming languages like Java or C#. The first line is obviously a comment, and the second says we want to use classes from UIKit, the iOS user interface framework. The third line assigns the text "Hello, playground" to a variable called str. The "Hello, playground" in the right pane lines up with the variable assignment, because it represents the result of evaluating that line of code.

The way the playground works is that we can type code into the left pane and see any results in the right. So that's what we'll do now: we'll write some code and see what happens.

We're putting off our formal introduction to Swift and frameworks like UIKit until the next few chapters, so take our code on faith for the moment. We're going to start by asking UIKit to start creating some UI objects. On the next blank line, write the following code:

```
var myLabel = UILabel (frame: CGRectMake(0.0, 0.0, 200.0, 100.0))
myLabel.text = str
```

This creates a UILabel, a non-interactive view that shows some text. We have to give it a "frame" that represents an x,y origin point and a width-by-height size, which we do with the embedded CGRectMake() function. Then on the second line, we set the label's text to the str variable, which was set earlier to "Hello, playground".

So what? The evaluation pane just says UILabel. But mouse over that and notice that two small buttons appear: an "eye" and a circle. The eye icon only appears when the playground knows that the object it has evaluated has a graphic representation, so click that. The result is a popover like the one shown here:

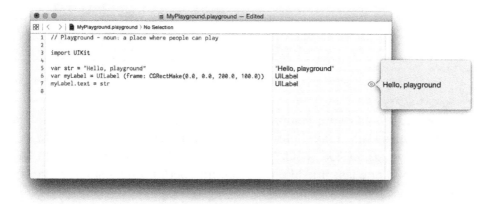

OK, fun, we can create UI components in the playground. We can customize it further. Add two more lines of code to set the background and foreground colors:

```
myLabel.backgroundColor = UIColor.redColor()
myLabel.textColor = UIColor.whiteColor()
```

Again, click the eye icon on the last line. This time a little label pops up, but it just says "(2 times)." That tells us that it has executed these two lines of code. But it doesn't give us a preview of the result, because evaluating these lines doesn't give a different result for myLabel. We haven't replaced myLabel; we've just changed what it looks like.

Fortunately, we can see our changes another way. Click the round button on each line to split the window in two, with a new right pane showing the clicked line of code and its result. This lets us walk through the history of our changes and compare them side by side, rather than in ephemeral popovers. Here's what that looks like if we click the buttons for each myLabel, from top to bottom:

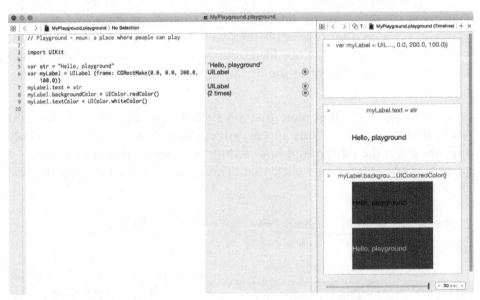

For a kicker, let's have our computer actually do some computing. Swift lets us build strings from smaller parts, and uses the sequence \(expression) to say "evaluate that *expression* inside the parentheses, and insert that into the string." So add one last line like the following, performing whatever mathematical expression suits you:

```
myLabel.text = "Math is easy: \(6454 + 24323)"
```

Click the eye icon next to the "(3 times)" result string, and we'll see all three subsequent versions of myLabel, concluding with the red-and-white version with the text Math is easy: 30777, or whatever the answer to our math problem ended up being.

Playgrounds are a fun way to test out ideas in code. When we find new classes in the documentation or online, we can always jump into a playground and throw a few lines of code at it to see how stuff works.

But playgrounds are limited, too. What we're doing looks nothing like a real app; it takes five lines of code just to create a label (with some manual coordinates to set the sizing), it doesn't have anything we can touch or interact with, and didn't we say there were special tools to build our GUIs without code? There's no icon, there's no screen…it seems like we're a long way from having a real app!

Our next step is going to be to figure out how to move past playing around in the playground, and start building real apps.

My First Computer (Chris)

Messing around in the Xcode Playground reminds me of how computers used to dump you into an interactive programming environment by default. My first computer was a Texas Instruments TI-99 4/A, bought by my father because the saleswoman at K-Mart was really persuasive, and maybe because it cost $400 when the Apple II's we had at school were over $1,000 (*Plus ça change, plus c'est la même chose*).

When you turned it on, the menu gave you two choices by default: TI BASIC, or whatever cartridge (if any) was in the slot. With no cartridge, all it could do was BASIC. Back in those days, messing around with some flavor of BASIC was what every home computer did. For a while, the idea was that anyone could program—and would actually want to—and pretty much any student in our school at least knew enough to do 10 PRINT "SARA IS GREAT" 20 GOTO 10.

In the TV documentary *Triumph of the Nerds*, Steve Jobs once recalled that for every one person who wanted to hack on hardware in that era, there were another thousand who wanted to hack on software. And beyond Jobs's observation, it seems that for every one person who wanted to hack on software, another thousand just wanted to run the stuff, without necessarily knowing how it works. Inevitably, computers got away from writing programs as being the primary user experience, and coding eventually became a specialist skill and no longer accessible to the layperson, despite the occasional programming renaissance like Hypercard.

Having a playground is like going back to those summer nights of the 1980s, with mosquitos banging off the window screen (attracted by the glow of the TV that served as a monitor), a Styx cassette playing on the tape player that was used to load and save programs, and a blinking cursor inviting me to write some code…just to see what happens.

Digging Into the Docs

Throughout the book, we're going to build out a single application, a Twitter client that gradually gains more and more features: sending tweets, getting the user's timeline, getting details about a tweet or a user, and so on. One reason this makes sense as a sample project is because the process of getting data from the Internet, presenting it to the user, handling user input, repeat...this is the heart and soul of many iOS apps, and reconciling web service APIs with the iOS frameworks is an essential skill for iOS developers to master.

The ability for apps to send tweets has been in iOS for a while—most of us have used apps that offer to tweet on our behalf—but how would we know how to use it in our app? This calls for some documentation.

Xcode's documentation viewer is available via the menu item Help → Documentation and API Reference, also accessible via the keyboard shortcut ⇧⌘0. However, when we try to browse the documentation, we may be challenged to sign in with an Apple ID. If you haven't joined the developer program at http://developer.apple.com/, the only way to see the docs is to download a local copy. This is a good thing for all of us to do anyway, so we'll have a local copy to refer to when we don't have Internet access. In Xcode's preferences, click the Downloads icon and then the Documentation tab. This pane, shown below, lists the available doc sets and versions of the iOS Simulator and whether they're installed or need to be downloaded. If the current version of iOS—8.1 as of this writing—doesn't say Installed, then just click the Install button to download it to your Mac.

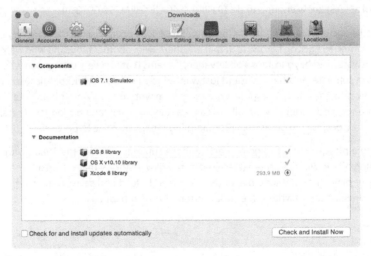

Let's go back to the documentation viewer, seen in the following figure. This window is organized around a search bar at the top, with a content pane below it. There are also optional Bookmarks and Table of Contents panes on the left side that can be shown and hidden with toolbar buttons, similar to the ones used for hiding and showing panes in the project workspace window. A magnifying glass icon on the search bar lets you choose whether to search iOS or OS X documentation (or both, or just let Xcode choose automatically). When we type a search term, the best results are shown as a pop-up list under the search bar, and we can choose one of these results, or just pick Show All Results to present all matches as clickable links in the content pane.

What are we looking for exactly? Since we want to send a tweet, we can enter twitter as the search term, and we'll find a whole Twitter Framework Reference. Tempting, but take it from us that that's old news—it was a Twitter-only framework for iOS 5 that has been supplanted by a new framework that works with multiple social networks. Keep looking and one of the results will be the constant SLServiceTypeTwitter. Select this result and the documentation will follow the link to the middle of a class called SLRequest, with SLServiceTypeTwitter defined as follows:

> A string constant that identifies the social networking site Twitter

Scroll to the top of this file to see the essential traits of this SLRequest class: what class it inherits from (NSObject), what versions of iOS provide it (iOS 6 and up), and what framework it's a part of. Search again for social framework, and select the result for Social Framework Reference. This document begins:

The Social framework lets you integrate your application with supported social networking services. The framework provides a template for creating HTTP requests and provides a generalized interface for posting requests on behalf of the user.

"Posting requests on behalf of the user"? Perfect, this sounds like just what we need. Scroll down to the class listing and discover that there are just four classes, including the SLRequest in which we found the SLServiceTypeTwitter constant and an SLComposeViewController. Click the link to the latter and take a look at its documentation, which begins like this:

The SLComposeViewController class presents a view to the user to compose a post for supported social networking services.

This looks particularly promising. We can use this SLComposeViewController to post to Twitter, and presumably our same code will work just as well for other social networking services.

It's highly tempting to figure out how to use this in our playground, but it turns out to be impractical to do so. The SLComposeViewController needs to be presented by another "view controller," and we don't have one of those in our playground or a reasonable way to get one. At this point, it's going to make more sense to start building our first project, which will be the task of the next chapter.

Wrap-Up

Now let's tally up what we've learned so far. We've downloaded and installed Xcode, and we've tried out its playground feature. In a playground, we can try out little bits of Swift code to see what they do, making them a good place for experimentation and discovery. We've also familiarized ourselves with looking up documentation on the iOS SDK, so we can find the classes and methods we'll need to build our apps.

We're now ready to start building our Twitter app, so let's move ahead and see how to create Xcode projects.

CHAPTER 2

Building Adaptive User Interfaces

We're going to kick things off with a little secret about iOS development, something it inherited from Mac development: *You're supposed to create the user interface first.* This is totally backward for a lot of seasoned developers. A lot of us think through an application's requirements and immediately start thinking of our data models and strategies and...*nuh-uh.* Build the UI first. Build what users are going to see, what they're going to interact with, and start to understand how they'll experience it. Then figure out how the heck you're going to do that.

That philosophy is reflected in the tools provided to us for iOS development. If we built the user interface by writing code, it would be natural to code the functionality and then put buttons and views on top of it. Instead, the iOS SDK provides distinct tools for building the user interface graphically and for coding its functionality. The tools let us see our interface first, and then make it work.

We're going to begin work on our Twitter app with a super-simple UI: a button that sends tweets. From there, we'll revise our appearance and the code behind it, to the point where our app will approach the functionality of the Twitter clients on the App Store today.

Our First Project

To begin work on a new app, we need to start a new project, which we can do with the menu sequence File→New→Project (⇧⌘N). There was also a button on the Xcode greeting window for starting a project, so that's another way to do it.

When we create a new project, a window opens and out slides a sheet that asks us what kind of project we want to create. This project template sheet, seen below, has a list on the left side of project categories divided into iOS and Mac OS X sections. Since we're building an iOS application, we'll select Application from the iOS section and then look at the choices in the main part of the frame. We can click each to see a general description of what kind of app to start on. For our first example, we'll select Single View Application.

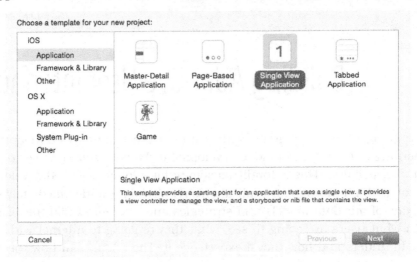

After we click Next, the sheet then asks us for details specific to the project, as shown in the following figure. Some of these change based on the project type; in general, this is where we need to provide names and other identifiers to the app, indicate which device formats (iPhone and/or iPad) it's for, and so on. For our first app, here's how we should fill out the form:

Choose options for your new project:

Product Name:	PragmaticTweets
Organization Name:	Pragmatic Programmers, LLC
Organization Identifier:	com.pragprog.yourhandle
Bundle Identifier:	com.pragprog.yourhandle.PragmaticTweets
Language:	Swift
Devices:	Universal
	☐ Use Core Data

Cancel   Previous   Next

- *Product Name*—A name for the product with no spaces or other punctuation. Our product will be called PragmaticTweets here.

- *Organization name*—This can be a company, organization, or personal name, which will be used for the copyright statement automatically put at the top of every source file.

- *Organization Identifier*—This is a reverse-DNS style stub that will uniquely identify our app in the App Store, so if someone else creates a PragmaticTweets the two apps won't be mistaken for each other because they'll each have a unique *Bundle Identifier*, which is the auto-generated fourth line of the form. If you have your own domain, you can use it for the company identifier; otherwise, just invert your email address, such as in com.company.yourhandle.

- *Language*—There are two choices for this pop-up menu: *Swift* and *Objective-C*. Swift is a new language introduced by Apple in 2014 for iOS and OS X development, which is meant to clean up some of the cruft that has accumulated around C and Objective-C over the decades. We'll have a lot more to say about Swift in the next chapter. For now, since we're starting a new project, with no need to support old code, we'll choose Swift here.

- *Devices*—This determines whether the template should set us up with an app that's meant to run on an iPhone (and iPod touch) or iPad or be a "universal" app with a different layout for each. Not all templates offer all three options. For iOS 8, Apple is pushing hard for developers to build Universal apps that run and look good on a variety of screen sizes, from iPhones to iPads and perhaps some new product sizes in between, so select Universal here.

After clicking Next, we choose a location on the filesystem for our project. There's also an option for creating a local Git source code repository for our files; we'll look at source control in *Protecting Our Code with Source Control*, on page 241, so we can leave it unchecked for now. Once we specify where the project will be saved, Xcode copies over some starter files for our project and reveals them in its main window.

The Xcode Window

Xcode 6 provides a single window for a project. This window provides our view into nearly everything we'll do with a project: editing code and user interfaces, adjusting settings for how the project is built and run, employing debugging tools, and viewing logged output.

The window is split into five areas, although some of them can be hidden with menu commands and/or toolbar buttons. These areas are shown in an "exploded" view in the following figure:

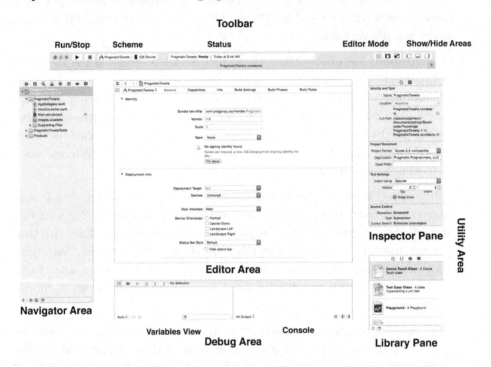

The window is split up as follows:

Toolbar

> The toolbar at the top of the window offers the most basic controls for building projects and working with the rest of the workspace. The leftmost buttons, Run and Stop, start and stop build-and-run cycles. Next are two borderless buttons collectively known as the scheme selector, which chooses which "target" to run (currently PragmaticTweets) and in what environment (a simulated "iPhone 6," or the name of an actual iOS device connected to the Mac). Next comes an iTunes-like status display that shows the most recent build and/or run results, including a count of warnings and errors generated by a continual background analysis of the code. Further right, the Editor Mode buttons let us switch between three different kinds of editors, which we'll describe shortly. Finally, three View buttons allow us to show or hide the Navigator, Debug, and Utility areas. These areas perform the following roles:

Navigator Area

The left pane (which may be hidden if the leftmost View button in the toolbar is unselected) offers high-level browsing of our project's contents. It has a mini-toolbar to switch between eight different navigators. The File Navigator (⌘1) shows the project's source and resource files and is therefore the most important and commonly used of the seven. Other navigators let us perform searches (⌘3), inspect build warnings and errors, inspect runtime threads and breakpoints, and more.

Editor Area

The main part of the window is the Editor area. This view cannot be hidden. Its contents are set by selecting a file in the Navigator area, and the form the editor takes depends on the file being edited. For example, when a source file is selected, we see a typical source code editor. But when a GUI file is selected, the Editor area becomes a visual GUI editor, and when an image file like a .gif or .jpeg is selected, the Editor area displays the image.

The Editor Mode buttons in the toolbar switch the editor pane between three modes: standard, which is the default editor for the type of file that's selected; assistant, which shows related files side by side; and version, which uses source control to show current and historical versions of the file side by side, a "blame" mode that shows the committer of each line of code, or a log of commit comments alongside the code. The Editor area also contains a *jump bar*, a breadcrumb-style strip at the top that shows the hierarchy of the thing being edited; for a source file, this might go "project, group, file, method." Each member of the jump bar is a pop-up menu that navigates to related or recent points of interest.

By default, a new project comes up with its top-level settings selected in the Navigator area, which means that the Editor area defaults to showing settings for things like the app version number, the targeted SDK version and device families, and so on. There may also be a scary-looking "No matching provisioning profiles found" warning, which just means we're not set up to run our app on a real device yet; we'll deal with that in *Provisioning the App*, on page 247.

Utility Area

The right side of the window is a utility area that provides detailed viewing and editing of specific selections in the Editor area. Depending on the file being edited, the toolbar atop this area can show different tools in its Inspector pane. Basic information about a selected file and quick help on the current selection are always available. For GUI files, there are inspectors to work with individual UI objects' class identities (⌥⌘3), their settable attributes (⌥⌘4), their size and layout (⌥⌘5), and their connections to source code (⌥⌘6). We'll be using all of these shortly. At the bottom of the Utility area, a library pane gives us click-and-drag access to common code snippets, UI objects, and more.

Debug Area

The bottom of the window, below the Editor area and between the Navigator and Utility areas, is a view for debugging information when an app is running. Its tiny toolbar has a segmented button that lets us switch between the debugging-oriented *variables view* that allows us to inspect memory when stopped on a breakpoint, a textual *console view* of logging output from the application, or a split view of both. We'll make use of the right-side console view in a little bit, while the left-side variables view will be our focus in Chapter 14, *Debugging Apps*, on page 227.

So that's how Xcode presents our initial project to us, but what can we do? Well, there's a nice big Run button, and it's not like it's disabled. Let's try running the app. Make sure the scheme is some flavor of "iPhone" from the "iOS Simulator" section (and not "iPad" or the name of an actual device); in Xcode 6, our choices range from the iPhone 4s to the iPhone 6 Plus. Click the Run button. The status area will shade in with a progress bar that fills up as it builds all the files and bundles them into an app, and when it's done, it will launch the iOS Simulator. The Simulator is another OS X application, which looks and behaves more or less like a real iPhone or iPad. When our app runs in the Simulator, the main screen disappears and is replaced by a big white box that fills the Simulator screen.

Building Our User Interface

That white box in the Simulator is our app. It's not much, but then again, we haven't done anything yet. Let's start building our app for real. Press Stop in Xcode to stop the simulated app, and then take a look at the project in Xcode.

If the File Navigator isn't already showing on the left side of the project window, bring it up with ⌘1. The File Navigator uses a tree-style hierarchy with a blue Xcode document at the top, representing the project itself as the root. Under this are files and folders. The folder icons are *groups* that collect related files, such as the views and logic classes for one part of the app; groups don't usually represent actual directories on the filesystem. We can expand all the groups to see the contents of the project, like this:

Different project templates will set us up with different files. For the view-based app, we get two source code files in the PragmaticTweets group, along with a Main.storyboard, a Launch-Screen.xib, and an Images.xcassets. These are the files we'll be editing. The files in the Supporting Files group help build and run our app, but we won't need to edit them directly. The Prag-maticTweetsTests group is where we will write unit tests to validate our code, something we'll do much later in Chapter 4, *Testing Apps*, on page 61. Finally, the Products group shows the files our build will create: in this case, PragmaticTweets.app for the app and PragmaticTweetsTests.xctest for the

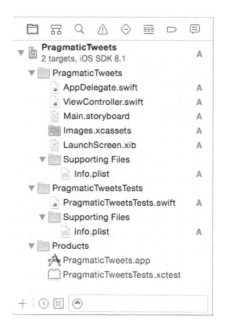

runnable unit tests. Files shown in red indicate they haven't been built yet; PragmaticTweets.app is red in the figure because although we've run it in the Simulator, we haven't built it for the actual device yet.

We said at the outset that iOS development traditionally starts with the user interface. By focusing on what the user sees and how he or she interacts with it, we keep our focus on the user experience and not on the data models and logic behind the scenes. On iOS, we typically build our user interfaces visually and store them in *storyboards*. The project has one such file, Main.storyboard, so let's click it.

Storyboards

When we click on Main.storyboard, the Editor area switches to a graphical view called *Interface Builder*, or IB for short. In iOS, IB works with user interface documents called *storyboards*. Just like in movie-making, where a storyboard is a process used to plan out a sequence of shots in a movie or TV show, the storyboard of an iOS app shows the progression through the different views the app will present. The initial storyboard looks like the following figure:

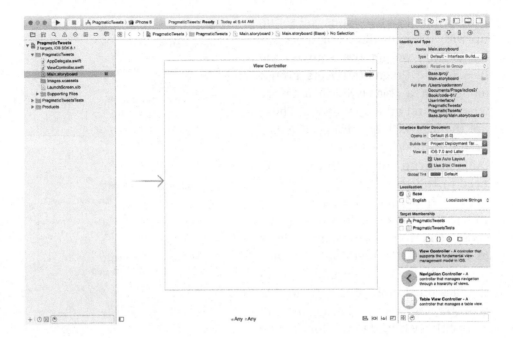

Our app uses a single view, so we follow the right-pointing arrow (which indicates where the app starts) into a square that represents the visible area of the screen. This is our app's one view; if we were building a navigation-style app, there would be one view rectangle for each screen of the navigation. Click the view to show a header box with three icons. These are *proxy objects* that represent objects that will work with the view at runtime: a *view controller* that contains logic to respond to events and update the view; a *first responder* that represents the ability to handle events; and an *exit segue*, used for when we back out of views in navigation apps (something we'll visit in Chapter 9, *Navigating Between View Controllers*, on page 139).

At the bottom left of the Editor area, IB shows a little view disclosure button. Click this to show and hide the scene list (already showing in this figure), which shows each "scene" of the storyboard and its contents as a tree structure. Currently, our one scene has the proxy objects discussed earlier, and inside the view controller, we find two layout objects and a "view." This view is the big square in the UI; as we add UI elements like buttons and labels, the scene's tree list will show them as children of this view.

But wait a minute!, you might say, *iPhones aren't square, and neither are iPads!* Quite right. What we're seeing in our startup view is Apple pushing developers to "think different" about device sizes. At the bottom of the IB pane, a label indicates our current layout as "w: Any h: Any." This is actually a button that allows us to try our user interface layouts in different sizes and orientations. Click the label to show the sizing popover, which looks like the one in this figure:

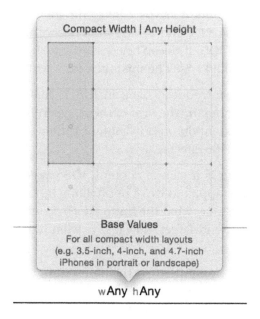

As we mouse over the grid of boxes in this popover, we can switch the height and width previews between Compact, Any, and Regular, and the popover titles will give us a hint of the class of sizes we're previewing, like "iPhone in landscape orientation." Click on the box to change the preview to see the main view change to this size and shape. Once we start laying out some contents for the view, this is how we will preview how they'll be laid out on different device sizes, and when we rotate from portrait to landscape, or vice versa.

Adding Buttons

So let's start adding some UI elements to our view. We'll begin by adding a button to send a tweet telling the world that our first app is running. To add components to our storyboard, use the toolbar to show the Utility area on the right (if it's not already showing), and find the Library pane at bottom right. There's a mini-toolbar here that should default to showing user interface objects; if not, click the little icon of a square in a circle (or press ^⌥⌘3). The bottom of the pane has a button to toggle between list and icon views for the objects, and a search filter to find objects by name. Scroll down through this pane to find the icon that just says "Button"; we can tap once on any of the objects to get its name, class, and description to appear in a popover. Drag the button from the Object library into the iPhone-sized view in IB. This will create a plain button.

 It kind of leaves a lot to the imagination, huh? Without the edge and background decorations of earlier versions of iOS, it doesn't necessarily look like a button at all. It could easily be mistaken for a text label.

The new look of iOS, introduced back in iOS 7, has three stated themes: *deference, clarity,* and *depth.* The first of these, deference, means that the UI appearance focuses attention on our content rather than competing with a bunch of pseudo-realistic effects.

So maybe our problem is a lack of content. iOS expects us to tell the user what's going on in our app, and we're not holding up our end of the deal yet. Let's fix that. First, we'll say what the button does. Double-click on the button to change its name to Send Tweet. Now it says what it does, but it still doesn't exactly feel button-y.

Maybe we can fix that by contrasting the blue text of the button with a plain label. Back in the Object library at the lower right, find the Label object, and drag one above the button. Change its text to "I finished the first project." Drag both objects so that they're centered in the view; a dashed blue line will appear when we're centered, and the drag will snap to this position. The view should now look like the following figure:

Go ahead and click the Run button to run this app again in the iOS Simulator. We should just see the label and the button, right? Sure, but...there's a problem.

When we run the app in the Simulator, we typically start in portrait orientation. And right now, that's going to be a problem, because our label and button are not centered in portrait; in fact, they're cut off on the right edge, as seen in the following figure. Rotate to landscape with Rotate Left and Rotate Right items in the Hardware menu (⌘← and ⌘→, respectively), and it looks a little better, but it's still clearly not centered on tall models like the iPhone 5. What happened?

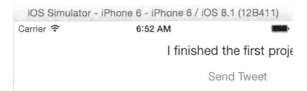

The problem is that we've been designing against a hypothetical square shape, and we never explicitly said these labels were supposed to be centered. What's happened instead is that they've kept a constant distance from the top and left sides of their parent view. In a way, it makes sense: iOS doesn't know what matters to us: a constant distance from the top or bottom, or being centered, or some other relationship entirely.

Stop the Simulator, go back to Xcode, and select the label. On the right side of the workspace, show the *Size Inspector*, by clicking the little ruler icon (or pressing ⌥⌘5). This inspector tells us about the size and location of elements in our UI. There's a section called Constraints, which currently reads:

> The selected views have no constraints. At build time explicit left, top, width, and height constraints will be generated for the view.

Autolayout

In iOS, our UI elements are placed onscreen with an *autolayout* system that lets you determine where objects should go and how big they should be based on *constraints* that we set on them. This allows our interfaces to adapt to being rotated between portrait and landscape, and to handle the differing screen sizes of the 3.5-inch models (original iPhone through iPhone 4s), 4-inch models (iPhone 5, 5c, and 5s), the 4.7-inch iPhone 6, and 5.5-inch iPhone 6 Plus. Constraints allow us to express what matters to us—the size of components, their alignment with or distance from other components, etc.—and to let other factors vary as needed. In this example, we want our label and button to be horizontally centered, and we don't care what the resulting x and y coordinate values are.

Interface Builder puts a floating set of buttons at the bottom right of the pane to give us access to autolayout features. These buttons display a popover or pop-up menu when tapped.

From left to right, these buttons are as follows:

- *Align popover*: This lets us create constraints that align a view's edges or horizontal or vertical center with another view, or horizontally or vertically center it within its containing view (its *superview*).

- *Pin popover*: This lets us create constraints that specify a fixed value for spacing from one or more edges to another view (possibly the superview), and/or a fixed width or height.

- *Resolve menu*: The options here will adjust a view position or size so it matches its constraints, or do the opposite and create constraints based on its current position and size. We can also clear all constraints and start over with this menu.

- *Resizing Behavior menu*: This menu determines which views get their constraints adjusted when we drag handles to resize a view. By default, only its subviews get updated, but this menu lets us update sibling and ancestor views too.

Storyboard Zooming

Perhaps surprisingly, Xcode 6 removes zoom in/out buttons that used to be located alongside the autolayout buttons. With a trackpad, we can pinch zoom in and out to show more of the storyboard. Without a trackpad, there are zoom menu items available via a control-click in the Editor area, or the menu item Editor→Canvas→Zoom.

So what we need to do is to just tell our label and button to be centered. Click the label and then click the Alignment button. This shows the popover in the figure. Click the checkbox next to Horizontal Center in Container. This will change the button at the bottom of the popover to say Add 1 Constraint. Click this button to dismiss the popover (note that if we tap outside the popover instead of tapping the button, the popover will dismiss *without* creating the constraint).

This causes an orange line to appear down the middle of the view, and an orange box around it, when the label is selected. In Interface Builder, orange is a warning color, meaning *there aren't enough constraints*. The label is *under-constrained* because although we've provided a horizontal constraint, we haven't provided a vertical constraint, meaning autolayout can't know for sure how high or low on the screen to place the label.

Since we're happy with what the label looks like in Interface Builder, let's just tell it to keep this same distance from the top of the container view. We do that by *pinning* its distance from the top. With the label selected, click the Pin button to show the popover seen here.

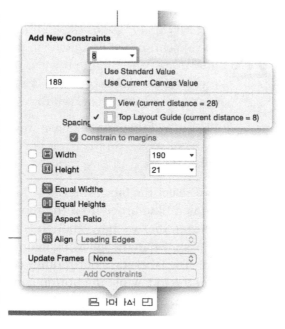

The pinning popover lets us lock down values such as width and height or distances from containers or other views, or force sides of multiple components to stay aligned. The top section is called "Spacing to nearest neighbor," and if we click the top pop-up menu in this part, we can select the value Top Layout Guide, meaning we want to lock the distance between the top of our label and the area at the top of the screen reserved for the status bar (where the battery level, signal strength, clock, and other indicators appear), or any other menus at the top of the screen (like the navigation bar we'll introduce much later). When we select this menu item, the "brace" graphic under the menu becomes solid, and the button in the popover again says Add 1 Constraint. Click this button to add the new constraint.

One other thing to watch for is orange markers indicating that an object is not in its correct position. Typically, these warnings will also show a size or distance number in a little bubble. When you see this, you can correct the problem by selecting the object, going to the resolve pop-up menu at the lower right, and choosing Update Frame. The only problem is that if the object is out of position *and* underconstrained, the update could send it all the way to one edge of the view, or radically change its size. If this happens, just undo (⌘Z), and think about what other constraints you might need.

Size-specific constraints

When creating constraints, it's important that the sizing bar at the bottom of the pane is in "w:Any h:Any" mode. Although this creates somewhat unrealistic square views, the danger is that constraints created with any other sizes set for width or height *will only apply for those sizes*. If we set width to Compact to preview the appearance of an iPhone in portrait and add a constraint like horizontal centering, that will only apply for compact width, so there will be *no* constraint for landscape, or on an iPad, since those aren't cases of compact width.

We learned this one the hard way, when one of our buttons went flying offscreen on the iPad. We'll talk about the underlying size concepts later, in *Size Classes*, on page 173.

Now when we select the label, Interface Builder shows the centering line as blue, and adds a blue brace from the top of the label up to the status bar area. Blue means that we have enough constraints to not be ambiguous to autolayout, as shown in the following figure. Try running it again, and rotate the Simulator. The label stays horizontally centered and maintains a constant distance from the top, while the button continues to be uncentered in landscape orientation.

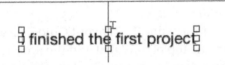

We can repeat the same steps to fix the button. First, select the button, click the Alignment button, choose Horizontal Center in Container, and click Add 1 Constraint. This again gives us the orange line to tell us we're not quite done. Now click the Pin button, and show the menu for the top spacing. This time we have a choice: we can pin either the distance to the Top Layout Guide as before, or the distance from the top of the button to the label. This is the power of constraints: we get to indicate what matters to us. Do we care about the button's distance to the top, or its relation to the label? In this case, the label helps explain what the button does, so it makes more sense to keep them together and pin the distance from the button to the label, rather than the button to the top. So, select "Label - I finished the ..." and click Add 1 Constraint. This gives us blue guides in Interface Builder, indicating that all is well, including a blue brace between the button and the label.

Run the app again and both our components are centered regardless of orientation. We can also change the device type between 3.5-inch and 4-inch iPhone models in the scheme selector to see the effect of the larger screen; it doesn't matter much now because our buttons' vertical positions are measured from the top of the screen, but it would be a big deal if we had anything pinned to the bottom, since we'd be losing a half inch of space in the middle as we go from an iPhone 5 to an older iPhone.

Also, think back to when we created the label in the playground, explicitly setting its position and size in code. With autolayout, we get to describe size, shape, and position with constraints, whereas if we build our UI in code, we would be doing a bunch of math to set the position and size, using logic like "subtract the label's width from the superview's width and then indent half of that space to center up." For complex layouts on devices with different sizes and shapes, all of which can be rotated at any time, autolayout ends up being both easier and more dependable.

Connecting User Interface to Code

It's great that our UI handles resizing and orientation changes, but it still doesn't, y'know, *do anything* yet.

And that raises an interesting question: how do we get the button tap to do something? After all, we've been creating the user interface in the Main.storyboard file, but it doesn't look like there's any place in this editor to start writing code.

In iOS, we use Interface Builder *connections* to tie the user interface to our code. Using Xcode, we can create two kinds of connections:

- An *outlet* connects a variable or property in code to an object in a storyboard. This lets us read and write the object's properties, like reading the value of a slider or setting the initial contents of a text field.

- An *action* connects an event generated by a storyboard object to a method in our code. This lets us respond to a button being tapped or a slider's value changing.

What we need here is an action connecting the button tap in the UI to a method in our code, which we'll write in a little bit. To create either kind of connection, we need to declare an IBOutlet or IBAction in our code, and then create the connection with Interface Builder. Fortunately, IB makes this pretty easy by giving us a way to combine the steps.

With the storyboard showing in the Editor area, go up to the toolbar and click the Assistant Editor button, which looks like two linked circles. This brings up a side-by-side view with the storyboard on the left and a source file on the right. If there's not enough horizontal room on the screen to see things clearly, use the toolbar to hide the Utility area for now.

The pane on the right side has a jump bar at the top to show which file is shown in that pane. After a pair of forward/back buttons, there's a button that determines how the file for this pane is selected: Manual, Automatic, Top Level Objects, etc. Set this to Automatic and the contents of the file ViewController.swift should appear in the right pane. We'll have more to say about why ViewController.swift is the file we need in the next few chapters, but for now, let's take the filename at face value: this is the class that controls the view.

Xcode's template prepopulates ViewController.swift with trivial implementations of two methods, viewDidLoad() and didReceiveMemoryWarning(). We'll be adding a new method to this class.

Creating the action turns out to be pretty easy. Control-click on the button in Interface Builder, and control-drag a line over into the source code, anywhere between the set of curly braces that begin with class ViewController : UIViewController and end at the bottom of the file, and not within the curly braces of an existing method. Don't worry; a blue drop indicator and the tooltip Insert Outlet or Action will appear only when we mouse over a valid drop zone. A good place to target is the line right before the final curly brace, as seen in the figure on page 25.

When we let up the mouse in the source file, a popover appears, asking us for the details needed to finish the method declaration. On the first line, change the Connection from Outlet to Action. Next, we need to provide a name for the method, so type handleTweetButtonTapped in the Name field. Next, the Type field 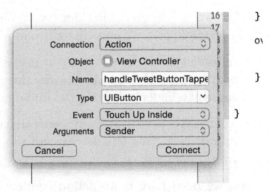 determines what kind of object will be passed to the method as an argument identifying the source of the action. The default, AnyObject, represents any kind of object and works well enough, but we can save ourselves some typing later by switching it to UIButton so we know that the object calling us is a button.

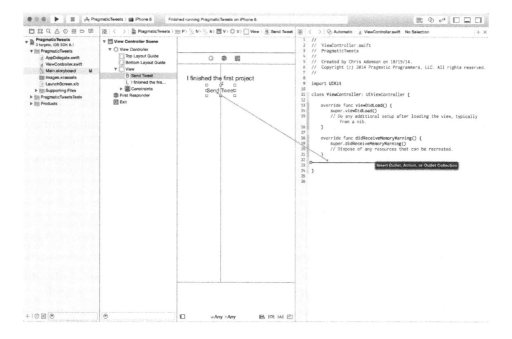

For the Event and Argument fields we can take the default values. Click the Connect button to create the connection.

We're done with the Assistant Editor, so click the Standard Editor button in the toolbar to return to one-pane mode. If we select ViewController.swift in the Navigator area, we can see that Xcode has stubbed out a method signature for us:

UserInterface/PragmaticTweets-2-1/PragmaticTweets/ViewController.swift

```
@IBAction func handleTweetButtonTapped(sender: UIButton) {
}
```

Xcode has also made a change to the storyboard, but it's not as easy to see. Switch to Main.storyboard and bring the Utility area back if it's hidden. Click on the button to select it. Then, in the Utility toolbar, click the little circle with the arrow (or press ⌥⌘6) to bring up the *Connections Inspector*. This pane shows all the connections for an object in Interface Builder: all the outlets from code to the object, and all actions sent by the object into the code. In this case, one connection appears in the Sent Events section, from Touch Up Inside to View Controller - handleTweetButtonTapped:. This connection, shown in the next figure, is editable here; if we wanted to disconnect it, we could click the little "x" button, and then reconnect to a different IBAction method by dragging from the circle on the right to the View Controller icon in the scene.

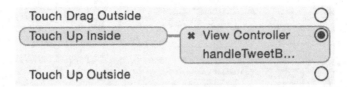

Honestly, we don't break and remake connections very often, but if a connection ever gets inadvertently broken (for example, by renaming the method in the source file), looking in the Connections Inspector is a good approach for diagnosing and fixing the problem.

Coding the App

Now that we've added a button to our view and wired it up, we can run the app again. The app now has the Send Tweet button, and we can even tap it, but it doesn't do anything. In fact, we don't even know if we've made our connections correctly. One thing we can do as a sanity check is to log a message to make sure our code is really running. Once that's verified, we can move on to implementing our tweet functionality.

Logging

On iOS, we can use the function println() to write a string out to the system's log file. We can implement our action to just log a message every time the button is tapped and thereby verify that the connections are working. Select ViewController.swift in the File Navigator (⌘1) to edit its source code and rewrite handleTweetButtonTapped() like this:

```
UserInterface/PragmaticTweets-2-1/PragmaticTweets/ViewController.swift
@IBAction func handleTweetButtonTapped(sender: UIButton) {
  println ("handleTweetButtonTapped")
}
```

Run the app again and tap the button. Back in Xcode, the Debug area automatically appears at the bottom of the window once a log or error message is generated, as seen in the following figure. Every time the button is tapped, another line is written to the log and shown in the Debug area. If the Debug area slides in but looks empty, check the two rightmost buttons at the bottom of the Debug area, next to the trashcan icon; the left one enables a variables view (populated only when the app is stopped on a breakpoint), and the right (which we want to be visible) is the console view where log messages appear. Another way to force the console view to appear is to press ⇧⌘C.

So now we have a button that is connected to our code, enough to log a message that indicates the button tap is being handled. The next step is to add some tweeting!

Calling Up the SLComposeViewController

Back in *Digging Into the Docs*, on page 6, we discovered the SLComposeViewController class, which provides a fly-in view that lets the user compose and send a tweet. Armed with this class, we're ready to lay down some code. In ViewController.swift, rewrite the handleTweetButtonTapped() method as follows:

UserInterface/PragmaticTweets-2-1/PragmaticTweets/ViewController.swift

```
Line 1  @IBAction func handleTweetButtonTapped(sender: UIButton) {
    -     if SLComposeViewController.isAvailableForServiceType(SLServiceTypeTwitter){
    -       let tweetVC = SLComposeViewController (forServiceType:
    -         SLServiceTypeTwitter)
    5       tweetVC.setInitialText(
    -       "I just finished the first project in iOS 8 SDK Development. #pragsios8")
    -       presentViewController(tweetVC, animated: true, completion: nil)
    -     } else {
    -       println ("Can't send tweet")
    10    }
    -   }
```

Getting in Trouble on Purpose

You will probably see some little error icons appear in the left gutter while typing this code. Sometimes these go away, as Xcode figures out that an incomplete line that wouldn't be valid code is in fact legitimate once it's completed. In this case, however, we're going to get in trouble on purpose, as will be explained and resolved shortly.

We've replaced our one-line logging statement with several lines of Swift, which is what iOS uses for most of its high-level APIs, such as UIKit and the Social framework. We'll have much more to say about the language in the next chapter, but for now, let's try to tease out how this code works. To start with, on line 2 we ask the SLComposeViewController class if it's even possible to send tweets: it might not be if a given social network isn't set up to post.

If we can send tweets, then we initialize a new SLComposeViewController on lines 3-4, and we assign it to the variable tweetVC.

On lines 5–6, we set the initial text of the tweet to "I just finished the first project in iOS 8 SDK Development. #pragsios8" by calling the setInitialText() method on tweetVC.

This is all we need to do to prepare the tweet, so on line 7, we show the tweet composer by telling self (our own ViewController) to presentViewController() with the newly created and configured tweetVC, setting the animated parameter to true, which makes the tweet view "fly in." The third parameter, completion, specifies code to execute once the view comes up; we don't need that, so we send nil.

Finally, if isAvailableForServiceType() returned false, the else block on lines 8–10 logs a debugging message that we can't send tweets. As our skills improve, we'll want to actually show the user a message in failure cases like this.

And that's it. We did all the work in IB to create the button and have it call this method when tapped, so we should be able to just build and tweet at this point, right? Let's try running the app. Click the Run button and see what happens.

Disaster—the project doesn't build anymore! Instead, we get a bunch of error messages in red displayed alongside our code, as seen in the following figure. Worse, depending on the width of the window, the errors are likely truncated. What are we supposed to do?

```
25
26    @IBAction func handleTweetButtonTapped(sender: UIButton) {
27        if SLComposeViewController.isAvailableForServiceType(SLServiceTypeTwitter) {    ⊙ Use of unresolved identifier 'SLComposeViewController'
28            let tweetVC = SLComposeViewController (forServiceType: SLServiceTypeTwitter  ⊙ Use of unresolved identifier 'SLServiceTypeTwitter'
29            tweetVC.setInitialText(
30                "I just finished the first project in iOS 8 SDK Development. #pragsios8")
31            presentViewController(tweetVC, animated: true, completion: nil)
32        } else {
33            println ("Can't send tweet")
34        }
35    }
36
```

Broken Builds

Let's get a more detailed look at what's going on. Visit the report navigator using the rightmost button in the Navigator area toolbar, or just type ⌘8. This replaces the list of files with a list of our builds and runs, with the most recent at the top. Click the top Build, and the Content area shows a build log, as seen in the next figure. By default, the selected filter in this view is All Issues, and aside from a possible warning about CODE_SIGN_ENTITLEMENTS (which you'll see so long as you aren't set up to build for actual iOS devices), most of the actual errors are Use of undeclared identifier 'SLComposeViewController' and Use of undeclared identifier 'SLServiceTypeTwitter', which in turn cause the later errors.

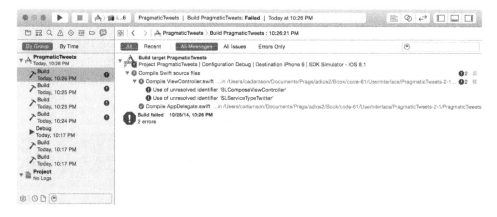

This error means that the compiler doesn't know we're using the Social framework, and therefore it doesn't recognize the SLComposeViewController. Xcode project templates only set us up to use the most common frameworks: Foundation, Core Graphics, UIKit, and XCTest. Anything else has to be added manually. So to tell the compiler about the Social framework, add the following line near the top of ViewController.swift, after the import UIKit line:

UserInterface/PragmaticTweets-2-1/PragmaticTweets/ViewController.swift
```
import Social
```

The import directive tells the compiler to pull in another framework. This tells the compiler and the linker about our dependency on the Social framework. Once we add the import Social declaration, the red error icons on the side of our code disappear. This is a good sign, so let's try running again.

Tweeting at Last

This time the build completes without errors, and the app will launch in the Simulator. Try clicking the button; either the Xcode log will say Can't send tweet, or the Simulator will show an error alert saying that no Twitter accounts have been configured, with buttons offering to take you to Settings or to cancel.

To fix this, we use the Simulator as we would a real iPhone: tap the Settings button in the alert, or use the Home button (menu item Hardware→Home or keyboard shortcut ⇧⌘H) to switch out of the app and launch the Settings app. In the Twitter settings, configure a Twitter account with a valid Twitter username and password. If you don't have one, create a disposable one for free on http://twitter.com/, since we'll be using it throughout the book. With username and password entered, tap the Sign In button. Once the checkmarks appear to indicate the credentials have been accepted, use the Home button menu item again and switch back to PragmaticTweets. This time when you tap the button, the tweet composer should come up, like the one below. Edit the text if desired and then click Post. Go visit your Twitter page on the Web with a browser—for style points, go ahead and use Safari in the Simulator—to see your brand-new tweet, posted for all the world to enjoy and admire.

Wrap-Up

In this chapter, we've gotten our first project built, launched, and sending data to the Internet. We downloaded and installed Xcode, created a view-based project, and started customizing it. We customized the user interface, and set up autolayout constraints to deal with different device sizes and orientations. We connected the UIButton in the storyboard to a method in our ViewController by way of an action. Then we implemented that action method to show iOS's default tweet-composer UI. When it was all done, with just a little bit of code and UI tweaking, we ended up with an app that sends tweets. Not bad for one chapter's work.

Now that we've had our first experience with the tools that the SDK gives us, we're going to use the next chapter to learn more about the Swift programming language that iOS uses for its high-level frameworks, and in the process we'll make our app more interesting and more functional.

CHAPTER 3

Programming in Swift for iOS

In a single chapter, we've learned enough about the iOS SDK to write a simple app that can send tweets on our behalf to the Internet. Still, we did have to take it on faith that the code we used to create the SLComposeViewController would do what we needed it to. Now that we've gained some familiarity with our tools, it's time to do the same with the language and libraries.

In this chapter, we're going to look at the fundamentals of coding an iOS app: programming with Swift and calling the default frameworks, UIKit and Foundation. As we go, we'll make a series of enhancements to our Twitter app. We'll add the ability to see our twitter.com page, internationalize the app for other languages and locales, and see how the language and tools work together to make us more productive. Each time we need to change the UI, we'll edit the storyboard, and when we need new functionality, we'll write more Swift code.

Introducing Swift

So what is Swift and why are we using it? In the previous chapter, we had a choice of using Swift or Objective-C for our project, and we chose Swift. There's a story there, of course. Objective-C has been the primary language of iOS development since the iPhone's debut in 2007, and goes way back from there: through Mac OS X's Cocoa in the early 2000s, and the NeXTStep environment of the 1990s. It started as a means of adding object-oriented features to C, and while it was enhanced in many clever and compelling ways over the years, various C legacies held back efforts to make Objective-C faster, safer, and easier to program.

So, in June 2014, Apple surprised the developer community by announcing they had created a new language as a successor to Objective-C on Apple platforms, one that could build on Objective-C's strengths while eliminating its weaknesses, and drawing on good ideas in other languages. According to Swift creator Chris Lattner, Swift took inspiration from "Objective-C, Rust, Haskell, Ruby, Python, C#, CLU, and far too many others to list."[1]

Swift is:

- *Compiled*, meaning that we perform an up-front conversion of source to bytecode when we build our project, rather than interpreting the source at runtime as with many scripting languages like JavaScript or Ruby.

- *Strongly typed*, meaning objects are clearly identified as strings, floats, integers, and so on. Types are *static*, meaning they can't change, and these two traits help the compiler build safer and faster code. However, the compiler also uses *type inference*, so we don't have to explicitly indicate a type when the compiler can figure it out unambiguously for us.

- *Automatically reference-counted*, meaning that every object keeps track of how many other objects own references to it, and immediately frees the memory of any object that has zero incoming references (since this object can no longer be used, given that no other object knows about it anymore). This is different from *garbage collection*, popular in many modern languages (Java, C#, most scripting languages), in which a distinct system (the garbage collector) scans memory for objects it can free. *Automatic Reference Counting* (ARC) is implemented by the compiler and makes objects themselves responsible for freeing their memory *immediately* when they are no longer needed.

- *Name-spaced*, like many modern languages but significantly unlike Objective-C. This makes it easier for our code to coexist with others, because it's very unlikely our class and method names will get confused with those provided by Apple or other third parties. For example, the compiler and runtime won't mistake our ViewController class for some other ViewController, because our project settings indicate that our class is part of the com.pragprog.yourname namespace, and not some com.apple namespace. Since Objective-C couldn't do this, we used to have to put two- or three-letter prefixes on all our class names; this explains why all the Apple classes we'll see in this chapter start with NS or UI—for compatibility reasons, we're stuck with the old Objective-C names.

---

1.   http://nondot.org/sabre/

Joe asks:

Why Didn't They Just Use Ruby?

With the transition from Objective-C to Swift, Apple is transitioning developers from one language under its control to another that is, if anything, even more proprietary. Why not use the opportunity to adopt a popular language like Ruby or Python?

One important reason is that compatibility with the existing frameworks—a mixture of Objective-C, C, and even some C++—was required. Reworking thousands of classes and tens or hundreds of thousands of methods and functions would be a mammoth undertaking. It was easier to create a new language that could feel modern, even while adapting to old C conventions like enumerations and structures, and Objective-C's various idiosyncrasies.

In fact, Apple did try adopting Ruby and Python once before, in Mac OS X 10.5, which offered first-class support for using these languages with Cocoa, the predecessor to iOS's Cocoa Touch. But it didn't take off (nor did support for Cocoa-Java, offered way back in OS X 10.0), so it was retired. You can't say they didn't try.

Swift Classes

We've already got some Swift code in our project, courtesy of the Xcode template we started with. Our project starts with two files, AppDelegate.swift and ViewController.swift. We did a little work in the ViewController in the last chapter, so let's start there. After the import that tells the compiler to use UIKit (the user interface framework we'll discuss later in this chapter), the class is defined like this:

```
class ViewController: UIViewController {
```

This says that we are creating a class called ViewController, as a subclass of the UIViewController exposed to us by the UIKit framework, meaning we inherit all the functionality of UIViewController, and all of its superclasses. The line ends with an open curly brace; any functions and properties between this and the matching closing curly brace are part of the class.

Let's look at the corresponding line at the top of AppDelegate.swift:

```
class AppDelegate: UIResponder, UIApplicationDelegate {
```

What's going on here…does AppDelegate have two superclasses? No, only one, the UIResponder. The second term after the colon, UIApplicationDelegate, is a *protocol*, which is just a declared list of methods. The idea is that the UIApplicationDelegate protocol describes methods that can be called to tell us that the app is being backgrounded, is being launched via a URL from another app, and so forth, and our code can implement one or more of these methods to act on that call.

We'll do some of those things much later, in Chapter 13, *Launching, Backgrounding, and Extensions*, on page 207.

Swift Methods

In the previous chapter, we control-dragged in the storyboard to create an action connecting a tap on our button to a method in the file ViewController.swift. The method has the following signature:

```
@IBAction func handleTweetButtonTapped(sender : UIButton);
```

Let's break this down into parts:

- @IBAction is an *attribute* indicating that the GUI-builder tool, Interface Builder, can create or change connections to this method. If we wanted to drag a second kind of event to a method in this class, only methods with the @IBAction attribute could receive the drop. There are lots of other attributes, such as the override on some of the methods that Xcode already included in the file. We'll see other attributes that affect our methods' behaviors later.

- func indicates that we are declaring a *function*, a self-contained chunk of code with some distinct purpose. Inside a class (or an enumeration or structure), a function is a *method*. Methods operate on object instances by default; to create a *type method*, which is called on the class as a whole, we would use class func instead. Type methods are like class methods in other languages, but in Swift they can be created for non-class types, like structures and enumerations.

- handleTweetButtonTapped is the name of the method, followed by its parameters in parentheses. This method takes one parameter, sender, of type UIButton. A method that takes no parameters would have empty parentheses, whereas methods taking multiple parameters would separate each name-type pair with commas. For example, if we had asked Interface Builder to send us both the sender and the event for the button tap, the argument list would be (sender : UIButton, event : UIEvent).

- After the parameters, we indicate the return type, in the form -> *type*. Since this method does not return a value, that part of the declaration is absent (optionally, we could also write -> Void to indicate that there is no return value).

Let's look again at the entire method body to see how we called methods.

```
     /Programming/PragmaticTweets-3-1/PragmaticTweets/ViewController.swift
Line 1  @IBAction func handleTweetButtonTapped(sender: UIButton) {
    2      if SLComposeViewController.isAvailableForServiceType(SLServiceTypeTwitter) {
    3          let tweetVC = SLComposeViewController (forServiceType: SLServiceTypeTwitter)
    4          tweetVC.setInitialText(
    5             "I just finished the first project in iOS 8 SDK Development. #pragsios8")
    6          self.presentViewController(tweetVC, animated: true, completion: nil)
    7      } else {
    8          println ("Can't send tweet")
    9      }
   10  }
```

Our first method call is on line 2, in which we ask whether we can even send tweets at all. This is a type method, called on the SLComposeViewController class rather than any specific instance. Indeed, we need to get a true response here to even bother creating an instance.

On line 3, we create an instance of SLComposeViewController by calling its *initializer*, a method with the name of the class, which returns a new object of that class. For this particular class, initializing requires passing in a parameter, which is indicated by the label forServiceType:, and the value SLServiceTypeTwitter, which is a constant provided by the Social framework.

This initializer returns a new object of type SLComposeViewController. We assign it to a local variable called tweetVC. Declaring the local variable requires one of two keywords: let, if the value will not change, or var if it will. We're not going to change the value of tweetVC within this short method, so using let allows the compiler to treat it as a constant, which can make for faster code.

Notice there's no semicolon at the end of line 3! Semicolons are only needed in Swift for multiple statements on the same line. It doesn't hurt to have them, but they're not needed, so out they go, much as our muscle-memory from C, Java, and other languages insists otherwise.

Lines 4–5 call setInitialText() on the tweetVC instance to prepopulate the Tweet composer UI with the given string. We've split this into two lines solely for the book's formatting; you can write it all on one line if you want.

Line 6 tells self, the object we're currently in, to call the presentViewController() method (inherited from the UIViewController superclass) to show the tweet composer. Look at how this takes three parameters, and the second and third are labeled. The first is effectively named by the method name, so we know it's a view controller. The second and third parameters are labeled as animated: and completion:, respectively. These labels are *mandatory*, and make the code more readable by making it clear what each parameter does: one indicates whether the appearance of the tweet composer is animated, and the second provides any completion code to be run when the composer is done. It may feel like extra typing, but it really isn't when we have auto-complete, and it's arguably preferable to C functions that have a half dozen or more parameters that we can't easily tell the purpose of.

Actually, this line is a little more verbose than necessary. The self is not required, because if it's absent, the compiler can figure out that we mean to call presentViewController() on this object. We'll start eliminating self after this, except in cases where it does turn out to be necessary.

Finally, look at line 8 and notice what's missing: there's no object associated with the call to println()! Instead of being an instance method called on an object or a type method called on a class, this is just a function, which we can call from *anywhere*. In Swift, the println() method logs text to the output console, similar to print() in PHP or System.out.println() in Java.

So, with just a few lines of Swift code, we handle the button tap, determine if we're configured to tweet, and either set up and present the UI for that, or log an error message if we can't. If this were C or older versions of Objective-C, we would have to worry about cleaning up the memory allocated to tweetVC at the end of the method, but in Swift with its Automatic Reference Counting, that's not our problem. Instead, we can go on to adding more functionality to our app!

Managing an Object's Properties

Now that we've gone back and figured out how our object allocation and method calls work in the last chapter's code, let's put this knowledge to work and add some new functionality to the app. Our original app lets us send a tweet, but there's no way to tell if we were successful. We'll gradually improve that throughout the next few chapters. For starters, let's use iOS's built-in web browser to bring up our Twitter page inside the app.

Adding a UIWebView

Select Main.storyboard to bring up the UI in Interface Builder. We're going to add a Reload button at the top and a web view (a subview that renders web content) to fill up most of the bottom of our view. While we're at it, we can get rid of the "I finished the first project" label; having a second button named Show My Tweets, with an active verb, should provide enough context for users to know that these are both buttons.

Reworking GUIs in autolayout can be tricky, so let's go through the steps carefully. Select the label and press the backspace key or use the Cut or

Delete menu items. Before we add our new button, select the Send Tweet button and look at its constraints. The centering constraint is now orange because the surviving button's layout is now underconstrained: it depended on the distance to the label above it to know where it should go vertically. We'll have to fix that.

Using the Object library (^⌥⌘3) at the bottom right, drag a new button above the existing one, and give it the title Show My Tweets. Drag it until the center guide appears. Now drag it toward the top of the view until the top margin guide—another dashed blue line—appears. Click the autolayout Align button at the bottom of IB and use its popover to add a Horizontal Center in Container constraint. Then click the Pin button and add a constraint pinning the distance to the Top Layout Guide as 0, which should be the value that pops up automatically because we dragged up to the top margin.

That's enough to fully specify the new button's constraints, but we still have our old Send Tweet button. Drag it up or down to position it under the other button, until a horizontal dashed appears between it and the Show My Tweets button. Use the autolayout Pin button's popover to pin a distance from this button to Show My Tweets, at either the current distance or Standard. This should turn the bottom button's constraints blue, indicating it is now adequately constrained.

Now we're ready for the web view that will show our tweets. Drag out a web view—as seen in the figure, its icon in the Object library resembles the Safari app icon—and put it on the bottom portion of the view. Use its handles to drag the bottom and sides of the web view all the way to the bottom and sides of the
parent view, and drag the top until a horizontal guide appears between it and the Send Tweet button. It may be easier to set the web view all the way at the bottom first, then fix the sides, and then drag up.

We want this view to always fill the entire width of the screen, always stay at the bottom, and always respect the distance to the Send Tweet button, so we will need four constraints, all from the Pin button.

- 0 distance to the left and right sides of the parent View. Be sure to turn off the Constrain to Margins checkbox to get all the way to the container's edges (the distance will initially come up as -16 points otherwise).

- 0 distance to the Bottom Layout Guide

- Standard (or the current value, 8) distance to Button - Send Tweet

Click Add 4 Constraints and the web view will be properly constrained for autolayout. It should look like the following figure:

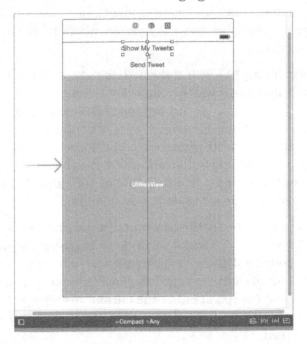

It's also possible to verify that our layout will work in landscape. From the blue sizing strip, select a rectangle that is one box tall and two boxes wide. The popover window describes this as "any width | compact height," and says it is for iPhones in landscape orientation. The layout should now look like the figure on page 39. Notice that both buttons maintain their expected spacing from the top, the web view, and each other. We don't have a lot of vertical space to work with in landscape, but for now, the design is holding up. Just make sure to go back to Any/Any mode, so we don't inadvertently create any compact-specific constraints, a problem explained back in *Autolayout*, on page 19.

Connecting the UIWebView to Code

Now let's get back to our original goal of showing tweets in the web view. For this to work, we need to write another event-handler method, one that handles a tap on Show My Tweets. That method will need to load the user's Twitter page in the web view. But wait: How do we make a call from this event-handler method into the web view we just created in the storyboard?

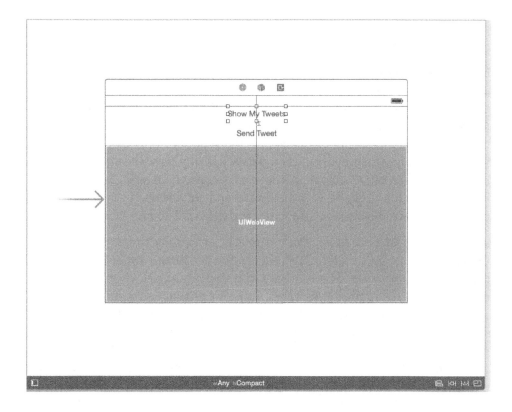

In the previous chapter, we talked about outlets, which are used to connect objects in our code to objects in the storyboard. In Swift, those objects are called *properties*. Preceding a property with the @IBOutlet modifier tells Interface Builder that a property can serve as an outlet.

Declaring Properties

So that begs the question of how to declare properties in Swift. But it turns out, we've already done that: in their simplest form, properties are just variables or constants within a class. So we can declare a property as simply as this:

```
class MyClass: NSObject {
  var myVariableInt: Int = 999
  let myConstantString: String = "myConstantString"
  // methods or other class contents
}
```

In this example myVariableInt and myConstantString are properties of a hypothetical MyClass. These are different from the tweetVC variable we used earlier, since that existed only inside the scope of a method, whereas these are defined on the class as a whole.

Notice that in these declarations, we explicitly indicate the type of each property, by providing a colon and then the type of the property. We actually could have done that with tweetVC, but we didn't have to because of *type inference*: the ability of the compiler to figure out the type of the variable on the left side of an assignment based on the type returned by the right side. When we declare the property, we don't necessarily have a value to assign to it, like we do here. In that case, we need to declare the type we will eventually be using. For this book, we've adopted the style of always declaring types for properties, instead of mixing and matching when we do and don't need them.

It's important to remember that in Swift, *properties aren't variables.* To understand this, let's make a distinction: the properties we declare here are called *stored properties*, which means that there is indeed a variable to store the value, but it's managed by Swift and we can't access it directly. Callers will get and set the property through getter and setter methods that Swift sets up for us, and this introduces another kind of property. A *computed property* is one that doesn't have a backing variable, but instead has get() and set() methods that we provide to compute the property's value on the fly. We'll use these fancy property tricks much later, in *Property Setters*, on page 147; for now, all we need are the more conventional stored properties.

We're ready to create our first property, and to make things easy, we're going to let Xcode do it for us.

Creating IBOutlet Properties in the Storyboard

Select Main.storyboard and switch back to Assistant Editor (via the "linked rings" button on the toolbar, ⌥⌘↩, or the View menu). To make room for the split view, we may want to hide the Utility area on the right. This will show the storyboard on the left and ViewController.swift on the right; if this isn't the case, check the ribbon above the right pane and make sure it's set to Automatic, which picks the most appropriate counterpart file in the right pane given the selection on the left.

To create an outlet property, we do the same thing we did to create the action method for our button: control-drag from the storyboard into the code. Start a control-drag from the web view in the storyboard and drag over to the source code in the right pane, as shown in the figure on page 41:

Drag over different parts of the source file without releasing the button; notice that the tip "Insert Outlet" only appears when our drop target is inside the

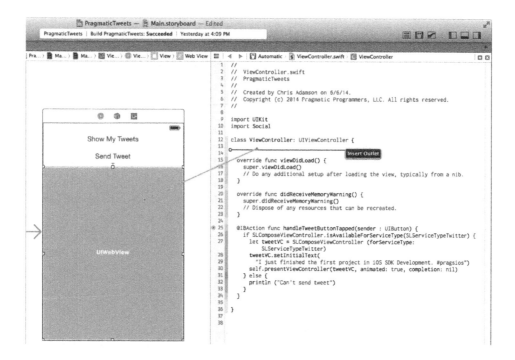

curly brace that defines the class, and not within a method inside the class. Anywhere in here, but ideally in the whitespace just below the class declaration, release to end the drag. Xcode shows a popover to specify the outlet, much like it did when we created the action in the last chapter. Make sure Connection says Outlet and Storage says Weak, and give it the name twitterWebView. When we click Connect, the following declaration is inserted into the source at our drop point:

Programming/PragmaticTweets-3-1/PragmaticTweets/ViewController.swift

```
@IBOutlet weak var twitterWebView: UIWebView!
```

This line is a lot like the hypothetical instance variable mentioned earlier: it declares the attribute IBOutlet (which lets us connect to it with Interface Builder), the weak keyword, the var keyword to indicate the property's value can change, the name twitterWebView, and the class UIWebView. It also has an exclamation point character (!), which we'll explain in a little bit.

So now we have a property called twitterWebView. To access the property, we use dot notation, similar to calling a Swift method, just without arguments in parentheses. That means we can read the property with a call of the form object.property and set it with object.property = value. Since twitterWebView is a property of ViewController, within the class we'll refer to it as self.twitterWebView. For properties that themselves have properties, we just chain dot operators. For example,

UIWebView has a canGoBack property, so our view controller class can test this with self.twitterWebView.canGoBack.

> **⌣ Joe asks:**
> # What the Heck Is the weak Keyword?
>
> Earlier, we mentioned how Automatic Reference Counting (ARC) solves all our memory problems. Well, not *quite*. There are a few problems it can't figure out for itself. One is *retain cycles*, a problem that works like this:
>
> - Our ViewController knows about the twitterWebView, so ARC can't free the web view from memory as long as the view controller exists. Otherwise, the view controller might go looking for the web view and it would be gone.
>
> - But if the twitterWebView also requires the ViewController to hang around in memory, then neither can ever be freed from memory, even if we don't need them anymore.
>
> The way to break this is to declare one side of the arrangement as weak, meaning that we don't require an object to hang around in memory if ours is the only one that knows about it.
>
> The reason it works in this case is that the top-level view has strong references to all its children (including the web view), and the view controller has a strong reference to the view, so having an additional strong reference from the view controller to the twitterWebView would be overkill. The rule of thumb is that only "top-level" objects in a storyboard scene (like the view) need strong references, and everything else can be weak. Xcode defaulted to this behavior when we made the connection, and it solves the problem for us.

Calling into the UIWebView Property

Now that we've created the twitterWebView property, we're ready to use it in our code. We'll write an event handler for Show My Tweets that loads the user's Twitter page into the web view. How do we do that? Well, if we look up the UIWebView in the documentation viewer, the docs tells us that UIWebView has a loadRequest() method that we can use, provided we use a string to create an NSURL (which we assume to be an object that represents a URL), and from that create an NSURLRequest.

But let's start with getting the button-tap event in the first place. Select Main.storyboard and again switch to the Assistant Editor. Make sure the right pane shows ViewController.swift. Control-drag from the Show My Tweets to anywhere inside the class's curly braces, as long as it's not within an existing method's curly braces. When the drag passes over a viable area of the source file, the drag point will show the pop-up tip "Insert Outlet or Action," which is what we want to do.

End the drag and fill in the popover, like we did in the previous chapter for Send Tweet. Change Connection to Action, enter handleShowMyTweetsTapped for the method name, and change the type from AnyObject to UIButton. Leave the defaults for event (Touch Up Inside) and Arguments (Sender). Click Connect, and Xcode will stub out a method for us:

Programming/PragmaticTweets-3-1/PragmaticTweets/ViewController.swift
```
@IBAction func handleShowMyTweetsTapped(sender: UIButton) {
}
```

Switch back to Standard Editor mode and select ViewController.swift. The method that Xcode built for us with the drag says @IBAction, which just means that Interface Builder, the storyboard editor, can work with it. It takes one parameter, sender, which is the UIButton that sent the event (that is to say, the button that was tapped). There's no return type stated, so the method doesn't return a value.

We sketched out a plan to implement this method above: we just have to work up a call to the UIWebView's loadRequest() method. Fill in the method like this:

Programming/PragmaticTweets-3-1/PragmaticTweets/ViewController.swift
```
Line 1  @IBAction func handleShowMyTweetsTapped(sender: UIButton) {
     2      let url = NSURL (string:"http://www.twitter.com/pragprog")
     3      let urlRequest = NSURLRequest (URL: url!)
     4      twitterWebView.loadRequest(urlRequest)
     5  }
```

On line 2, we create an NSURL from its initializer that takes an argument called string:. We've used http://www.twitter.com/pragprog here, but feel free to put in your own Twitter username. Next, line 3 takes this NSURL and makes a new NSURL-Request from it; the ! character here is new in iOS 8.1/Xcode 6.1, and will be explained soon. At any rate, the resulting urlRequest is the object we need on line 4 to tell the URL to load up that page, by using its loadRequest() method.

We wrote this example in a verbose way, so it's easier to follow. As with most languages, Swift lets us chain the results of one statement as parameters to another—a technique called *function composition*—so we could have written this in a more terse form, like this:

Programming/PragmaticTweets-3-1/PragmaticTweets/ViewController.swift
```
@IBAction func handleShowMyTweetsButtonTapped(sender : UIButton) {
  twitterWebView.loadRequest(NSURLRequest (URL:
    NSURL (string: "http://www.twitter.com/pragprog")!))
}
```

Either approach is fine, of course. Also, the line breaks in the terse version are only present to accommodate the book's formatting; this could all be written on one line in Xcode.

Now that we've written this simple method, we're ready to go, so click the Run button to launch the updated app in the Simulator, and then click the Show My Tweets button. The event sent by the new button goes to the handleShowMyTweetsTapped() method, and its code makes a reference to the self.twitterWebView property to load up the Twitter page in the web view, as shown in the following figure:

Note that since the UIWebView is a real live web client, it acts just like Safari, so the first time we use it, we might get intercepted by an advertising page asking us to download the Twitter app for iOS, or worse yet a redirect; just look for a close button or link to dismiss it, as we would do in any other browser. Still, real live web browser component with just a little clicky-draggy and a couple lines of code...*not bad!*

The iOS Programming Stack

Now we're rolling: we can visually create automatically resizing GUIs in the storyboard, connect them to methods and properties in the view controller class that owns the view, and write code in Swift to do stuff. Life is good.

Except that we're still taking a lot on faith when it comes to actually calling stuff in our code. We can search the documentation for cool-looking methods all day, but first we should make sure we understand where all these classes are coming from and how they're organized.

The iOS SDK divides its functionality into a set of frameworks. We saw this in the last chapter when we used import Social to add Social.framework to the frameworks used by the project. Conceptually, we can divide the SDK's frameworks into four layers:

Cocoa Touch Layer
> The top-level abstractions over applications and their UIs (UIKit) and integration with system-provided UI features like mapping (MapKit), and Notification Center

Media Layer
> Graphics, sound, and video frameworks

Core Services Frameworks for essential, non-UI functionality, like filesystem access, in-app purchase (StoreKit), health-tracking device integration (HealthKit), and so on

Core OS
> Low-level frameworks and libraries needed by the upper layers, including the BSD libraries that are the core of iOS and Mac OS X

In this book, we will spend most of our time working with the frameworks that are included by default in the Xcode project templates: Foundation and UIKit.

Building Views with UIKit

The UIKit framework provides the building blocks of touch-based applications for iOS. That means it's responsible both for the concept of what an app *is* and how it interacts with the rest of the system, as well as for providing a suite of user interface views. Every user interface control we add to the app comes from UIKit, as well as the systems for sending user interface events to our code, how we draw things, fonts, colors, gestures, and so forth.

UIKit's UIApplication class is the point of contact between our code and the rest of the system. By accessing its sharedApplication() method, we can open other apps by URL, receive remote events from Apple's Push Notification service, and set a number for our app icon's badge. But a lot of apps don't do any of these things, so we don't often use UIApplication directly. Instead, the Xcode template sets up a UIApplicationDelegate class for us to customize; this class gets callbacks when common events occur, like the app being started up or opened via a URL from another app, or when it's sent to the background by the user tapping the home button.

The *delegate pattern* is frequently used in the iOS SDK, often as an alternative to subclassing. The idea is that for certain responsibilities, usually the custom behaviors specific to an app, an object can delegate its behaviors to another object. In this case, the UIApplication class handles the activities that are common to all applications, but for cases where different apps will want to do different things, it makes callbacks to our AppDelegate. Delegates don't need to be their own classes like this: they are often classes with other purposes that just implement one or two methods (usually collected as a protocol) in order to serve as a delegate.

As for the app delegate itself, we'll be revisiting it in Chapter 13, *Launching, Backgrounding, and Extensions*, on page 207, when we look into what apps can do in iOS 8 even when they're not running.

Many of the UIKit classes are views, which are the onscreen touch objects in our user interface. We've been using these in our Twitter example: our UI has a single view that fills the screen and has three subviews: two buttons and the web view. Many other view classes are available, like switches, tables, and sliders.

The top-level UIView defines the common functionality of all views. All views have visual properties, such as a backgroundColor, an alpha variable, and hidden and opaque flags. As we've already seen, a view can contain other views; these are accessible via a subviews property and can be added with convenience methods like insertSubview(). A child view can access whatever view it's a subview of via the superview property. Subviews are layered on top of one another by drawing them in the order of the subviews array, with the view at index 0 at the bottom, then index 1 on top of it, and so on. For visual styling needs, UIView also has a tintColor property that applies to all subviews, which makes it easier to apply custom theming to all the UI components on the screen.

Views also have frame and bounds properties that indicate their size and location. Each of these properties is a CGRect, a structure that defines an *x-y* origin (of type CGPoint, inherited from the *Core Graphics* framework) and a width-by-height size (of type CGSize, another structure). The difference is that the bounds values are in the view's own coordinate system, while the frame is in its superview's coordinate system. So a subview's frame's origin is its top-left corner, relative to its parent's top-left corner at (0,0). Setting either property changes the other as needed, and these interact with two related visual properties, transform and center.

Swift Structures

Notice that the CGRect used for a view's frame is not a class. Classes typically have both state, expressed as properties, and functionality, expressed as methods. What if we only care about the state? For this, Swift provides *structures*, a very straightforward layer atop the C struct. Structures are useful in cases where we just want to pass a related set of values around.

We saw the CGRect back when we were messing around in the playground, manually setting the frame of our UILabel. Here's what that struct really looks like:

```
struct CGRect {
  var origin: CGPoint
  var size: CGSize
}
```

The CGPoint and CGSize are also structures, the first having an x and y, the second a width and height.

The other thing that's important to know about structures is that when we pass them to a function or method, Swift uses *pass-by-value* semantics, rather than *pass-by-reference* as it would with an object. This means the recipient is getting a copy of the values, and changing them inside the method won't change them anywhere else. It's more like receiving an Int as a parameter than receiving an object.

Along with views, UIKit provides the UIViewController class, which is meant as the place where we put the logic for our user interfaces. The view controller also has a number of life-cycle callbacks, telling it when its view is loaded from the storyboard and when the view will appear or disappear as a result of navigating to different parts of the app. We will look more at this relationship in Chapter 9, *Navigating Between View Controllers*, on page 139.

Finally, UIKit provides classes for objects that are commonly needed by user interfaces, such as UIFont and UIImage. Taken together, the UIKit classes provide an extensive and extensible user interface toolkit.

Accessibility in UIKit

UIKit offers deep support for accessibility, the ability of a user interface to adapt to a user's needs, such as limitations in vision, hearing, and touch. Every UIView has accessibilityLabel and accessibilityHint attributes, along with accessibilityTraits that describe the view's behavior, that the system uses to render it to users who need help. For example, blind users can turn on the Voice Over feature to have the iOS speech synthesizer speak the names of UI elements, using the provided accessibility values if they have been set. These attributes can all be customized in the storyboard or in code.

Unfortunately, many developers don't customize their UIs for accessibility. The good news is, they often don't need to: the default behavior of iOS makes typical UIKit applications highly accessible. But it's good karma—and a legal requirement in some cases—to test the accessibility of our apps and customize these accessibility properties as necessary. And if we were to create our own views, we would have to implement these attributes on our own, so the system would know how to present our custom view to a disabled user.

Strings

The other major framework we import by default in iOS projects is *Foundation*, which provides fundamental data types for common concerns like dates and times, regular expressions, file I/O, and so on. We've already used two classes from Foundation: the NSURL and NSURLRequest that we used to populate the UIWebView.

Foundation also provides strings (as the NSString class) and collections (NSArray and NSDictionary), and in Objective-C, we would work with these as we would with any other class. However, in Swift, the language has taken more responsibility for strings and collections, and we can do a lot of common tasks without having to explicitly call methods on object instances. This makes Swift a lot easier to just get in and use.

Let's start with the String. We can create a string as we do with any other variable or constant, assigning a value with var or let. The value to assign on is enclosed in straight quotes and can include any Unicode characters.

```
let myConstantString = "iPhone"
var myVariableString = "iPad"
```

We can also build strings by using the concatenation operator, +:

```
var shoppingList = "I need to buy an " +
        myConstantString + " and an " + myVariableString
```

Strings defined with var are mutable, so we can append to them:

```
shoppingList += ", and maybe an Apple TV"
```

It's also possible to build up strings by performing in-line evaluations of expressions in the form \(*expression*), like this:

```
var shoppingListCountString = "This list has \(1 + 1 + 1) items"
```

One rather surprising fact about Swift strings is that that they are *pass-by value*, rather than *pass-by reference*. This means that a method that takes a string as an argument gets the contents of the string, rather than a reference to a string object. It's a subtle difference but it means, among other things, that a function or method can count on the value of a string not being changed by code running at the same time and with a shared reference to the string object. In Objective-C, developers typically copied strings they received from callers just to prevent such problems. It's another way that Swift eliminates entire categories of subtle bugs.

Collections

As with strings, Swift moves support for the most common collections directly into the language, which makes them significantly easier to work with than the Objective-C approach of calling methods on objects.

Arrays

Swift provides direct language support for two essential collections: *arrays* and *dictionaries*. Arrays, as in most languages, are ordered lists of objects.

```
var musicGenres = ["Pop", "Rock", "Jazz", "Hip-hop", "Classical"]
```

Because of type inference, Swift knows this is an array of Strings. We could make that explicit by making the declaration var musicGenres: [String].

We can access array members by a zero-based index, inside square braces. We can also get a sub-array by using the *range operator*, where ..< includes the first index but not the second, and ... includes both the first and last index.

```
let pop = musicGenres[0]
let popRock = musicGenres[0..<2]
let popRockJazz = musicGenres [0...2]
```

If the array was declared with the var keyword, then it is mutable and we can add to it with the append() method, or change values in-place.

```
musicGenres.append("J-Pop")
musicGenres[1] = "Rock and Roll"
```

Arrays also have several self-descriptive methods for mutating their contents, such as insert(), removeAtIndex(), removeFirst(), and removeLast().

What do you suppose happens if we try to add something that isn't a String to musicGenres? The following produces a build error:

```
musicGenres += 2.99
```

Since the original contents of musicGenres were all strings, Swift inferred that it was an array of Strings, effectively making the declaration var musicGenres: Array<String>, where the type to the right of the colon explicitly declares what musicGenres is: an Array of Strings. Since 2.99 is a Double, it can't be added. If we really needed to do something like this, we could instead use the special type Any in our declaration, like this:

```
var musicGenres2 : Array<Any> = ["Pop", "Rock", "Jazz", "Hip-hop", "Classical"]
musicGenres2.append(2.99)
```

Any supports, well, pretty much anything: strings, numeric types, objects, and so forth. If we know we're dealing solely in objects—keeping in mind that String and collections are *not* objects in Swift—then we could use the somewhat more restrictive type AnyObject.

Swift also allows us to declare an array with the more concise syntax [Any], which is functionally identical to Array<Any>.

Dictionaries

Swift also provides *dictionaries*, which map from one object to another. These are commonly used in "lookup"-style scenarios. As with arrays, we can create a dictionary by assigning some values into it (by putting *key-value* pairs in square braces like an array, each pair separated by commas), and let Swift figure out the types.

```
var planetaryMass = [
        "Mercury"       : 3.301E+23,
        "Venus"         : 4.867E+24,
        "Earth"         : 5.972E+24,
        "Mars"          : 6.417E+23,
        "Jupiter"       : 1.899E+27,
        "Saturn"        : 5.685E+26,
        "Uranus"        : 8.682E+25,
        "Neptune"       : 1.024E+26,
]
```

In this example, Swift will infer the declaration var planetaryMass :Dictionary <String, Double> (although we gave it help by using scientific notation for the large numeric values, without which it might have inferred the value type to be Int).

As with arrays, there's a more compact way to write this declaration: [String:Double], though for now we'll use the more verbose form for clarity.

As with arrays, we use square braces to access members of the dictionary by name. The simplest use of this syntax is to add a member to the dictionary.

```
planetaryMass["Pluto"] = 1.471E+22
```

Of course, Pluto isn't a planet anymore, so this example is purely hypothetical. Anyway, we can also use square braces to look up a value by its key...or can we? Consider the following:

```
println ("Earth's mass is \(planetaryMass["Earth"]) kg")
```

This code won't even compile. But why not? The answer is a little tricky...

Optionals

To see what the problem is when we fetch a dictionary member by name, let's imagine if we added the following line:

```
var mass = planetaryMass["Gallifrey"]
```

Considering that "Gallifrey" is a fictional planet (and was, for a time, erased from history even within that fiction), it's not in our dictionary, so there's no valid answer here. So what value should be returned for a value that doesn't exist? Double is a numeric type, not an object, so we can't just have it be nil as a means of saying "no object." Can it be 0? No, 0 is a perfectly good value for a floating-point number. So what do we do here?

Swift uses a concept called *optionals* which encapsulate both knowing whether or not there *is* a value, and if so, what the value is. Dictionaries return optionals, so planetaryMass can return nil when there is no value for a key.

We make a type into an optional by adding a ? character to the type. Then we expose the optional to an if statement; if the optional has no value, this will evaluate to false. So here's a safe way to print a value from the dictionary:

```
let mass : Double? = planetaryMass["Earth"]
if mass != nil {
        println ("Earth's mass is \(mass) kg")
} else {
        println ("No such planet")
}
```

The only problem with this is that, well, optionals can be a little burdensome. In this case, the println() output is

```
Earth's mass is Optional(5.972e+24) kg
```

Ick. The println() puts that "Optional" stuff around the value. How do we get rid of it? Swift gives us an expedient way to work around cases like this: we can try to assign an optional to its non-optional base type inside an if statement, and the if evaluates to true or false based on whether the assignment works:

```
if let unwrappedMass : Double = planetaryMass["Earth"] {
      println ("Earth's mass is \(unwrappedMass) kg")
} else {
      println ("No such planet")
}
```

This prints Earth's mass is 5.972e+24 kg, without the Optional(...) stuff, because unwrappedMass is a real Double, and not a Double? (that is to say, a Double optional).

Converting an optional to its base type is called *unwrapping*. We can do this carefully, as with the if let... construction. But that can be burdensome if we have to nest a bunch of if statements, just to get at the underlying types of some optional variables or properties.

Swift also provides the as operator for casting between classes, and as? for an optional cast that may or may not succeed. So the following two if statements are equally valid ways to unwrap an optional:

```
if let unwrappedMass : Double = planetaryMass["Earth"]
if let unwrappedMass = planetaryMass["Earth"] as? Double
```

For cases where we "just know" that the value isn't nil, we can accelerate the unwrapping with the ! operator. So in our earlier example of getting Earth's mass, we can unwrap the optional within the println(), without an if test, by using the ! operator.

```
let optionalMass : Double? = planetaryMass["Earth"]
if optionalMass != nil {
      println ("Earth's mass is \(optionalMass!) kg")
} else {
      println ("No such planet")
}
```

This unwraps optionalMass within the println(), so we don't get the Optional(...) junk in our output.

Doing a fast unwrap is great, but the problem with the ! operator is that whole part about assuming the optional isn't nil. If we were to foolishly write the else case like this:

```
println ("Failed to get planet's mass: \(optionalMass!)")
```

then we would crash on the second line with unexpectedly found nil while unwrapping an Optional value. So much for what we "just know," huh?

We've actually seen the ! character much earlier in this chapter, back when we dragged over a connection to create the twitterWebView property. When we apply the ! to a type, it becomes an *implicitly unwrapped optional*, meaning we can unwrap its value without the ! operator. In other words, we can just refer to twitterWebView and not have to write twitterWebView! or a bunch of if let unwrappedWebView : UIWebView = twitterWebView code every time we want to touch it. The unwrapping is implicit, hence the name.

Cool, right? But since it's still an optional, there is no guarantee that it even *has* a value. So it's inherently unsafe and should only be used when we really know the variable or property will always have a value when we reference it. Since Xcode is responsible for connecting our storyboard elements to our code, it can confidently use the implicitly unwrapped optional instead of the more burdensome optional type.

In fact, we'll see this a lot in the iOS code we're going to call. On http://devforums.apple.com, Apple's engineers have explained that implicitly unwrapped optionals are needed when bridging to old Objective-C code, where nil is always a possible value for Objective-C types, and they couldn't immediately audit every method in all the frameworks to guarantee that a given parameter can *never* be nil. Yet, on the other hand, if every parameter were a full-blown optional, we'd be writing lots of defensive "if not nil" code. So, for now, it's a trade-off between safety and usability, and most of Apple's methods currently work with implicitly unwrapped optionals. That said, Apple engineers are indeed auditing the iOS frameworks, and some implicitly unwrapped optional parameters and return types are changing to either plain types or full-blown optionals with each new release of Xcode. We can plan on this being an ongoing process for a while.

Failable Initializers

Xcode 6.1 and iOS 8.1 introduce a new use of optionals, the *failable initializer*. These are used for cases where we call an initializer and get *nothing* back.

We saw this earlier when we created an NSURL from a string. If the string is garbage, the NSURL class now reserves the right to give us back nil, rather than a useless object. With a failable initializer, the initializer returns NSURL?, which is an optional type. This explains why we had to put a ! on the returned url object when we passed it to the NSURLRequest initializer.

Internationalization

We've talked a lot about the potential uses of strings, collections, and classes in the UIKit and Foundation frameworks, which in turn means we've spent a lot of mental time away from our code. Let's pull together some of their combined strengths to improve our app.

The Swift language, along with the Foundation and UIKit frameworks, do their part to support *internationalization*, the ability of code to adapt to local conventions in different parts of the world. These concerns include things like language, time and date formatting, and currency symbols and separators. If we properly adopt internationalization—often abbreviated as i18n for the first and last letters of the word and the 18 in between—then our Twitter-sender will be as useful to a French-speaking user as an English one. We'll wrap up this chapter by doing exactly that.

Let's identify what parts of our app are currently English-only. When the UI appears, there are two buttons in English, and when the user taps the first button, we fill in the tweet composer with an English message. Both of those need to change.

When we internationalize an app, we create a *localization* for each *locale* we want to support. The locale is a combination of language and geographic region (which lets us distinguish between, say, the variants of Portuguese spoken in Brazil and Portugal), though we can omit the region and focus only on language issues for things that are consistent in the language. The localization is a collection of strings, currency formats, graphics, sounds, and other resources that are specific to one locale.

In Xcode, we declare supported localizations at the project level. Choose the PragmaticTweets project icon from the top of the File Navigator. This gives us a view of the project as a whole, along with the various targets it builds, such as the app executable and its unit tests. We need to inspect the project itself, so find the small hide/show button in the strip atop the editor area,

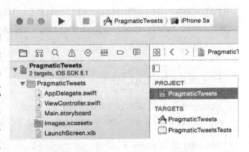

and use it to show the list of projects and targets on the left side of the editor area. Select the PragmaticTweets project (as opposed to the target of the same name), as shown here.

Click the Info tab at the top, and look down to the Localizations section to show the project's current localizations. This should show that for your default language, one file is currently localized. Click the plus (+) button at the bottom of this section to show a list of common locales and choose one. For our screenshots, we'll use French (locale fr)—choose any language you're familiar with. If you don't know another language, one useful technique is to use a made-up language like Pig Latin or Ubbi Dubbi. Either way, we'll be able to find text that needs internationalization by switching the runtime language and looking to see that all the onscreen text changes.

Once we've picked a language, a sheet slides out showing the files in the project that are internationalizable—currently just Main.storyboard and LaunchImage.xib—and asks for a "reference language" for each. The only choice for now is the Base language of the project, so just click Finish. This adds French to the list of project localizations, as this figure shows:

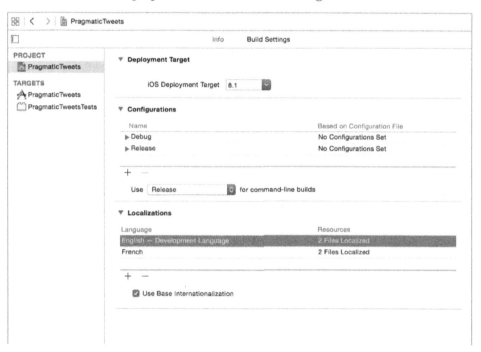

Once a language has been added to the list of localizations, the project navigator shows any files we localized as containers with disclosure trian-

gles, like in the following figure. The language we started in —English in this case—is shown as Main.storyboard (Base), and then each localization is shown below it. In this case, that means we see a second file, called Main.storyboard (French) Select this file to show that its contents are just a list of strings to be localized:

```
/* Class = "IBUIButton"; normalTitle = "Send Tweet"; ObjectID = "H7b-6b-5eJ"; */
"H7b-6b-5eJ.normalTitle" = "Send Tweet";

/* Class = "IBUIButton"; normalTitle = "Show My Tweets"; ObjectID = "sbN-Jq-Jl8"; */
"sbN-Jq-Jl8.normalTitle" = "Show My Tweets";
```

Xcode copies over the English labels for everything textual in the storyboard, so localizing is just a matter of changing these strings. For French, change "Send Tweet" to "Envoyer Tweet" and "Show My Tweets" to "Voir mes Tweets."

Does it work? We can actually check it in Xcode. Select Main.storyboard and switch to the Assistant Editor (with the "linked rings" button, or ⌥⌘↩). On the right pane, change the jump bar from Automatic to Preview. This shows how the layout will look on different devices, which can be selected via the plus button at the bottom left of the pane. On the bottom right, there's a language selection menu that defaults to our development language (English, in our case). Switch this to French and you'll see our UI layout as a French-speaking user would, as shown in the next figure:

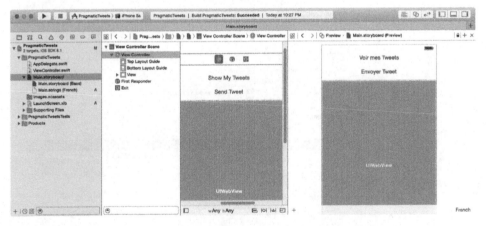

That internationalizes our user interface...almost. When the user composes a tweet, we still set up the tweet composer with an English string. That's something we do in code, with an NSString. So we need a way to internationalize that too.

Foundation gives this to us with the function NSLocalizedString(). This goes into our *application bundle*—the collection of our app's code and assets like images, storyboards, and multi-lingual string resources—and finds a match for the string we need in the user's current language. The function takes five arguments, but only the first (key) and the last (a comment seen only by localizers and not by end users) is required. So, in ViewController.swift, replace the line that calls tweetVC.setInitialText() with the following:

Programming/PragmaticTweets-3-2/PragmaticTweets/ViewController.swift

```
let message = NSLocalizedString(
  "I just finished the first project in iOS 8 SDK Development. #pragsios8",
  comment:"")
  tweetVC.setInitialText(message)
```

The way this works is pretty surprising the first time you see it. The key we ask for is the string we want, *in the development language.* In other words, we take the English string we had hard-coded before, and ask for a localized string corresponding to that. The missing value parameter is what we get back if no match is found; since it defaults to nil, we get back our original key. That's perfectly reasonable behavior: if there's no localized string, we default back to our original development-language string.

So, having written this, all we need is a Localizable.strings file for French, and we'll be all set.

In the project file, click the Supporting Files group and use the menu command File→New→File... (⌘N). In the dialog, choose the Resource group and select Strings File. When prompted for a filename, we *must* use the name Localizable.strings for Foundation to find our localizations. In the list of Targets at the bottom of the file dialog, make sure PragmaticTweets is checked but PragmaticTweetsTests is not.

This creates a Localizable.strings file for our default language, which we don't actually need localizations for. What we need to do now is to add a French localization to the strings file. Select Localizable.strings, show the Utility Area and bring up the File Inspector (click the little document-shaped icon, use the View menu, or press ⌥⌘1), and in the Localization section, click the Localize button. This pops up a dialog asking, "Do you want to localize this file?" and offering a pop-up menu of languages. Choose Base to create a base localization and click Localize. This alone only gives us a baseline version of Localizable.strings, but the Localize button in the File Inspector is now replaced by checkboxes for all the localizations defined in the project. Click French to add the French localization.

As with the storyboard, the Localizable.strings file will now have a disclosure triangle that exposes baseline and French versions of the file. Edit the French version as follows, with the English string in quotes, an equals sign, a French equivalent, and a semicolon. We've added a line break to suit the book's formatting; this isn't necessary for the file to work.

Programming/PragmaticTweets-3-2/PragmaticTweets/fr.lproj/Localizable.strings
```
"I just finished the first project in iOS 8 SDK Development. #pragsios8" =
"Je viens de terminer le premier projet en iOS 8 SDK Development. #pragsios8";
```

Let's try this out. Using the Simulator, visit the Settings application and switch languages by navigating through General →Language & Region→iPhone Language and then choosing Français. Go back to Xcode and run the app in the Simulator. When the app comes up, the buttons will now be in French. Tap "Envoyer Tweet" and the tweet composer will appear, pre-populated with French text, like in the next figure.

Components provided by UIKit should be automatically localized as well—the Cancel and Send buttons become "Annuler" and "Envoyer," respectively.

From here on out, we won't necessarily call attention to providing translated text for all our storyboard elements, but we will continue to use localizedStringForKey(), because it's an easy enough habit to adopt. And it's straightforward to localize a project when we're ready to do so: localize the storyboard, and add any strings from the application code to Localizable.strings.

Wrap-Up

In the first chapter, we had to take a lot on faith about Swift and the iOS frameworks in order to get started with the tools. In this chapter, we've dug deeply into the language and libraries, revealing how they work and why. We started by learning about the Swift programming language and how it handles variables, classes, and methods. Then we looked at the two most important frameworks in the iOS SDK, UIKit and Foundation, along with Swift's built-in support for strings, arrays and dictionaries, all of which we'll use heavily from here on out. Finally, we brought the power of UIKit and Foundation to bear on a cross-cutting concern, internationalization, using UIKit's localized storyboard loading ability to bring up a locale-appropriate GUI and Foundation's localized string support to let us call up i18n'ed strings at runtime.

It's great that our app works, but how can we be sure it will keep working? In the next chapter, we'll look at how Xcode supports automated testing, so we can programmatically put our code through its paces.

Internationalization broken in Xcode 6.1

This example worked great in Xcode 6.0, but if you don't see the French text in the app, it may be from a bug introduced in Xcode 6.1. From Apple's Xcode release notes:

> Localization and Keyboard settings, including 3rd party keyboards, are not correctly honored by Safari, Maps, and developer apps in the iOS 8.1 Simulator. [NSLocale currentLocale] returns en_US and only the English and Emoji keyboards are available. (18418630, 18512161)

In short, this means that the *only* localization supported by the 6.1 Simulator is U.S. English, which means that localizations for any other locale will be ignored. We hope Apple will restore i18n to Xcode quickly, but it's been a couple months since this broke, and it is still broken in Xcode 6.1.1, the current version as we write this. If it's still a problem by the time you read this, we wanted you to know what's going on.

CHAPTER 4

Testing Apps

We have come a long way in a short time. We've got an app that can send tweets and show our Twitter web page. We now have a stable app that isn't going to crash on us, right?

Well, how do we know that? We have run the app a few times, but have we really pushed the limits of the app? Have we really tried everything that anyone could possibly do to our app? How do we prove that our app is not going to crash before we ship it off to Apple?

And as we start adding features, what proves that those changes work, or that they're not going to have weird side effects that break the stuff that had been working?

The way we deal with this is to use *unit tests*.

Unit Tests

Unit tests are exactly what they sound like. Unit tests are small, self-contained segments of code that test very small, targeted units of functionality. Rather than check to see if the whole application works, we can break the functionality into pieces to pinpoint exactly where errors and bugs are occurring.

Unit tests are designed to either pass or fail. Is this feature working the way you want it to, yes or no?

The Parable of the Dinosaur
Here is an example of unit testing gone bad.

In *Jurassic Park* (the book, not the movie), Dr. Grant asks the scientists how they can be sure that the dinosaurs are not breeding.

The scientists assure Dr. Grant that every precaution has been taken. They engineered the dinosaurs to all be female. They had the island blanketed with motion detectors to count each and every dinosaur every five minutes. They created a computer algorithm to check the number and types of dinosaurs found by the motion sensors and the number only changed when a dinosaur died. There had been no escapes. They knew everything happening on the island and they were completely in control.

Dr. Grant asks them to change the parameters of the computer program to look for more dinosaurs than they were expecting to have. The scientists humor Dr. Grant and change the algorithm to search for more dinosaurs. Lo and behold! There are more dinosaurs. After running the program several more times with increasing numbers they eventually discovered there are over 50 extra dinosaurs on the island. Oops!

The program had been set up with the expectation that the number of dinosaurs could only go down, never up. Once the program reached the number of dinosaurs it was expecting to find, it stopped counting and the scientists never knew there was an issue. The program anticipated the outcome of dinosaurs dying or escaping the island, but never the possibility that life could find a way.

Reasons We Unit Test

Bugs, like life, do find a way. The first thing to remember in computer programming is that the computer is stupid. The computer only does what you tell it to do. It can't infer what you meant. It is important to verify that you are giving the right directions to the computer and the best way to do that is to test your apps.

One major reason to unit test an application is to eliminate crashes. The single biggest reason that most app submissions are rejected by Apple is because they crash. Even if Apple doesn't catch your crash, users have a talent for finding the one combination of things that will cause your app to crash. These are the users who tend to leave one-star reviews on the store, which is something we want to avoid if at all possible.

Unit tests also expose logic errors in our code. In the Jurassic Park example, the code being run had a logic error that prevented the scientists from discovering the problem until it was too late. We don't want that to happen to you.

Writing tests also helps you write your code. Have you ever started writing a piece of code only to figure out that one feature you spent days working on wasn't really going to work out in your project? By thinking critically about what specifically you want your application to do, you can avoid writing overly complicated and unnecessary code. They can inform the design of our code: what part of the code has what responsibilities, and how we recover if something unexpected happens.

Designing Good Unit Tests

As we will soon discover, writing a unit test is not difficult. Writing a good unit test is another story altogether.

There are generally three types of unit tests:

- *Debugging:* These tests are built around bugs to ensure that when you change the code these bugs do not reappear. Sometimes when we are coding we make changes to the code that affect bugs that we have already resolved. Since we do not want to see that bug again, we need to write tests to make sure that the bug has not reappeared when we change anything.

- *Assert Success:* We are testing to make sure you are getting a result you want.

- *Assert Failed:* We are testing to make sure you are not getting a result you don't want.

We might wonder why you would need a test to assert failure. Isn't the point of testing to make sure that features we created work properly?

Think back to the Jurassic Park example. The scientists created tests to make sure they were finding all of the dinosaurs they were looking for. They asserted success once the number of dinosaurs they were looking for was reached.

Sometimes it is as important to write a test that we expect to fail to make sure that we are not getting a result we don't want. Had the scientists also included a failure assertion test, they would have discovered that they were getting results that made no sense: there are more dinosaurs in the park than there are supposed to be.

Creating Tests in Xcode

Testing functionality was introduced in Xcode 5. Apple based many of its built-in functions on accepted and open source frameworks and has been working very hard to make testing a vital and useful tool in your developer utility belt.

We are going to go over several aspects of testing in Xcode in this chapter. Since you have spent a great deal of time creating and developing your PragmaticTweets app, let's run it through some tests to see how it works.

Let's direct our attention to the File Navigator, shown in the figure. There is a group titled PragmaticTweetsTests. Xcode has conveniently created this group and sample template class, PragmaticTweetsTests.swift, for our first two tests.

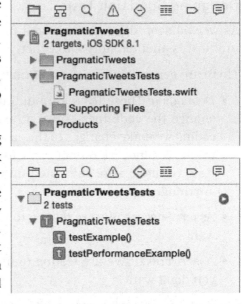

Before we move on to actually looking at the included test file, let's also look at the Test Navigator (⌘5). Rather than showing test files, this shows the tests themselves, and whether they passed or failed the last time they ran. This is another location in Xcode that makes it easy for you to get an overview of what tests you have and whether or not they are passing.

Click on the PragmaticTweetsTests.swift file in either the Project or the Test Navigator. There are four methods within this class: setUp(), tearDown(), testExample(), and testPerformanceExample(). Every test class that we create will have a setUp() and a tearDown() method. setUp() is used to instantiate any boilerplate code you need to set up your tests, and tearDown() is used to clear away any of the setup you needed to do for your tests. Whenever we find ourselves repeating code in multiple tests, it's a candidate for moving into setUp() and tearDown(). This is the principle of DRY: Don't Repeat Yourself.

Every test method we create will start with the word "test," just as the testExample() and testPerformanceExample() methods demonstrate. Additionally, every method in a test class will have no return type. We are doing this to make sure that our tests are found by the test compiler and that they get run. A test passes if it returns normally, and fails if it fails an assertion method before it returns.

For fun, let's just run the test included in the template. There are several ways to run your unit tests:

- Keyboard command: ⌘U
- Main Menu: Product→Test
- Clicking on the diamond icon next to either the test class or the specific test in Xcode

The first two ways of running tests will run all of your tests, whereas the third way will allow us to run selected tests. This is useful if you have one test that is failing and we want to focus on that one without having to run all the others.

Run the test in the manner of your choice.

Let's take a closer look at testExample().

Testing/PragmaticTweets-4-1/PragmaticTweetsTests/PragmaticTweetsTests.swift
```
func testExample() {
  // This is an example of a functional test case.
  XCTAssert(true, "Pass")
}
```

Just for fun, go in and change the first parameter in the method to false from true to see what happens.

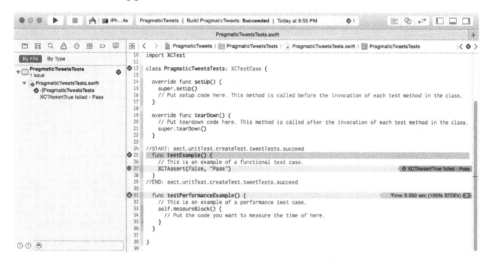

Oh no! The test stopped working! What happened?

Well, we just changed the conditions of the test. XCTAssert must pass a true condition through the test to pass. Since we programmed the condition to false, the test fails. Option-clicking on XCTAssert doesn't give us nice documentation like most Swift methods, but we'll cover the most useful XCTest assertions later in *OCUnit and XCTest,* on page 66.

At first blush this might seem like a useless exercise. Why would we want to write a test that always fails when you run it?

We run a test that is designed to fail so that we verify that the testing framework itself is working properly. If we simply create nothing but tests that are supposed to pass, we can't know for certain that the tests are passing because the code is correct. There could be an error and the tests would pass regardless. By prompting a failure, we now verify that when we write a test that passes that our code is, in fact, working correctly. As one wise person put it, "How do you know your smoke detector works if it never goes off?"

OCUnit and XCTest

At this point you may be wondering where we got XCTAssert() and the other testing methods from.

Prior to iOS 6, unit testing was done using an open source framework called OCUnit. As of iOS 8, OCUnit is deprecated, and as of Xcode 5, the preferred testing framework is XCTest. XCTest is built on top of OCUnit, so anyone already familiar with OCUnit should find translating from OCUnit to XCTest simple and straightforward.

As we saw earlier, the method in XCTest to assert a true condition is XCTAssert(). In OCUnit, the assertion call for a failing method was STAssert(). It is a convention that any method you have in OCUnit can be converted to XCTest() by changing the ST at the beginning to XCT. So, what was STFail() is now XCTFail().

There are about twenty different assertion methods in XCTest, but the ones we will be using most often are

- XCTAssert()

- XCTAssertFalse()

- XCTAssertEqual()

- XCTAssertNotNil()

- XCTAssertThrowsSpecificNamed()

There is a complete list of every assertion in the "Testing with Xcode" programming guide in your Xcode documentation, if you want to see how deep the rabbit hole goes.

Test-Driven Development

Now that we have a good handle on how to create a unit test, we are going to delve into the realm of test-driven development (TDD). TDD, in a nutshell, is figuring out the least number of objects you need to create in order to get your application to work the way you want it to. TDD utilizes the idea that you will write your tests first rather than after you have already completed your application.

If we write tests for the app now, we'll just be checking functionality we already know works. In TDD, we write the test first, fail for lack of any working functionality, then press ahead and actually create the functionality.

Why do we want to do all this extra work before we write a line of code? Let's jump in the Way Back machine and visit your elementary school English class. Remember back when you were learning how to write stories your teacher told you to write an outline. We write outlines for our stories so that we have an idea about how our story is going to go. We want to figure out the beginning, middle, and end so that we can write a tight and cohesive story that follows a path and has an ending that makes sense. If you go into a story not sure about what is going happen, you'll wind up writing lots and lots of plot where nothing happens.

Our time is valuable. It is in our best interest to figure out exactly which features are important and which ones are not before you spend a week trying to figure out and debug a feature that we figure out later doesn't fit in with what we want our app to do.

So let's add a new feature, TDD style. Let's say we want to have the web view load itself when the app starts up, without having to tap Show My Tweets. We'll start by writing a test to make sure the web view got populated, initially failing because it's not being populated, then go back and add the feature. When the test passes, our feature is good to go.

We'll start by creating a new test class. Before you create this class, click on the PragmaticTweetsTests group. Use the menu item File→New→File to bring up a template of file types. Choose iOS Source from the left pane, and on the right, select the Test Case Class template. Name our new class WebViewTests. Make sure this class is a subclass of XCTestCase and that it is attached to the PragmaticTweetsTests target before creating the class, as shown in the following figure:

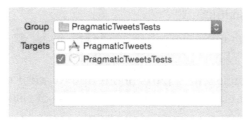

Creating Tests

The WebViewTests class contains the same setUp(), tearDown(), testExample(), and testPerformanceExample() methods we saw in the other class. We can delete the latter two methods, since they're just meant as examples and we will be writing our own.

> ## Xcode Targets
>
> In Xcode, it is possible to create multiple applications based on the same codebase. If we wanted to make, for example, a game where we had "full" and "lite" versions where the only difference is how many levels are included, we could create two targets that mostly differed by which level files were or weren't included.
>
> Since the primary application does not know what to do with a testing class, we don't want to include it in the codebase for that application; it would just take up space on the end user's device. Putting the test classes in their own target help us segregate them out.
>
> Targets can also be used for other sophisticated build tasks, like running arbitrary shell scripts prior to or after building our code. They can also be set as dependencies of one another. For example, the tests target is dependent on the main app target, so any time we run tests, any changes to the app's code will be built first.

Visibility Modifiers

What we need to do is to write a test method that can access the twitterWebView property of the ViewController class. This actually presents a little bit of a hassle that we haven't had to consider before. Swift considers all the classes in the PragmaticTweets target to be one *module*, and classes in a module can see each other's properties and methods by default. However, PragmaticTweetsTests is a different target and thus a different module, so it cannot see the methods or properties of our app's classes. We'll have to fix that before we can test anything.

Start in WebViewTests.swift by adding an import statement, just like the default ones that pull in the UIKit and XCTest frameworks. In our case, we need to import the PragmaticTweets module:

Testing/PragmaticTweets-4-1/PragmaticTweetsTests/WebViewTests.swift
```
import PragmaticTweets
```

Now, we have to decide which parts of our app we want to expose to outside callers, like the test classes. Swift has three levels of visibility, set by special keywords:

Access modifier	Visibility
public	Visible everywhere
internal	Visible within the same module
private	Visible only within the class itself

So, for the sake of testing, we need to make the ViewController public, as well as its twitterWebView property. So, edit the top of the ViewController.swift file as follows:

Testing/PragmaticTweets-4-1/PragmaticTweets/ViewController.swift

```
public class ViewController: UIViewController {

    @IBOutlet public weak var twitterWebView: UIWebView!
```

As a side effect, as soon as we declare the class public, Xcode will give us an error saying all the methods marked with the override keyword have to have the same accessibility as their class. So put a public modifier right before or after (the order doesn't matter) the override on the viewDidLoad() and didReceiveMemoryWarning() methods. Then build the project again to make sure everything's OK.

Writing Unit Tests

Now we're ready to write our test. What we want to do here is to look at the contents of the twitterWebView. To keep things simple, we won't go scraping for any specific text—Twitter could always change their web page—and instead we'll just make sure it isn't blank.

The test is really an outsider, so it doesn't have direct access to the views on the screen or the logic behind them. However, we can ask the UIApplication object for the first view controller it's showing (luckily, we only have one in our app) and drill down from there. So let's write a testAutomaticWebLoad() class like this:

Testing/PragmaticTweets-4-1/PragmaticTweetsTests/WebViewTests.swift

```
Line 1  func testAutomaticWebLoad() {
   -      if let viewController =
   -        UIApplication.sharedApplication().windows[0].rootViewController
   -          as? ViewController {
   5            let webViewContents =
   -            viewController.twitterWebView.stringByEvaluatingJavaScriptFromString(
   -              "document.documentElement.textContent")
   -            XCTAssertNotNil(webViewContents, "web view contents are nil")
   -            XCTAssertNotEqual(webViewContents!, "", "web view contents are empty")
  10      } else {
   -        XCTFail("couldn't get root view controller")
   -      }
   -  }
```

Lines 2–4 are how we get to the ViewController object. The shared UIApplication object has an array of UIWindows (one per screen, so usually just one unless we're doing AirPlay), and each window has a rootViewController. So we use an if let statement to try to get that object as our ViewController class.

If that works, then we want to inspect the contents of the twitterWebView. There's no method on UIWebView to just give us its contents, but there is the method stringByEvaluatingJavaScriptFromString(), which lets us run any JavaScript string on the contents of the UIWebView (seriously!). So on lines 5–7, we evaluate the DOM property document.documentElement.textContent to get the text of the web page.

We are now ready to test whether or not this got anything. On line 8, we use XCTAssertNotNil() to make sure the webViewContents is not nil. And then on line 9, we use XCTAssertNotEqual() to make sure it's not an empty string. If we survive both of those test methods, the method executes normally and we pass the test.

Notice that we will also fail the test on line 11 if we can't get the rootViewController as our ViewController class. If we start getting reckless with the storyboard, and change how the app even works, this test will let us know.

We now have a test and no feature. So what do we do? This is test-driven development, so we run the test of course! Click the diamond to the left of testAutomaticWebLoad() to run just this test.

And we fail. We knew we'd fail, because we know the feature isn't there. The error message from the XCTAssertNotEqual() assertion appears next to that line in the source to show us where the test failed. Our pass/fail results also appear in the test navigator, and in the Report Navigator (⌘8), which has a nice summary of all tests run, the simulator or device we ran them on, and which tests failed and where. See the following figure:

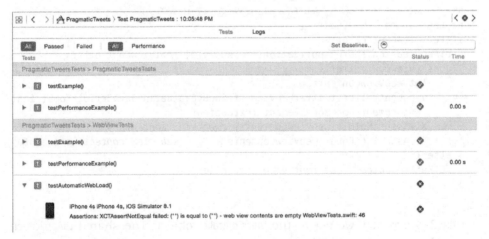

Finishing the Feature

We are following proper TDD practice: we built a test, we watched it fail. Now we can build the feature, and when the test stops failing, we know we have a working feature.

Go back to ViewController.swift. We want the web view to come up when the app does, so all the things we do in handleShowMyTweetsButtonTapped() should happen in viewDidLoad() too. A good way to do that is to have them both call the same thing. Copy everything currently in handleShowMyTweetsButtonTapped() into a new method called reloadTweets(), and then make handleShowMyTweetsButtonTapped() just be a call to reloadTweets(), like this:

Testing/PragmaticTweets-4-1/PragmaticTweets/ViewController.swift
```
@IBAction func handleShowMyTweetsButtonTapped(sender : UIButton) {
  reloadTweets()
}

func reloadTweets() {
  let url = NSURL (string:"http://www.twitter.com/pragprog")
  let urlRequest = NSURLRequest (URL: url!)
  twitterWebView.loadRequest(urlRequest)
}
```

Now, add the line self.reloadTweets() to the viewDidLoad() method. This will do our automatic web-page loading.

Testing/PragmaticTweets-4-1/PragmaticTweets/ViewController.swift
```
override public func viewDidLoad() {
  super.viewDidLoad()
  reloadTweets()
}
```

Run the app (not the test) with the Run button or ⌘R to make sure it works. The app comes up, the web page loads. We are good to go! Now run the test and we will have finished our first TDD development.

But wait, the test is still failing! What's wrong?

Testing Asynchronously

Take another look at running the app. After the app appears, it takes a second or two for the web page to load. But from the test's point of view, as soon as the app is up and running, it is ready to be tested. What's happening is that we are testing too soon. We need a way to wait before we run our test.

What we need is *asynchronous testing*, the ability to test things that happen at unpredictable times. If we wanted to test that 2 + 2 == 4, or that a string has a certain value, we could do that right away, because the value would be there right when we asked for it. But with the web view, we don't know when (or if) its contents will be set. Asynchronous testing lets us test these kinds of unpredictable events.

Prior to iOS 8, you could not run asynchronous unit tests using XCTest, so it was impossible to do testing on the network calls, background tasks, or anything else where the value to be tested was not immediately available.

iOS 8 introduces a new testing class called XCTestExpectation. XCTestExpectation creates expectation objects that describe events that you expect to happen at some point in the near future. We tell it how long it can wait, and then perform test assertions elsewhere—in parts of the code that run asynchronously—finally notifying the expectation when we're done. And if we fail to do so, that's considered a failure.

Joe asks:
What the Heck Is an "Expectation Object?"

There is a wonderful quote by the late John Pinette that goes: "Salad isn't food. Salad comes with the food. Salad is a promissory note that food will soon arrive."

Expectation objects are like salad. They are not the test; they are the promise to your program that something is going to happen a little later.

If you went to a restaurant and got a salad, then waited for an hour for food that never arrives, you would realize something is terribly wrong. You were set up to expect that another part of your meal was coming and if it never arrived, your meal would be a failure.

That, in a nutshell, is how asynchronous testing with expectation objects works.

The first thing we will do is to create an XCTestExpectation object in the WebViewTests class:

Testing/PragmaticTweets-4-2/PragmaticTweetsTests/WebViewTests.swift
```
var loadedWebViewExpectation : XCTestExpectation?
```

We'll need to create this expectation object when we start the test, and then when we know the web view has loaded, we can tell it that we're done by calling its fulfill() method.

We'll also need a way to know when the web view has loaded. Some general-purpose techniques for doing asynchronous tasks are discussed in *Do-It-Yourself Concurrency*, on page 120, but for now, UIWebView can help us out. It has a delegate object that gets notified when web pages load or fail to load, when the user submits a form, and other events. We can use that to know that the web page has loaded, and then pass or fail the test.

To be a delegate, we have to declare that our class implements the UIWebViewDelegate protocol, which declares the methods that the web view can send to the delegate.

Testing/PragmaticTweets-4-2/PragmaticTweetsTests/WebViewTests.swift
```
class WebViewTests: XCTestCase, UIWebViewDelegate {
```

We are going to rewrite the testAutomaticWebLoad() to do two things. The first is to become the web view's delegate. The second is to create our expectation object so that the tests know to wait a little while and don't just return a test fail. Here's how we do that.

Testing/PragmaticTweets-4-2/PragmaticTweetsTests/WebViewTests.swift
```
Line 1  func testAutomaticWebLoad() {
    -      if let viewController =
    -        UIApplication.sharedApplication().windows[0].rootViewController
    -          as? ViewController {
    5            viewController.twitterWebView.delegate = self
    -            loadedWebViewExpectation =
    -              expectationWithDescription("web view auto-load test")
    -            waitForExpectationsWithTimeout(5.0, handler: nil)
    -      } else {
    10       XCTFail("couldn't get root view controller")
    -      }
    -    }
```

On line 5, our test class becomes the web view's delegate, so it can be notified of events from the twitterWebView.

Next, lines 6–7 create the loadedWebViewExpectation and give it the name web view auto-load test. If we have many expectations, the name helps us figure out which one failed. We create as many expectations as we need—just one for now—and kick them off with a call to waitForExpectationsWithTimeout() on line 8. If we don't call fulfill() on the expectation within 5 seconds we'll get a timeout test failure.

Now that we have created our expectation object, we need to implement the UIWebViewDelegate protocol. If you look in the documentation, you will see this protocol has four methods that it can call: one to ask if it should start loading, one to report an error, and one each when the page starts and stops loading. We will implement two of these: if the web page load fails, our test fails, and if it succeeds, we use the JavaScript call to see if the web view has any contents. Let's start with the easier failure case.

Testing/PragmaticTweets-4-2/PragmaticTweetsTests/WebViewTests.swift
```
func webView(webView: UIWebView, didFailLoadWithError error: NSError) {
  XCTFail("web view load failed")
  loadedWebViewExpectation!.fulfill()
}
```

If the web page doesn't load, we use the always-fail XCTFail() to tell the test suite we failed. Notice that we also have to fulfill() the expectation even though we've already failed; if we don't do this, we'll get a timeout that looks like a second failure.

Now we can look at the possible success case.

```
Testing/PragmaticTweets-4-2/PragmaticTweetsTests/WebViewTests.swift
func webViewDidFinishLoad(webView: UIWebView) {
  if let webViewContents =
    webView.stringByEvaluatingJavaScriptFromString(
      "document.documentElement.textContent") {
        if webViewContents != "" {
          loadedWebViewExpectation!.fulfill()
        }
    }
}
```

This is like our first version in how it gets at the twitterWebView and runs the JavaScript to get the web document's contents as a string. The difference is that all we do this time is fulfill() the expectation if we ever get contents that aren't an empty string. (It turns out we don't want to fail on an empty string because this will be called with an empty string when the app starts up...by not failing then, we give the web view more tries to call us back with some contents.)

Whew! That was a lot of code. Congratulations, you are now capable of doing something that wasn't possible before. Now click the diamond next to testAutomaticWebLoad(). This time, we pass the test, as shown by the green icon in the Test Navigator in the following figure:

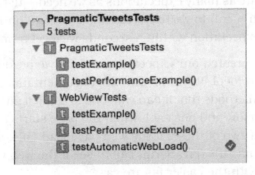

Testing Frameworks

Beyond Apple's built-in unit test framework, some further internal and external frameworks exist to make your testing life easier. We are just going to touch on these briefly so that you are aware of what they are and what options are available to you to make the best app that you can.

OCMock

At this point, you might be wondering how to test any functionality that requires a call to the network when we don't have Internet, or a request for which we always want the exact same response. For this kind of testing, you would need to employ a mock object. A mock object is like a Patronus from Harry Potter. Like Harry Potter's Patronus, a mock object is an imaginary object we conjure into existence as a stand-in for a real being.

A mock object is a file, object, or piece of code that we create to fill in for the actual data we will be using in our application. We create it to stand in for something we would rather not muck around with in our production code.

Unit tests are supposed to be small and test one unit of functionality. If we want to test our Tweet parser without a mock object, that would require us to make an API call. Since the API call would require us to make a network call, there would be many things that would need to happen correctly for our test to pass. It is possible the server could be down or that there is an error in our networking code. Without having it be clear exactly which of those possibilities is the root reason for a test failure, we would be unable to proceed with fixing the issue.

OCMock is a third-party framework created to solve the issues associated with testing networked apps or any apps that have dependencies on external parameters. OCMock is an Objective-C implementation of mock objects. OCMock provides the following functionality:

- Stub objects that return predetermined values for specific method invocations

- Dynamic mocks that can be used to verify interaction patterns

- Partial mocks to overwrite selected methods of existing objects

OCMock has a rich repository of documentation and a great deal of user support. If you are interested in utilizing their functionality in your app, go to http://www.ocmock.org and read through their tutorials to get your mock objects up and running.

UI Automation

UI Automation is different than the types of unit tests we have been doing so far. UI Automation, as its name implies, simulates user interactions with your app. The parts of the app that we have been testing have been its internal logic. We did not set up any tests to see what happens when a user presses a button or interacts with the app in any way. UI Automation is the ideal way to test your app without having an army of monkeys pressing every single button and interaction you have programmed into your app. (If you do have an army of monkeys, they could probably be better used sitting at typewriters trying to re-create the works of Charles Dickens.)

UI Automation is best used to do the following:

- Access its UI element hierarchy
- Add timing flexibility by having timeout periods
- Log and verify the information returned by Instruments
- Handle alerts properly
- Handle changes in device orientation gracefully
- Handle multitasking

To use UI Automation you need to use Instruments, one of the tools that comes with Xcode (available through the Product→Profile menu item, ⌘I).

The fact that UI Automation is not integrated into Xcode's unit testing targets or XCTest illustrates the big pitfall of doing test-first development on iOS: many of the things we want to expose to unit tests are user interactions that are difficult to turn into automated tests. We were only able to do TDD in this chapter because it was kicked off by the application's startup and not by a user interaction. It's because of this that few iOS developers we know do true TDD, and those who do usually limit it to the models and logic of their apps, not the user interface.

For now, UI Automation is the best option we have for testing user interactions, but its features are beyond the scope of this chapter. If you are interested in utilizing UI Automation in your app, please check out the excellent book by Jonathan Penn.[1]

---

1. *Test iOS Apps with UI Automation: Bug Hunting Made Easy*, https://pragprog.com/book/jptios.

Wrap-Up

In this chapter we have gone on a nice tour of unit testing and gotten a taste for the fundamentals of test-driven development. We walked through the TDD process from idea to implementation.

We have explored Apple's built-in unit testing suite XCTest. We also touched on some of the most common tools in your toolbox for testing your application. You now have the tools to go forth into the world and test your apps so that you can be sure your users will not have to deal with a crash or erroneous behavior.

Now that we know how to write tests to ensure our features work as designed, we're going to start reworking those features. In the next chapter, we'll begin moving to the table view style of presentation that is so common on iOS.

CHAPTER 5

Presenting Data in Table Views

For organizing and presenting many of the kinds of data we see in iPhone and iPad apps, it's hard to beat a table view. Thanks to the intuitive flick-scrolling provided by iOS, it's comfortable and convenient to whip through lists of items to find just the thing we need, with each item visually presented in whatever way makes sense for the app. In many apps, the table view is the bedrock of the app's presentation and organization.

In this chapter, we're going start turning our Twitter application into one that's based around a table view. However, it's going to take us a few chapters to completely move away from the web view. First, we'll put some fake data into a table view, and then in the following chapters we'll get real data from the Twitter API and load it into the table view.

Tables on iOS

Coming from the desktop, one might expect a UITableView to look something like a spreadsheet, with rows and columns presented in a two-dimensional grid. Instead, the table view is a vertically scrolling list of items, optionally split into sections.

The table view is essential for many of the apps that ship with the iPhone, as well as popular third-party apps. In Mail, tables are used for the list of accounts, the mailboxes within each account, and the contents of each mailbox. The Reminders app is little more than a table view with some editing features, as are the alarms in the Clock app. The Music app shows lists of artists or albums, and within them lists of songs. Even the Settings app is built around a table, albeit one of a different style than is used in most apps (more on that later).

And while our Twitter app currently displays a web view of all the tweets we've parsed, pretty much every Twitter app out there (including the official Twitter app, as well as *Twitterrific*, *Tweetbot*, and *Echofon*) uses a table view to present tweets.

So our task now is to switch from the web view to a table view–based presentation of the tweets. We'll build this up slowly, as our understanding of tables and what they can do for us develops.

Table Classes

To add a table to an iOS app, we use an instance of UITableView. This is a UIScrollView subclass, itself a subclass of UIView, so it can either be a full-screen view unto itself or embedded as the child of another view. It cannot, however, have arbitrary subviews added to it, as it uses its subviews to present the individual cells within the table view.

The table has two properties that are crucial for it to actually do anything. The most important is the dataSource, which is an object that implements the UITableViewDataSource protocol. This protocol defines methods that tell the table how many sections it has (and optionally what their titles are) and how many rows are in a given section, and provides a cell view for a given section-row pair. The data source also has editing methods that allow for the addition, deletion, or reordering of table contents. There's also a delegate, an object implementing the UITableViewDelegate protocol, which provides method definitions for handling selection of rows and other user-interface events.

These roles are performed not by the table itself—whose only responsibility is presenting the data and tracking user gestures like scrolling and selection—but by some other object, often a view controller. Typically, there are two approaches to wiring up a table to its contents:

- Have a UIViewController implement the UITableViewDataSource and UITableViewDelegate protocols.

- Use a UITableViewController, a subclass of the UIViewController that is also defined as implementing the UITableViewDataSource and UITableViewDelegate protocols

It's helpful to use the second approach when the *only* view presented by the controller is a table, as this gives us some nice additional functionality like built-in pull-to-refresh, or scrolling to the top when the status bar is tapped. But if the table is just a subview, and the main view has other subviews like buttons or a heads-up view, then we need to use the first approach instead.

Model-View-Controller

The careful apportioning of responsibilities between the view class and the controller comes from UIKit's use of the *model-view-controller* design pattern, or MVC. The idea of this design is to split out three distinct responsibilities of our UI:

- *Model*—the data to be presented, such as the array of tweets

- *View*—the user-interface object, like a text view or a table

- *Controller*—the logic that connects the model and the view, such as how to fill in the rows of the table, and what to do when a row is tapped

This pattern explains why the class we've been doing most of our work in is a "view controller"; as a controller, it provides the logic that populates an onscreen view, and updates its state in reaction to user interface events. Notice that it is not necessary for each member of the design to be have its own class: the view is an object we created in the storyboard, and the model can be a simple object like an array. At this point in our app's evolution, only the controller currently requires a custom class.

Creating and Connecting Tables

We're going to need to make some major changes to our user interface to switch to a table-driven approach. In fact, we're going to blow away our original view entirely. We'll get all our functionality back eventually, and we'll be in a better position to build out deeper and more interesting features. Eventually, we'll have an app that looks and feels like a real Twitter client.

We'll start by preparing our view controller to supply the table data. We can do this by either declaring that we implement UITableViewDataSource, or by becoming a subclass of UITableViewController. Since the table will be the only thing in this view, let's do the latter. In ViewController.swift, rewrite the declaration like this:

Tables/PragmaticTweets-5-1/PragmaticTweets/ViewController.swift
```
public class ViewController: UITableViewController {
```

Adding a Table View to the Storyboard

Now switch to Main.storyboard and look through the Object area at the bottom right for the Table View Controller object, shown in the figure. Drag one into the storyboard, anywhere where it won't collide with the existing view controller. This adds a new Table View Controller Scene to the list of scenes in the storyboard.

Select the view controller from the previously existing scene and press ⌫ to delete the old scene. This leaves the storyboard with no entry point. Select the Table View Controller, bring up its Attributes Inspector (⌥⌘4), and select the Is Initial View Controller checkbox. The view gets an arrow on its left side, showing our app once again has a place to start. The view itself shows a status bar that says Prototype Cells above a Table View that has a single Table View Cell as a subview, as seen in the following figure:

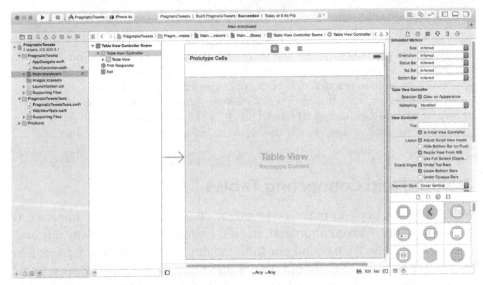

We can run this app...but it shows an empty table! That's because the table is not yet connected to a data source that can provide it with cells or even a count of how many sections and rows there are. Let's get to work on that.

Providing a Temporary Table Data Source

As it is, the table in the storyboard doesn't know to use our class; it expects to create a generic UITableViewController for the table. We want it to use our View-Controller instead. So, while still in Main.storyboard, choose the Table View Controller and visit its Identity Inspector in the right-side pane (⌥⌘3). In the Custom Class section, for the Class, enter ViewController. This should autocomplete, since we declared that our ViewController class is a valid UITableViewController, although we've done nothing to implement that behavior yet.

While here, control-click on the table view, or visit its Connections Inspector (⌥⌘6), and notice that table view's connections to the dataSource and delegate properties are already wired up, connected to the view controller.

As a warm-up, let's provide a trivial implementation of the data source methods, just to ensure the new storyboard and its connections are good to go. To do this, our data source needs to provide a minimum of three things: the number of sections, the number of rows in a given section, and a cell for a given section and row. In ViewController.swift, provide the following trivial implementations of the UITableViewDataSource methods numberOfSectionsInTableView(), tableView(numberOfRowsInSection:), and tableView(cellForRowAtIndexPath:), as well as the optional tableView(titleForHeaderInSection:), which will let us see the section breaks.

Tables/PragmaticTweets-5-1/PragmaticTweets/ViewController.swift

```swift
override public func numberOfSectionsInTableView(tableView: UITableView)
    -> Int {
  return 5
}


override public func tableView(_tableView: UITableView,
  titleForHeaderInSection section: Int) -> String? {
    return "Section \(section)"
}


override public func tableView(_tableView: UITableView,
numberOfRowsInSection section: Int) -> Int {
    return section + 1
}


override public func tableView (_tableView: UITableView,
  cellForRowAtIndexPath indexPath: NSIndexPath) -> UITableViewCell {
    let cell = UITableViewCell(style: UITableViewCellStyle.Default,
      reuseIdentifier: nil)
  cell.textLabel!.text = "Row \(indexPath.row)"
  return cell
}
```

Notice that in our quick-and-dirty table code, three of our methods are called tableView(). The reason these methods don't get confused with one another is because they're differentiated by their named parameters: one takes titleForHeaderInSection, another takes cellForRowAtIndexPath, and so on.

By convention, all these methods take the table view in question as their first argument, so if we had multiple tables, a method would be able to figure out which table it's working with.

But as for why it has to be the *first* parameter, that's more of a legacy of Objective-C, where it was somewhat more natural to incorporate the name of your first parameter into the method name, and differentiate with the rest of the parameters. Swift came later, so we're stuck with the old naming schemes, at least for now.

In this book, when we encounter cases where the method name by itself isn't unique, we'll include the parameters for clarity. That way, we'll call out the difference between tableView(numberOfRowsInSection:) and tableView(cellForRowAtIndexPath:), but we won't feel the need to write viewWillAppear(animated:) when there's only one method that starts like that, so it can be written as just viewWillAppear().

Anyway, while we're in the ViewController.swift file, let's delete the line that declares the twitterWebView that no longer exists, and all of the handleShowMyTweetsButtonTapped() method that populated it. We won't need those anymore. Also, delete the contents of reloadTweets(), but leave the method definition; we'll rebuild that one shortly. Finally, with no twitterWebView, there's no need for the WebViewTests test class, so delete that entire file.

In this implementation, we are telling the table that there are five sections, that each section has one more row than the section index (that is to say, there's one row in section 0, two rows in section 1, etc.), and that any time a new cell is needed, it should create a new UITableViewCell, get its textLabel property (a UILabel), and set the text property of the label to a string that shows the row number. When run, the table will look like the image.

You may be wondering why the status bar overlaps the table. This is one of the more controversial aspects of the iOS 7 visual design—view controllers default into a full-screen mode. In fact, the property wantsFullScreenLayout was deprecated in iOS 7, and since then view controllers are assumed to *always* fill the screen with their views, even the space under the status bar.

It looks horrible at first, but the idea is that once we start scrolling and see content go under the status bar, the transparency of the status bar gives us a visual cue about information that is about to come fully into view. In later chapters, we'll add a navigation bar at the top and then it'll look and feel a lot better.

Notice that tableView(cellForRowAtIndexPath:) passes in an NSIndexPath. This is a class originally intended for representing paths in tree structures, things like "the third child of the second child of the root node." In iOS, it is pressed into service representing table entries. NSIndexPath is extended to add the properties section and row (which are implemented as just the first and second entries in the path), and the combination of section and row can uniquely identify any cell in UITableView.

Now we have a table and a way to get data into it. What we need to do next is to provide a nontrivial implementation of the data source, one that actually shows some tweets.

Filling In the Table

Let's think about how we're going to go from this to a table of real tweets. Since the table can demand the contents of any row at any time, we'll want to have a data structure representing all the tweets that we want to show in the table. This doesn't have to be anything fancy; in fact, an array will do just fine.

But an array of what? Well, one approach would be to just create a class including the parts of a tweet we care about—its text, the screen name of the person who sent it, etc.—and then have an array of those objects. We haven't had to create a new class of our own yet, so let's do that.

Creating a **ParsedTweet** Class

To create a new class in our project, we use File→New File (⌘N), which causes a sheet to slide out showing templates for new files, shown in the following figure. From the iOS group on the left, choose Source, and then from the icons on the right, choose the Cocoa Touch Class template and click Next.

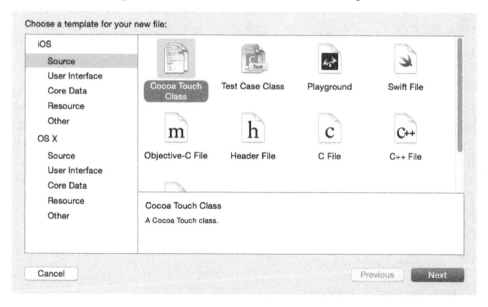

This takes us to the second page of the sheet, in which we set the class name, parent class, and language. For the class name, use ParsedTweet and for Subclass of, use NSObject. Make sure the language is Swift. Click Next to show a file dialog that indicates where to save the file, and which *targets* will build the class. The default will build it only for the PragmaticTweets app and not the PragmaticTweetsTests unit tests. This is what we want, so click Create to create a ParsedTweet.swift file in our project.

This class doesn't need to really *do* anything; it just needs to hold on to some values, so it'll be convenient to use in an array. For now, let's figure we'll want the tweet text, the username, a created-at string, and a URL for the user's avatar. So we define public properties for those, in ParsedTweet.swift.

Tables/PragmaticTweets-5-1/PragmaticTweets/ParsedTweet.swift

```
var tweetText : String?
var userName : String?
var createdAt: String?
var userAvatarURL : NSURL?
```

We'll make all of these optionals, since we are in no position to populate them when an instance of the class is instantiated. The alternative would be to assign a value like an empty string to one of these properties, but it's more expressive to use the absence of a value to say "this hasn't been set yet," even if it might be a bit more work later to defend against the optional and make sure the property isn't nil.

We can now create ParsedTweet instances in other classes by simply writing code like this:

```
let myTweet = ParsedTweet()
myTweet.userName = "@pragprog"
myTweet.tweetText = "Check out our new iOS book!"
```

But it seems a little burdensome to have to create the object and then set all its properties one by one. Fortunately, Swift lets us define initializer methods that can set some or all of an object's properties at initialization time. We do this by writing an init() method, specifying which arguments we want to take. After the properties in ParsedTweet.swift, add the following initialization method:

Tables/PragmaticTweets-5-1/PragmaticTweets/ParsedTweet.swift

```
init (tweetText: String?,
     userName: String?,
     createdAt: String?,
     userAvatarURL : NSURL?) {
  super.init()
  self.tweetText = tweetText;
  self.userName = userName;
  self.createdAt = createdAt;
  self.userAvatarURL = userAvatarURL;
}
```

Notice that in an initializer, we actually *do* have to use self, since the initializer's parameters have the same name as the corresponding properties. We could get around this by using different names, but that would make it confusing for callers to use two different names for the same property. It's easier for everyone if we just disambiguate with self here.

This initializer starts by calling its superclass's initializer, and then takes a value for every property in the class and simply assigns the property. Because it handles every property, we call it a *designated initializer*. We could also create initializers that only set some of the properties; these are called *convenience initializers*, and are declared in the form convenience init (...). There's a key difference in implementation: convenience initializers should call the designated initializer of their own class (typically passing in nil for properties being left unset), whereas designated initializers should call one of the *superclass's* initializers, as we do here with super.init().

Still, we might want to populate a ParsedTweet one property at a time, and by adding the initializer that takes four arguments, we lose the ability to call the no-argument version. Let's add that back in:

Tables/PragmaticTweets-5-1/PragmaticTweets/ParsedTweet.swift
```
override init () {
  super.init()
}
```

Notice that since there's a no-argument init() in the superclass (NSObject), we have to use the override modifier to tell Swift that we know we're overriding that initializer.

Building a Table Model of ParsedTweets

Until we're ready to get real tweets from the Twitter API, we'll have to make do with some *mock data*, predictable stand-in values that will let us figure out tables and put off dealing with network stuff. We can create an array of ParsedTweet objects, and just come up with our own values for the tweetText, userName, and createdAt strings.

Actually, let's start with the URL. Twitter's new user "egg" icon lives at a set of URLs like https://abs.twimg.com/sticky/default_profile_images/default_profile_0_200x200.png, where the 0 after profile_ can be any number between 0 and 6 inclusive, each showing a different color, and the 200x200 has several replacements for different sizes. For now, we'll just use this one image over and over. At the top of View-Controller.swift, after the imports, add the following constant:

Tables/PragmaticTweets-5-1/PragmaticTweets/ViewController.swift

```
let defaultAvatarURL = NSURL(string:
  "https://abs.twimg.com/sticky/default_profile_images/" +
  "default_profile_6_200x200.png")
```

We had to split the URL string into two lines for the book's formatting; feel free to write it all on one line. We would if we could.

Now, we can create an array of ParsedTweet objects to serve as our data model. After the curly brace that begins ViewController's class declaration, declare an array of ParsedTweets, and then inside square braces, use the designated initializer to create as many tweet objects as you like (we'll just use three to save space). The beginning of the class should look like this:

Tables/PragmaticTweets-5-1/PragmaticTweets/ViewController.swift

```
public class ViewController: UITableViewController {

  var parsedTweets : Array <ParsedTweet> = [
    ParsedTweet(tweetText:"iOS 8 SDK Development now in print. " +
      "Swift programming FTW!",
      userName:"@pragprog",
      createdAt:"2014-08-20 16:44:30 EDT",
      userAvatarURL: defaultAvatarURL),

    ParsedTweet(tweetText:"Math is cool",
      userName:"@redqueencoder",
      createdAt:"2014-08-16 16:44:30 EDT",
      userAvatarURL: defaultAvatarURL),

    ParsedTweet(tweetText:"Anime is cool",
      userName:"@invalidname",
      createdAt:"2014-07-31 16:44:30 EDT",
      userAvatarURL: defaultAvatarURL)
    ]
```

For clarity, we defined parsedTweets as Array<ParsedTweet> here, but creating arrays of a given type is such a common task, Swift offers a more compact alternative: [ParsedTweet]. They mean the same thing; use whichever you like.

Now that we have an array that can serve as our data source, we can rewrite the UITableViewDataSource methods to use the ParsedTweets in this array to calculate the number of rows and the contents of each. Rewrite those methods as follows:

Tables/PragmaticTweets-5-1/PragmaticTweets/ViewController.swift

```
Line 1  override public func numberOfSectionsInTableView (tableView: UITableView)
   -       -> Int {
   -       return 1
   -     }
```

```
5  override public func tableView(_tableView: UITableView,
     numberOfRowsInSection section: Int) -> Int {
       return parsedTweets.count
   }
10
   override public func tableView (_tableView: UITableView,
     cellForRowAtIndexPath indexPath: NSIndexPath) -> UITableViewCell {
       let cell = UITableViewCell(style: UITableViewCellStyle.Default,
         reuseIdentifier: nil)
15     let parsedTweet = parsedTweets[indexPath.row]
       cell.textLabel?.text = parsedTweet.tweetText
       return cell
   }
```

Also, go ahead and delete the titleForHeaderInSection() method; we'll only have a single section from here on, so the title is superfluous.

In this new version, we have a single section (and therefore can eliminate the entire tableView(titleForHeaderInSection:) method), and the number of rows in this section is just the size of the parsedTweets array. Then we use the indexPath's row property to figure out which ParsedTweet to fetch from our parsedTweets array, and put its tweetText into the cell's text label.

There's another thing we've done differently here. Look at how we access the textLabel on line 16, using a ? operator instead of the ! to force-unwrap. What we're doing here is called *optional chaining*. The idea is that we can connect any number of properties or method calls that may return nil, using the ? operator to unwrap them, and if any of them actually are nil, the whole expression evaluates to nil, instead of crashing on a failed force-unwrap like the ! would do. Evaluating to nil is safe to do on the left side of an assignment, because it just becomes the meaningless expression nil = parsedTweet.tweetText.

Chaining optionals isn't always practical, but sometimes it's a nice alternative to deeply nested if lets or dangerous force-unwraps.

Anyway, run the app now and behold the tweets:

Look at that...we've got our tweets in a table view! And they scroll, so if we coded 200 in our mock data array, we could just flick through them.

Of course, the one line of text isn't big enough for most tweets. So now that we've got our data where it needs to be, let's start improving the table's appearance.

Reloading Table Contents

One thing that might not be immediately evident but that might come back to bite us later: the only reason we can see any table contents is that the app's startup will do a one-time presentation of the first view's contents. Later on, we'll be updating and changing the table's contents. So how do we refresh its contents?

We can add ParsedTweet objects to the parsedTweets array, or delete some of its contents, but the array doesn't have a way to tell the table that its contents have changed, so the table won't do anything if we just edit the array. As a controller, it's our job to keep the view and model in sync. UITableView offers methods to notify the table of distinct edits, like insertRowsAtIndexPaths() or removeRowsAtIndexPaths(). Sometimes, it's simpler to just do a full-on reload of the table, with reloadData(). So let's write a method to do that for us:

Tables/PragmaticTweets-5-1/PragmaticTweets/ViewController.swift
```
func reloadTweets() {
  tableView.reloadData()
}
```

Later on, this view won't be the first thing we see in the app, so let's make sure we reload the table automatically any time it appears, which we can do by editing the viewDidLoad() method to call reloadTweets():

Tables/PragmaticTweets-5-1/PragmaticTweets/ViewController.swift
```
override public func viewDidLoad() {
  super.viewDidLoad()
  reloadTweets()
}
```

Customizing Table Appearance

While it's great to have the Twitter data in our table cells, only having access to a single, one-line text label makes it impossible to show the various fields of the ParsedTweet; at this point, we don't even know who sent which tweet! We need to change what these table cells look like, to provide more room to show our data.

Table Cell Styles

When we create the UITableViewCell in tableView(cellForRowAtIndexPath:), our init method takes a style argument. As it turns out, this can allay our problems somewhat.

The available styles are collected in an *enumeration*, which declares both a type and a closed set of possible values for that type. Four cell styles are defined in the UITableViewCellStyle enumeration, of which we've been using UITableViewCellStyle.Default. Fortunately for our fingers, we don't have to write the whole type when we refer to an enumeration's value; we can just write the value itself, like .Default.

The cell class itself defines certain subviews—textLabel, detailTextLabel, imageView, and accessoryView—and this style determines if and where those subviews are laid out. The figure shows a four-row table with the row number in the textLabel, and the name of the style in the detailTextLabel. Notice that for the .Default style in row 0, the detailTextLabel is not shown at all.

This figure doesn't show the cell's other possible subviews; if an imageView is set, it appears on the left side of the cell, and an accessoryView (usually a Show Details button) appears on the right. Clearly, if all of those subviews are present, the cell is going to get pretty crowded, and that's something we'll have to deal with soon.

For now, we'll try out the two-line presentation of the UITableViewCellStyle.Subtitle, and along the way we're going to fix a problem we've created for ourselves.

Grouped Tables

Another appearance option is to use *grouped tables*, which is just an attribute we can set on the table view in the storyboard. This sets the table's style to UITableViewStyleGrouped, which in turn makes the table look like the following figure. The major differences with a grouped table are that header and footer views do not "stick" to the top or bottom of the screen when scrolling, and on iOS 6 and earlier, the cells have rounded edges that make them look more like buttons. The grouped table is what the Settings app uses, and users will be familiar with its appearance from that.

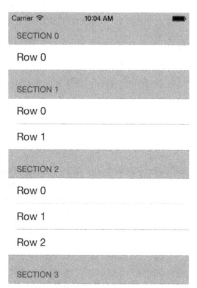

Cell Reuse

Right now, we create a new UITableViewCell in every call to tableView(cellForRowAtIn-dexPath:). If we flick through a really long table, that might mean we create a cell that will only appear for an instant before it goes off the screen and is no longer needed. As it turns out, creating views is fairly expensive, so if we can avoid doing that frequently, it will make our app faster and more responsive.

The UITableView class is actually built to cache and reuse cells. It provides a method, dequeueReusableCellWithIdentifier(), that takes a string identifying a cell to be reused. The idea is that we can create a cell in the storyboard as a sort of template and identify it with a known string. In code, we'll ask for a cell by this name. If the table has already created a cell with this name *and* it isn't currently being shown—meaning it has scrolled off the top or bottom of the screen—the table will give us the old cell and allow us to reuse it. Otherwise, it will create a new cell from the *prototype* in the storyboard. This way, we'll create only as many cells as we need to show on the screen at one time, and our scrolling performance will be much improved.

Go to Main.storyboard and select the table view. Notice that the table header is Prototype Cells, and the table has a single Table View Cell as a child. The table's Attributes Inspector also has a field for Prototype Cells, currently set to 1. We only need the one prototype cell, because new cells will be minted from this prototype—if we had different layouts for different rows (like advertising cells that were different from tweet cells), we could add more prototypes.

Select the Table View Cell, visit its Attributes Inspector (⌥⌘4), and set its style to Subtitle. Then, for the Identifier, we need a string value that we can use to fetch this cell from our code. Let's use UserAndTweetCell.

Now we need to fetch this cell in code and customize it. We do this in table-View(cellForRowAtIndexPath:), so go back to ViewController.swift and rewrite the method as follows:

```
Tables/PragmaticTweets-5-2/PragmaticTweets/ViewController.swift
override public func tableView (_tableView: UITableView,
  cellForRowAtIndexPath indexPath: NSIndexPath) -> UITableViewCell {
    let cell =
      tableView.dequeueReusableCellWithIdentifier("UserAndTweetCell")
      as UITableViewCell
    let parsedTweet = parsedTweets[indexPath.row]
    cell.textLabel?.text = parsedTweet.userName
    cell.detailTextLabel?.text = parsedTweet.tweetText
    return cell
}
```

The changes we make here are to get the cell via dequeueReusableCellWithIdentifier:() (on lines 3–5), and then to use two fields from the parsedTweet: its userName can go in the textLabel, and the tweetText can go in the detailTextLabel. The result is a lot more useful.

The result of dequeuing prototype cells instead of creating new cells every time doesn't have an immediate visual impact, although there is a subtle performance improvement when scrolling a few hundred cells on the simulator, and this effect is much more pronounced when running on a genuine iOS device.

Still, while it's nice to have both the tweet and its author, nearly all the tweets are still being truncated. Clearly we need a multiline label for those. How are we going to do that? It doesn't look like it's going to fit in the subtitle cell, and even if it does, we still would like to have a third label to show the tweet's timestamp.

Fortunately, we're not limited to the provided cell styles. We can create our own prototype cells with whatever views suit us—even tappable elements like buttons—and then use them in our table.

Custom Table Cells

To create a custom table cell, it usually makes sense to create a subclass of UITableViewCell and give it public properties for the fields that we'll need to update from tableView(cellForRowAtIndexPath:). So, in the File Navigator, select the Pragmatic Tweets group, go to File→New→File, and choose the Cocoa Touch Class template. In the next pane of the assistant, name the class ParsedTweetCell, and set the Subclass of: to UITableViewCell. We don't need to do anything with the code yet, but it will help us in the Storyboard to have this class already created.

Back in Main.storyboard, select the table view. We could edit the existing prototype cell, but just to prove that we can juggle multiple prototypes, let's create our custom cell as a second prototype. In the Attributes Inspector, tap the up button on the Prototype Cells field so the table has two prototypes. A second prototype is created, a copy of the first. Select the second and, in the Attributes Inspector (⌥⌘4), change its style to Custom and its identifier to CustomTweet-Cell, as shown in the following figure. Then, in the Identity Inspector (⌥⌘3), change its class to the ParsedTweetCell class that we just created; the Module should default to Current - PragmaticTweets.

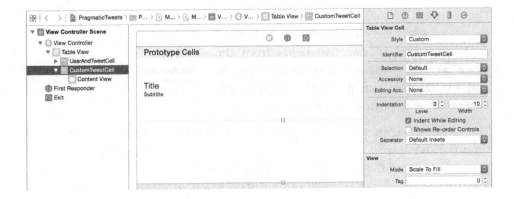

Switch to the Size Inspector (⌥⌘5) and notice that the first field is Row Height, currently shown with the placeholder text Default because the Custom checkbox is not checked. If we want to pack a bunch of fields in here, it's pretty clear that the default row height is not going to cut it for us, so click Custom and enter a height of 125. That should give us enough room.

Now we get to lay out a UI inside the cell pretty much the same way we built the app's original view with buttons and a web view in earlier chapters. Within the cell, we can add labels, image views, whatever we like...provided that we wrangle all the autolayout constraints to put them in their place (there had to be a catch, right?). We're going to add four subviews: labels for the username, tweet text, and created-at string, plus an image view for the user's picture. Feel free to play around; for the sample code, we've used the following views:

- An image view with height and width constraints to lock its size at 75×75 points, plus top and leading constraints of 0 points each from the margin. The image view will initially want to be much larger than this when you drop it, but once you set the constraints, using Update Frames in the autolayout Resolve Menu (⌥⌘=) will clean it up.

- A label for the username, with the font set to System - Bold, leading constraint of 8 points from the image view, 0 point top, and trailing space constraints from the margins.

- A label for the tweet text, Lines set to 3, with the font set to System 14-point, leading and top constraints of 8 points, and trailing constraint of 0 points from the margin.

- A label for the created-at string, with the font set to Caption 1, center-aligned text, a Horizontal Center in Container constraint, and a bottom constraint of 0 points to the margin.

Once we've created the layout (shown in the following figure), we're going to connect this prototype cell to the custom class we created earlier. Since we used the Identity Inspector to assign the cell to our ParsedTweetCell, the Assistant Editor will let us connect these subviews to new IBOutlet properties in that class. With the cell selected in the storyboard, switch to Assistant Editor mode via the rings icon or ⌥⌘↵ (it may help to hide the utility pane too). Ideally, Assistant Editor should bring up ParsedTweetCell.swift on the right, but sometimes it chooses ViewController.swift; in that case, use the jump bar at the top of the pane to load ParsedTweetCell.swift into the right side.

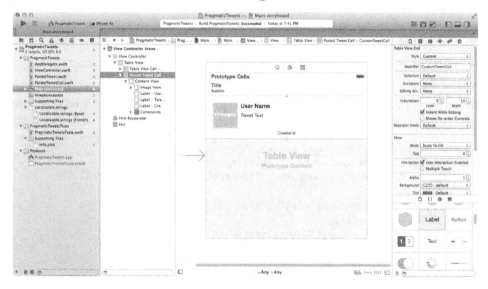

Control-drag from each of the subviews over to the ParsedTweetCell.swift code, just under the class declaration and before the first method. After releasing the drag, give each property an appropriate name. With all the connections established, the properties should look like this:

Tables/PragmaticTweets-5-3/PragmaticTweets/ParsedTweetCell.swift

```
@IBOutlet weak var avatarImageView: UIImageView!
@IBOutlet weak var userNameLabel: UILabel!
@IBOutlet weak var tweetTextLabel: UILabel!
@IBOutlet weak var createdAtLabel: UILabel!
```

Problems when connecting custom cell subviews

 When creating connections from subviews in the custom cell, be sure that the subview (the label, image view, etc.) is selected, and not the Content View that is a superview to all of them. If the pop-up that appears at the end of the drag wants to define the class

Problems when connecting custom cell subviews

of the outlet as UIView rather than UILabel or UIImageView or what have you, chances are the connection is being made to the Content View instead of the specific subview we're trying to connect. One way to be sure is to start the drag from the subview's item in the scene's tree list, rather than from the storyboard view itself.

There's one more thing we need to do in the storyboard: the cells know they're 125 points tall, but the table doesn't, and will continue to assume the default row height of 44. Return to the Standard Editor mode, select the table, bring up its Size Inspector (⌥⌘5), and set Row Height to 125. We could also provide this height in code, which would in turn also make it possible for rows to be of different heights, but this easy approach is fine for now.

Now it's time to start populating these custom cells. Back in ViewController, we again need to update our method that dequeues and populates cells. Rewrite tableView(cellForRowAtIndexPath:) as follows:

```
Tables/PragmaticTweets-5-3/PragmaticTweets/ViewController.swift
Line 1  override public func tableView (_tableView: UITableView,
   -      cellForRowAtIndexPath indexPath: NSIndexPath) -> UITableViewCell {
   -      let cell =
   -      tableView.dequeueReusableCellWithIdentifier("CustomTweetCell")
   5        as ParsedTweetCell
   -      let parsedTweet = parsedTweets[indexPath.row]
   -      cell.userNameLabel.text = parsedTweet.userName
   -      cell.tweetTextLabel.text = parsedTweet.tweetText
   -      cell.createdAtLabel.text = parsedTweet.createdAt
   10     if parsedTweet.userAvatarURL != nil {
   -        if let imageData = NSData (contentsOfURL: parsedTweet.userAvatarURL!) {
   -          cell.avatarImageView.image = UIImage (data: imageData)
   -        }
   -      }
   15     return cell
   -   }
```

The first big change here is on lines 3–5, where we dequeue the cell with the identifier string CustomTweetCell and since we know it's our custom cell, we can fetch it as the ParsedTweetCell class. Then, on lines 7–9, we set the values of the cell's properties that we connected.

Then we have the avatar image. The UIImageView has an image property we want to populate, of type UIImage. Unfortunately, UIImage can't be created directly from the contents of a URL. However, it will accept an NSData object containing image data, and we can initialize that with an NSURL, so we can chain those together. NSURL's contentsOfURL: requires a non-optional parameter, so we check the userAvatarURL against nil on line 10, make an NSData from it on line 11, and then load the image into the cell's image view on line 12.

While we're here, take another look at line 11, and how we test the assignment of imageData against nil. This is because the initializer NSData(contentsOfURL:) might not give us an NSData at all.

This is an example of a *failable initializer*, meaning an initializer that can return nil, rather than a new object of the specified type. Failable initializers were introduced in Xcode 6.1 for scenarios like populating the contents of an NSData from a URL. Should we really assume that the URL is valid, or that the user is always capable of downloading its contents? Of course not.

So, instead of giving us a possibly useless object, the failable initializer gives us back an optional of the specified type and makes us decide what to do if we get back nil.

Anyway, with the image loaded into the image view, we return cell to the caller, just as before. The result looks like the figure.

This is looking a *lot* better. The avatar image is there, and the author name is nicely set off from the tweet text and created-on date. The difference in fonts lets us easily distinguish between username and their tweet, and the smaller Caption 1 font downplays the timestamp label.

There is one problem right now, though, and it's our images. If we have enough cells that we need to scroll—copy-and-paste a bunch of ParsedTweet initializers into the parsedTweets array initializer if you want to see it for yourself—the scrolling performance is pretty choppy. It's nowhere near as smooth as on a real iPhone or iPad, and this is running on the Simulator, where the power of a full-blown computer tends to run apps *faster* than they will on the device. So why is this happening?

The culprit is how we're loading our images. Our approach of loading the image data from the NSURL right when the tableView(cellForRowAtIndexPath:) needs it means that everything in our app just stops while we load that image from the network. We can't draw the cell, continue scrolling, or update anything else in the UI until the image data loads. Just imagine how well that's going to go over with users who are only getting one bar of cellular signal. In the next two chapters, we'll fix this problem with a more sophisticated approach.

How I Gave Up Tables and Learned to Love Lists

One of the things we haven't talked about is the fact that UITableView looks a lot more like a *list* than a *table*. Isn't a table supposed to be two-dimensional? With columns and headers, like a spreadsheet? That's what a table is in most other UI toolkits.

This takes me back to a job I had back in 2002 or so, building a Java UI for a network operations center. The idea was it would feed out video clips, and the engineers there needed to see what was in the queue to go out, its priority, where it was going, and so on.

The first cut of the UI used a Java Swing JTable and, yeah, it did look like an Excel spreadsheet. I'd been playing with Mac OS X by this point—I was the only one in the office using it, and took a lot of crap for doing so—and realized that this was a lousy user interface. The wide table made it hard to trace a single item all the way across the window, and reading vertically down columns wasn't useful anyway. Also, JTable defaulted to making columns the same width, even when some of our fields were 4 characters and others were more than 40. It didn't need to be a table; it didn't work as a table.

So, I turned it into a list. I created custom cells that would group all the data together, using layout, fonts, and color to call out the stuff that mattered most, and how the items related to one another.

I liked it well enough that a decade later, with the company long gone, I still have screenshots. Here's one of the lists from the main status window:

The purple color scheme, programmer art, aliased text, and bland Windows NT fonts are hard on the eyes 10 years later, but at the time, this was a real breakthrough for us in how we thought about our in-house UI. You could easily see what was going out when, which items had priority, and why the queue was arranged the way it was. The cell layouts made the whole list more readable, and I've been a big fan of custom cells in lists and tables ever since.

Pull-to-Refresh

There's one other common table task we should attend to with our table: We haven't given the user a means of refreshing the tweets. We had this in the last chapter with the Show My Tweets button, but now that our whole view is a table (for now, anyway), there's no way to expose this functionality. It doesn't matter now with our mock data, but it will matter a lot if we can't get new tweets from the Internet. How are we going to fix that?

Many table-based iOS apps use a *pull-to-refresh* gesture, in which scrolling to the top of the table and then pulling down to scroll further is interpreted as a request for the app to refresh its data. There were a variety of third-party implementations of this gesture for a number of years, and in iOS 6, Apple provided a standard implementation in the form of the UIRefreshControl class.

The UITableViewController that our ViewController subclasses has a refreshControl property, meaning we inherit it, so all we need to do is to populate that with a refresh controller and default behavior will take care of the UI for us. In fact, the ease of using the refresh controller is one reason to choose to subclass UITableViewController, rather than have a plain UIViewController that also happens to implement the UITableViewDataSource protocol.

Looking at the documentation, the UIRefreshControl is a subclass of UIControl and acts somewhat like a button or another generic control; when triggered, it sends an event called UIControlEventValueChanged. For us to do anything with it, we need to get a callback when that event occurs. We do that with the UIControl method addTarget(action:forControlEvents:). This method takes an object to call back to (such as our view controller), a method to call (which we'll write), and the relevant events for this callback (UIControlEventValueChanged).

So let's create and set up a suitable UIRefreshControl when our view controller first comes to life, in viewDidLoad:

```
Tables/PragmaticTweets-5-4/PragmaticTweets/ViewController.swift
override public func viewDidLoad() {
  super.viewDidLoad()
  reloadTweets()
  var refresher = UIRefreshControl()
  refresher.addTarget(self,
    action: "handleRefresh:",
    forControlEvents: UIControlEvents.ValueChanged)
  refreshControl = refresher
}
```

The action, meaning the method that's invoked by the callback, is passed as a *selector*, a string that uniquely identifies a method signature. In this case, we're promising to write a method called handleRefresh() that will take one parameter, as indicated by the single colon character. By convention, these action methods take a single argument to identify the sender, and have a return type of IBAction, so they can be used for connections in the storyboard (so we could also connect it with the Interface Builder GUI rather than with code if we wanted to). So let's write this action method:

Tables/PragmaticTweets-5-4/PragmaticTweets/ViewController.swift

```
Line 1  @IBAction func handleRefresh (sender : AnyObject?) {
     2    parsedTweets.append(
     3      ParsedTweet (tweetText: "New row",
     4        userName: "@refresh",
     5        createdAt: NSDate().description,
     6        userAvatarURL: defaultAvatarURL))
     7    reloadTweets()
     8    refreshControl!.endRefreshing()
     9  }
```

This action method does three things:

- On lines 2–6, we append a new ParsedTweet to the parsedTweets array that serves as the table's data model. Notice that on line 5, we create a new NSDate object (which defaults to the current instant in time), and then use that class's description() method to turn it into a string.

- We call our existing reloadTweets() method on line 7.

- Finally, on line 8 we call endRefreshing() to tell UIRefreshControl to hide the spinning wheel. UIRefreshControl also has a beginRefreshing() method to show the spinner, but this is called for us automatically as UITableViewController processes the pull gesture.

When we run now, the spinner appears atop the table when we scroll to the top and pull again, as seen in the following figure. This starts a reload of the Twitter data and dismisses the spinner. If we're not following enough people for the reload to be obvious, we can temporarily comment out the reloadTweets() in viewDidLoad, so we'll have to pull to refresh when the app loads in order to see any tweets at all.

Wrap-Up

We've put our app through a radical makeover in this chapter, and in so doing we've turned it from a toy into something that's starting to resemble real-world Twitter clients. By switching to a table view, we've adopted what's arguably the most familiar and most useful iPhone user interface. We implemented the methods provided by UITableViewDataSource (which we inherited from UITableViewController) to structure our table data as sections, rows, and cells. We tried out the basic table cell styles, and then moved on to a custom cell approach that allows us to populate, lay out, and style the cell contents in whatever way best suits the contents.

Now that our user interface is ready, we're going to go out to the network to get real Twitter data to populate the table. This is going to introduce a bunch of new challenges with how (and *when*) our code runs, but along the way we'll solve the problem with how the image loading slows down our scrolling.

CHAPTER 6

Waiting for Things to Happen with Closures

It's very tempting to think of our code as a series of instructions, to be executed in order. But this falls down when any of these steps takes a long time, or worse yet, an *unknown* amount of time.

Imagine that instead of programming an iPhone, we're 50 years in the future, programming a household robot to do ordinary household tasks. Let's say we want to write a program to answer the phone (OK, and imagine there are still phones 50 years from now). We might write something like:

```
Pick up the phone.
Say "hello".
Wait for the other party to introduce themselves.
If they're a family member, let us know.
If they're a politician or an advertiser, hang up.
Otherwise, ask us what to do.
```

And so on. And this will be great, until we get a prank phone call that doesn't respond to our robot saying hello. The script will wait on step 3. If the robot is really literal-minded, it will get hung up there forever and won't attend to any of its other duties around the house.

We need the ability to express steps 4–6 as something to do once the waiting in step 3 is done. These tasks will be saved away for the future, to be performed when the other party finally responds (or maybe to be discarded when the call simply disconnects), while the robot can continue with other tasks in the meantime.

This is an example of *asynchronicity*, the occurrence of events in an unpredictable order or at unpredictable times. It's very important to us as developers, because it's a realistic model of how things happen in real life. We often don't know when things will happen or how long they will take. This is even true within the programming realm: we don't know when an event like a button tap or a rotation gesture will occur, or how long it will take to get data from the network or write a document to the filesystem.

It's very expressive to be able to say "when event *foo* occurs, do *bar*," or "do *foo*, and if and when that finishes successfully, do *bar*, but don't wait around for it."

A lot of the iOS APIs are written with an expectation of asynchronous behavior. In this chapter, we'll cover how to write "closures" that function as completion handlers, meaning they do their thing only when some long-running or indeterminately long task completes. To use the Twitter web services, we'll have to use them in two different scenarios: asking users to let our app use their Twitter account, and making the network call to Twitter, because one makes us wait for a user response and the other makes us wait for the network.

Setting Up Twitter API Calls

When we first set up our tweet-sending button, we found the documentation for the Social framework and made use of the SLComposeViewController. To start using the rest of Twitter's features (or any other social network supported by iOS), we'll need to use another class in this framework. SLRequest lets us call the various social networks' web APIs by just providing a URL, whose contents vary by service and are documented at their various developer sites (such as http://dev.twitter.com). For Twitter, we have an additional detail to work through first: as of May 2013, all Twitter requests need to be *authenticated*, meaning they need to come from a signed-in Twitter user.

Fortunately, iOS allows a user to sign in to her Twitter account from the Settings app, and the iOS SDK will allow us to use that authentication. The key to this is that the SLRequest includes an account property that represents an authenticated user. All we need to do is to set that property before we send off our request.

To use a social-networking account, we have to ask the ACAccountStore for access to it, by means of a requestAccessToAccountsWithType() method. And that raises an interesting question: what happens if the user says no? In fact, let's consider the worst case: that the user switches out of our app, goes to the privacy settings, and changes the permission setting for our app's access to Twitter *while our app is running*. We're basically going to have to plan on asking for permission to use Twitter every time we need to make a request. And as it turns out, that has some interestingly asynchronous behavior.

The first time we call requestAccessToAc-
countsWithType(), the user will be presented with
an alert asking if she wants to grant our app
access to her Twitter accounts, as shown in
the next figure. We have no idea whether the
answer will be Don't Allow or OK, and we
certainly don't want to hold up the whole app

waiting for an answer, so instead we'll make this call and move on with the
rest of our app. If and when the user approves our use of her Twitter account,
then we'll go ahead and call Twitter's web service. Actually, the user will only
ever see the alert once—after that, she can grant or deny access via the Settings app's Privacy settings—but our code won't behave any differently; the
decision about whether or not to run our asynchronous code will just be made
sooner.

Let's start by adding an import Accounts to the top of ViewController.swift, just like
we did when we added the Social framework.

Then look at the requestAccessToAccountsWithType() method. It takes an ACAccountType,
which has constants for Twitter, Facebook, and a few other services. The
second argument is a dictionary of options whose use depends on the service.
The third parameter is of type ACAccountStoreRequestAccessCompletionHandler. That's
new, so we click on its documentation and see this:

```
typealias ACAccountStoreRequestAccessCompletionHandler =
  (Bool, NSError!) -> Void
```

What...the...heck?

Encapsulating Code in Closures

Way back in *Swift Methods*, on page 34, we mentioned that functions use the
syntax -> to indicate the type of their return value. So, is that (Bool, NSError!) ->
Void stuff a function? Actually yes...kind of! What this syntax expresses is a
closure, a self-contained block of functionality. The syntax indicates what will
be passed in (a Bool indicating if permission was granted, and an NSError
optional in case the request for access totally failed) and what will be returned
(Void, that is to say, there is no return value). So it's not that this parameter
is a function; it's a closure...and in Swift, all functions (and thus all methods)
are just a special case of closures!

So what's so great about closures? Well, for one thing, it means we get to take
some code *and treat it as an object.* In this case specifically, we get to write
some code, give it to the ACAccountStore, and say "ask for permission to use the

Twitter account, and run this when done." That's precisely what we want to do here: we want to write a closure that makes a Twitter request if and when the user approves our use of her Twitter account.

Let's begin by rewriting reloadTweets to get the current Twitter account. We'll take it slowly and just concern ourselves for now with getting the Twitter account, not what to do with it yet.

Asynchronicity/PragmaticTweets-6-1/PragmaticTweets/ViewController.swift

```
Line 1  func reloadTweets() {
          let accountStore = ACAccountStore()
          let twitterAccountType = accountStore.accountTypeWithAccountTypeIdentifier(
            ACAccountTypeIdentifierTwitter)
     5    accountStore.requestAccessToAccountsWithType(twitterAccountType,
            options: nil,
            completion: {
              (granted: Bool, error: NSError!) -> Void in
              if (!granted) {
    10          println ("account access not granted")
              } else {
                println ("account access granted")
              }
            })
    15    }
```

On line 2, we create an ACAccountStore object, which we'll need for the next few steps. The requestAccessToAccountsWithType() will require us to get the Twitter ACAccountType, which we do with a call to accountTypeWithAccountTypeIdentifier() on lines 3–4. Once we have that, we can ask for access to Twitter accounts, passing in the type (line 5), a set of options that can be nil for Twitter accounts (line 6), and a completion handler closure that will be called with the result of our request, which receives a Bool to indicate if we were granted access, and an NSError that will describe any error associated with a failed request.

Our preliminary closure ranges from the opening curly brace on line 7 down to line 14, where it ends with a telltale sequence of characters—})—which are the curly brace to end the closure, and the close parenthesis that ends the parameters to the requestAccessToAccountsWithType() call that began back on line 5. Line 8 is the signature that indicates what's being passed into the closure (the granted Boolean and an optional NSError), the return type (Void, meaning nothing), and the keyword in that begins the closure's logic. Inside this closure, our first decision to make is whether or not we can proceed; if the variable granted that's passed into the block is false, then we don't have access to Twitter accounts and should just give up. For now, on lines 9–10, we will just log a failure message in this case. Later on we should come back add a proper alert so the user knows what has happened.

On the other hand, if granted is true, we will be able to start talking to the Twitter API, which means a lot more work! For now, we'll just log a success message (on line 12).

Using the Twitter SLAccount

Now let's fill out the empty else case, replacing the simple success println(). We're going to work with the accountStore that the user has graciously given us permission to use. Because it's a local variable in scope at the time of the closure's creation, we can use it within the completion handler closure.

On iOS, the user may have set up several accounts of a given type; a fancier app would show them and let the user pick one, but for now, we'll just make sure there's at least one. We can use the ACAccountStore's accountsWithAccountType() to get all configured accounts of type twitterAccountType.

Asynchronicity/PragmaticTweets-6-1/PragmaticTweets/ViewController.swift
```
let twitterAccounts = accountStore.accountsWithAccountType(twitterAccountType)
if twitterAccounts.count == 0 {
  println ("no twitter accounts configured")
  return
} else {
```

Once again, we're just bailing out with an println() message to the console if there are no Twitter accounts configured. We can come back later and give the user a helpful UIAlertController dialog in this case.

Let's assume the array contains at least one Twitter account. What do we do with it? A while back—before we had to work through getting access to the account—we noted there is an SLRequest class that accesses the web service APIs of the social networks like Twitter. Looking at its documentation, it doesn't have a lot of methods, and one that we should focus on is performRequestWithHandler:(), whose docs say it "performs an asynchronous request and calls the specified handler when done."

And look, it takes another closure! Well, actually it takes an SLRequestHandler, which if we click the link to its documentation, is defined as follows:

```
typealias SLRequestHandler = (NSData!, NSHTTPURLResponse!, NSError!) -> Void
```

So this is another closure, taking NSData, and NSHTTPURLResponse, and NSError as optional parameters and returning Void. We'll assume those parameters will give us everything we need to handle the response from the Twitter web service. But since we'll probably have a bunch of work to do for that, and since we're already tabbed in pretty far in this else block, let's stub out a method to take those parameters and deal with the response when it comes in. Somewhere outside all the existing methods' curly braces—right before the class's closing curly brace would be a great place for it—let's stub out the following method, empty but for a simple println() that at least lets us know we got this far:

Asynchronicity/PragmaticTweets-6-1/PragmaticTweets/ViewController.swift

```
func handleTwitterData (data: NSData!,
    urlResponse: NSHTTPURLResponse!,
    error: NSError!) {
  if let dataValue = data {
    println ("handleTwitterData, \(dataValue.length) bytes")
  } else {
    println ("handleTwitterData received no data")
  }
}
```

Now we'll be able to have our performRequestWithHandler() closure just call this method, allowing us to put off for now just what's in the Twitter response and how we're going to deal with it.

Making a Twitter API Request

But what goes in our request? If we take a look at the Twitter REST API 1.1 at https://dev.twitter.com/docs/api/1.1, we'll find the call statuses/home_timeline, which is called via an HTTP GET, and which returns "a collection of the most recent Tweets and retweets posted by the authenticating user and the users they follow." Not shown on this page, but fundamental to Twitter API calls, is the fact that we can append .json to get JSON-formatted results, or .xml to get XML. Foundation's JSON parser is far easier to use than its XML parser, so our URL will be https://api.twitter.com/1.1/statuses/user_timeline.json. Note that as of January 2014, all Twitter API calls must use SSL, so our URLs will always start with https://.

So now we need to create an SLRequest. The docs show us a single convenience initializer, which takes a service type, request method, URL, and a dictionary of parameters. We already know how to fill in these four parameters:

- serviceType: The constant SLServiceTypeTwitter.

- requestMethod: The Twitter docs say we need an HTTP GET, so we use SLRequestMethodGET.

- url: We already figured this out as https://api.twitter.com/1.1/statuses/home_timeline.json.

- parameters: This is a dictionary of name-value pairs. The Twitter docs tell us we need to provide the screen_name or user_id parameters, so that's what will go in our dictionary.

Now we can fill in this innermost else clause of reloadTweets(): we'll build up a call to performRequestWithHandler(), and have the handler block just call the handleTwitterData() method we stubbed out. Here's what goes inside the else:

/Asynchronicity/PragmaticTweets-6-1/PragmaticTweets/ViewController.swift

```
Line 1  let twitterParams = [
   -      "count" : "100"
   -    ]
   -    let twitterAPIURL = NSURL(string:
   5      "https://api.twitter.com/1.1/statuses/home_timeline.json")
   -    let request = SLRequest(forServiceType: SLServiceTypeTwitter,
   -      requestMethod:SLRequestMethod.GET,
   -      URL:twitterAPIURL,
   -      parameters:twitterParams)
  10  request.account = twitterAccounts.first as ACAccount
   -  request.performRequestWithHandler ( {
   -      (data: NSData!, urlResponse: NSHTTPURLResponse!, error: NSError!) -> Void in
   -    self.handleTwitterData(data, urlResponse: urlResponse, error: error)
   -  })
```

There's a lot going on here! Let's take it slowly.

- Lines 1–3 set up a dictionary of parameters to provide to the request. The available parameters depend on the web service's API. Twitter lets us send a count of how many tweets to return (the default is 20), so let's make things interesting and fetch 100.

- Lines 4–5 convert a String representation of the Twitter web service URL into an NSURL, the type needed by the SLRequest initializer.

- Lines 6–9 creates the SLRequest with the URL and parameters we've set up, along with the constant for the Twitter service type, and the SLRequestMethod enumeration value for GET requests.

- Line 10 gets the first object from the twitterAccounts array, and assigns it to the request's account property. Since the SLRequest wants an object of type ACAccount, and the array turns out to be of type AnyObject, we *cast* the value to the correct type with as ACAccount.

- Lines 11–14 finally performs our request. It takes a closure as its parameter, which is executed once the request finishes. We saw before that this closure is of type SLRequestHandler, which means it receives an NSData, NSHTTPURLResponse, and NSError as parameters. Inside the closure, we just pass these parameters to our handleTwitterData() method, to figure out later.

We've written a lot of code—and with closures two levels deep, this might be the hardest thing in the whole book so far—so let's run it to make sure it at least builds and starts up in the simulator. Nothing interesting will happen in the simulator, but the call from viewDidLoad() to reloadTweets() should produce a message like the following in the Debug area at the bottom of the Xcode window:

handleTwitterData, 71706 bytes

This means the request is being sent to Twitter's web service and being responded to. Now it's up to us to act on that response.

Parsing the Twitter Response

Inside our handleTwitterData() method, we receive the raw data from the Twitter API and can use it to update our UI.

We'll start by handing the raw data over to Foundation's NSJSONSerialization, which can easily produce either an NSArray or NSDictionary of the parsed data, an object that may itself be a deep structure of nested arrays and/or dictionaries. Let's do a quick sanity check by replacing the log statement with the following:

```
Asynchronicity/PragmaticTweets-6-1/PragmaticTweets/ViewController.swift
Line 1  func handleTwitterData (data: NSData!,
        urlResponse: NSHTTPURLResponse!,
        error: NSError!) {
          if let dataValue = data {
     5      var parseError : NSError? = nil
            let jsonObject : AnyObject? =
              NSJSONSerialization.JSONObjectWithData(dataValue,
                options: NSJSONReadingOptions(0),
                error: &parseError)
    10      println("JSON error: \(parseError)\nJSON response: \(jsonObject)")
          } else {
            println ("handleTwitterData received no data")
          }
        }
```

We're doing a bunch of new things here, so let's take it slowly again:

- Lines 1–3 are our method declaration. As explained a while back in *Optionals*, on page 51, the bang characters (!), indicate the parameters are implicitly unwrapped optionals: They're still optionals, but we can access their values directly without converting to a non-optional type if we're *sure* they can't be nil. When Apple's frameworks call back to us like this, they usually send implicitly unwrapped optionals.

- On line 4, we create the non-optional local variable dataValue from the data parameter, which is an optional, since a JSON parse error could result in no data. Notice that we can do this unwrapping in an if statement to save a step, compared to casting to a non-optional type on one line and then testing against nil on the next. If data is nil inside this if statement, we bail out to the else case on line 12.

- The JSONObjectWithData()'s third parameter is listed as an NSErrorPointer. This is a pattern used by the older frameworks that could only return one value in C or Objective-C, even though they wanted to send back both data and maybe an error object, so we pass in a nil error object, and if an error occurs, the reference is changed to become an NSError object describing the error. In Swift, this pattern is called an *in-out parameter* and has some different semantics. We don't pass an actual NSErrorPointer object. Instead, we create an NSError? optional on line 5, pass it to the method with a preceding & operator (syntactically the same as the "address of" operator in C), and the type will get converted for us when we pass it to JSONObjectWithData(). Note that since the point of this variable is to see if it changes from nil to having a value, we need to declare it with var to make it variable.

- Line 6 is the left side of an assignment that will be completed on the next few lines with our call to JSONObjectWithData(). That method returns AnyObject?, an optional, since it could give us an array, a dictionary, or nil, so that's the type we have to be prepared to receive.

- Lines 7–9 are the actual call to JSONObjectWithData(), passing in the data, behavior flags, and the error pointer. The behavior flags on line 8 are a Swift work-in-progress: the idea is to create a *bit-field* by mathematically OR'ing together behavior flags that each have one bit set, so multiple behaviors can be expressed with a single Int. This is a lot more natural in C and Objective-C than it currently is in Swift, but fortunately we don't need any of those behaviors, so we just pass 0 to the NSJSONReadingOptions struct. Meanwhile, the NSErrorPointer required on line 9 is the in-out parameter we mentioned earlier, so we pass a nil NSError, with the & character to mark it as an in-out, and if there is an error, parseError will have a non-nil value when the method returns.

- For the time being, we're done. On line 10, we'll use println() to print the parseError on one line, and the jsonResponse on a new line afterward.

Run this, wait for the table view to come up, and check the console at the bottom of the Xcode window. The result will be a deeply nested structure, set off by tabs and curly-brace blocks, showing each tweet as a set of name-value pairs. The top of it will look something like this:

```
JSON error: nil
JSON response: (
        {
        contributors = "<null>";
        coordinates = "<null>";
        "created_at" = "Wed Jun 11 14:02:42 +0000 2014";
        entities =          {
            hashtags =           (
```

In the response, the first curly brace sets off all the data for one tweet, which has keys named contributors, "created_at", and so on. Notice that the value for entities is a curly brace, with its own child set of keys and values.

We can pick out interesting data like text, which is a string containing the tweet's text, and user, which is a dictionary of name-value pairs with items like screen_name and followers_count. Everything we could want to know about each tweet is in these entries, meaning we now have the data we need to populate the UI.

Wrap-Up

Because of the complexity of closures and asynchronous code, let's take a break here and assess what we've done.

We want to get at the raw Twitter data, so we ask for access to the user's accounts and wait for that to happen (since they might be blocked on an Allow / Don't Allow alert). If we are allowed to use the Twitter account, we send off a request, wait for that to come back, and then use NSJSONSerialization to turn the received NSData into an array of dictionaries, one entry per tweet. Both of the waiting parts are done with closures, telling the iOS frameworks what work we want them to do once they're able.

We've written two closures, both using the "completion handler" pattern that is common in iOS. In the next chapter, we're going to use closures again, this time to update the user interface. But instead of waiting for things to finish, these closures will allow us to do multiple things at once, which opens the door to a lot of cool possibilities.

CHAPTER 7

Doing Two Things at Once with Closures

We started the last chapter with the example of a hypothetical household robot, who would answer the phone for us. We dealt with the problem of prank callers that never respond to "Hello" by batching together all of our instructions for how to handle the greeting until after the caller responds. That leaves the robot free to do other tasks in the meantime. Now let's think about how that would work.

Some tasks will require the robot's limbs, some need its eyesight, and others its voice and hearing. If we're careful about how we divvy up tasks, the robot can do several things at once: we can prepare dinner while talking on the phone, and our robot should be able to as well.

So let's imagine we have lists of what each part of our robot's abilities can be working on: a list of manual tasks; a list of visual tasks; a list of spoken tasks. When it's time for the robot to continue dealing with the phone call, it can continue working on the manual tasks like cleaning or cooking, uninterrupted by the voice task of handling the call.

Our robot is a multitasking genius. And, if we're smart, our iPhone can be too.

In this chapter, we'll learn how Grand Central Dispatch offers the ability to break up work into distinct units—closures—and parcel that work out to whichever CPU core is most able to perform it at that point in time. We'll also see where the iOS frameworks force us to deal with concurrency, and successfully do so. With this skill in our toolbelt, we'll be able to keep our user interface fast and responsive as we get long-running tasks out of the way of the UI processing.

Grand Central Dispatch

Just like our hypothetical robot has lists of tasks to do with its hands, tasks to do with its voice, and so on, iOS has "lists" of tasks to be performed. They're called *queues*, as part of a work-dispatching system called *Grand Central Dispatch*, or GCD. The idea of GCD is that there are multiple queues of work, each with tasks to execute. The tasks are C function calls, Objective-C blocks, or Swift closures. GCD can determine which tasks to execute based on the priority of the queue, whether the tasks are suitable for concurrent execution, how busy the CPU cores are, and other considerations.

Developers from other platforms will see an analogy to threading, and the queues are indeed performed by threads, but the difference in iOS is that the threads and their queues are managed by the system, which is in a unique position to best optimize the work. On other platforms, it's hard to reason about threads—if two threads are good, are four necessarily better? Maybe that's true on one CPU architecture, but not on another, and we can never know when we're coding. GCD takes responsibility for the problem and lets us off the hook: "Give me work to do," it says, "and I'll figure out how to best get it done."

GCD provides functions to create queues and to put work on them. The function we'll use the most is dispatch_async(), which takes a reference to a queue and a closure to execute on that queue. The async in the name means that the call doesn't wait for the closure to finish executing; the related dispatch_sync() will actually wait until the closure finishes. Mostly, we'll want to use dispatch_async() so our app doesn't wait and instead can move on to other work.

Concurrency and UIKit

In fact, GCD is already splitting our work onto multiple queues. All our user interface events run on the *main queue*, the queue that launches the app and is responsible for listening for user interface events. When we get a button tap, the call into our code is made on the main queue. When a table asks our code for the number or rows or the cell at a given index path, it's on the main queue. In fact, UIKit has a rule: calls to any method or property *must* be made on the main queue.

But when we perform certain other tasks, GCD will put that work on other queues. For example, since network calls are sometimes slow (and never predictable in how long they'll take), most of them are put onto other queues, which allows the UIKit queue to get back to work processing user events and redrawing the views.

Building a New Table Model

So let's think of where we stand right now. By the end of *Parsing the Twitter Response*, on page 110, we had used the NSJSONSerialization to convert the raw JSON (as an NSData) into an array. If we inspect the output from the println(), we see that each member of the array is a dictionary that contains the text of the tweet, a created_at time (as a string), and a user value that is its own dictionary to give us things like the user's name, screen_name, a profile_image_url for their avatar, and so on.

Back in Chapter 5, *Presenting Data in Table Views*, on page 79, we built a ParsedTweet class to hold some of these values and present them in our table view with the custom cells. So our job now is to pull values out of the array of tweets, put them into ParsedTweet objects, and use those objects to repopulate the parsedTweets array that serves as our table model.

First, since we'll finally be putting real values in the parsedTweets array, we can clear out the dummy values that we've used for the last few chapters. Replace its definition at the top of ViewController.swift with an empty array of ParsedTweets:

Concurrency/PragmaticTweets-7-1/PragmaticTweets/ViewController.swift
```
var parsedTweets : [ParsedTweet] = []
```

Also, since we're done with fake data, we can stop appending a fake tweet in our pull-to-refresh method. So we'll cut down our handleRefresh() method to just reload the tweets.

Concurrency/PragmaticTweets-7-1/PragmaticTweets/ViewController.swift
```
@IBAction func handleRefresh (sender : AnyObject?) {
  reloadTweets()
  refreshControl!.endRefreshing()
}
```

Now let's go back to our handleTwitterData() method, specifically the if block that called NSJSONSerialization.JSONObjectWithData and then just did a println() to dump the parseError and jsonObject to the debugging console. The first thing we'll do is to delete that println() and instead bail out if there was an error.

Concurrency/PragmaticTweets-7-1/PragmaticTweets/ViewController.swift
```
if parseError != nil {
  return
}
```

Next, we want to start walking the JSON array of tweets, but we can't know for sure that it's really an array, since NSJSONSerialization could have produced a dictionary, if that's what the root object in the encoding is. So we'll use an if let to cast it to what we expect, and only enter the if block if it's safe.

Concurrency/PragmaticTweets-7-1/PragmaticTweets/ViewController.swift

```
Line 1  if let jsonArray = jsonObject as? Array<Dictionary<String, AnyObject>> {
     2    self.parsedTweets.removeAll(keepCapacity: true)
```

It's not enough for something to be an array; Swift wants to know what's in the array. Put another way, it insists we say what it's an array *of*. We said above that the println() output shows us it's an array of dictionaries...which to Swift just begs the question "OK, buster, dictionaries of *what?*" We want to say it's a dictionary with strings for keys, but we really can't guarantee a consistent type for the values, since they can be strings, arrays, or dictionaries. So, our answer is "The array contains dictionaries with string keys and AnyObject values." This is what we're doing on line 1, but the syntax merits an explanation.

Swift's typing requires us to specify the type of members of a collection. These are written with angle braces, like Array<String> to represent an array of Strings. In this case, our array of parsed tweets is described as Array<Dictionary<String, AnyObject>>, meaning "an array of dictionaries, each of which has string keys and AnyObject-type values."

This is kind of a hassle, so we can write it in a more compact syntax: [[String : AnyObject]]. The outer square braces mean "an array...," and the inner square braces with the colon separator mean "...of dictionaries, with String keys and AnyObject values." We'll use this syntax in later examples; try it here if you like and see if it isn't easier to type and read.

Converting JSON Values to Swift Properties

Assuming this cast works, we enter the if block, and remove everything currently in the parsedTweets array, by use of the removeAll() provided for Swift arrays. Now we're ready to start walking the array.

Concurrency/PragmaticTweets-7-1/PragmaticTweets/ViewController.swift

```
Line 1  for tweetDict in jsonArray {
     2    let parsedTweet = ParsedTweet()
     3    parsedTweet.tweetText = tweetDict["text"]  as? String
     4    parsedTweet.createdAt = tweetDict["created_at"]  as? String
     5    let userDict = tweetDict["user"] as NSDictionary
     6    parsedTweet.userName = userDict["name"] as? String
     7    parsedTweet.userAvatarURL = NSURL (string:
     8    userDict ["profile_image_url"] as String!)
     9    self.parsedTweets.append(parsedTweet)
    10  }
```

Starting on line 1, we count over each tweetDict in the array, which we know is a dictionary because we only got into this if block by successfully casting as an array of dictionaries. The first thing we do in the loop, on line 2, is to create a new ParsedTweet. Instead of assigning its properties all at once with the designated initializer like we did before, we'll populate them one by one as we pull them out of the tweetDict.

Some of the values we want to put in our ParsedTweet are at the top level of the dictionary, so we assign tweetText and createdAt on lines 3 and 4, respectively. Unfortunately, the collections produced by NSJSONSerialization have values that can't always be cast directly to Swift types. Presumably for legacy reasons, the contents of these collections are the formal classes that the Foundation framework offered in Objective-C: NSString, NSArray, NSDictionary, and so on. Fortunately, these can all be cast to their Swift equivalents for free, so even if we asked for the tweet text as an NSString, we can simply assign it to our ParsedTweet's text property (defined as the optional type String?) with no additional effort. We'll chalk this up to iOS's growing pains as it changes languages, and hope it improves soon.

We face the same annoyance on getting the dictionary that describes the user who sent the tweet. On line 5, we have to get the value for the user key as an NSDictionary, but then we're free to use the resulting userDict local variable like a normal Swift Dictionary. We do so on line 6 to get the user's name, and on lines 7–8 to get their avatar URL as a string, and turn it into an NSURL.

Finally, with all the fields of the ParsedTweet populated, we add it to the parsedTweets array. This allows our table model to pick it up when it needs a cell for that row. Notice, by the way, that we've used self here. Because different objects can get pulled into the closure's scope, the compiler sometimes can't resolve property and method references; imagine if parsedTweets were a local variable or a parameter to the closure. We can always disambiguate these cases by just putting in a self, and we tend to do that a lot inside closures.

Refreshing the Table Model

In fact, after the for loop, all that's left to do is to tell the table to refresh its contents, and to close the if let jsonArray = jsonObject as? [[String:AnyObject]] { block that gave us the tweets as an array:

Concurrency/PragmaticTweets-7-1/PragmaticTweets/ViewController.swift
```
  self.tableView.reloadData()
}
```

This leaves us at the else from before, the one that just contains println ("handleTwitterData received no data"). So we should be good to go. Let's go ahead and run the app.

At first our empty table comes up; then we see in the Xcode window as the app logs the raw JSON and its array-of-dictionaries representation. *And then it just sits there.* After about 10 seconds, the table finally updates with the tweets from our request, as seen in the figure.

So, on one hand, it's a great success that our efforts of the last few chapters have finally paid off with a table of tweets pulled from the honest-to-goodness Twitter API. On the other hand, *why the heck is it so slow?*

Putting Work on the Main Queue

Early in this chapter, we were talking about queues and how they're used to keep the multiple cores of an iOS device busy. Maybe that's part of the problem.

Janie Clayton-Hasz

I think it is fun hearing so many stories about how people got into their special...

Sun Aug 31 14:31:57 +0000 2014

Janie Clayton-Hasz

New blog post: http://t.co/EVnT4MyLuO

Sun Aug 31 13:06:18 +0000 2014

Brian P. Hogan

#MonthOfMusic Day 30.

http://t.co/B0ynhMbVgy...

Sun Aug 31 04:32:43 +0000 2014

Matt Drance

RT @girltalk: #throwbackthursday http://t...

Unfortunately, Swift won't tell us which queue is running our code, so a definite answer will have to wait until we play with breakpoints in Chapter 14, *Debugging Apps*, on page 227. But for now, there's an easy way to see how we've gotten ourselves in trouble. The main queue is run by the lower-level "main thread," and NSThread provides a class method isMainThread() to tell us if the current thread (and therefore queue) is main.

To try it out, plop the following line of code in any of the app's methods:

```
println (NSThread.isMainThread() ? "On main thread" : "Not on main thread")
```

Inside reloadTweets(), this will print On main thread. But in handleTwitterData()—or the completion handler closure of performRequestWithHandler() that calls it—it will say Not on main thread. So, that's key to our problem.

Actually, we're kind of lucky. Back in Objective-C and iOS 7, this was a crashing bug. But crashing or suffering 10-second delays while updating will get us angry one-star reviews either way, so we need to fix it.

Our basic problem is that any calls to UIKit classes and their method must be made on the main queue, and handleTwitterData() is being called on some other queue. We're only doing one thing that touches UIKit—reloading the table—but that's enough to get us in trouble. We need a way to move at least that one line of code back to the main thread.

A Handy Concurrency Recipe

To do this, we need two things: a way to represent a chunk of code as an object, and a method that will take that code and put it back on the main queue. We already have the first of these: closures, which we used in the previous chapter. The other piece is the Grand Central Dispatch function dispatch_async(), which allows us to put work on a queue of our choosing, such as the main queue. So we have a recipe we can always fall back on:

```
dispatch_async(dispatch_get_main_queue(),
  {() -> Void in
    // code to be performed on main thread
  })
```

dispatch_async() takes two parameters: a queue to perform the work on, and a closure with the work to be done. For the first, the point of this recipe is to use dispatch_get_main_queue(), so all we ever have to change is the contents of the closure.

In fact, our recipe gets easier. In Swift's tradition of omitting empty or unnecessary syntax, a closure that takes no arguments and returns Void (that is, nothing) doesn't even need the signature. So our recipe can be written even more simply as

```
dispatch_async(dispatch_get_main_queue(),
  {
    // code to be performed on main thread
  })
```

So let's apply our recipe. Replace self.tableView.reloadData() with the following:

Concurrency/PragmaticTweets-7-1/PragmaticTweets/ViewController.swift
```
dispatch_async(dispatch_get_main_queue(),
  {
    self.tableView.reloadData()
  })
```

Run the app again, and the table should reload about a second after the app launches. This is *much* better. Our app does its network stuff on one queue so that it doesn't block the GUI; we can unpack our data on that other queue and only touch the main queue for an update when we're good and ready. It's concurrency in action, and when we're smart about it, our apps can stay nimble and responsive, which makes our users happy.

Do-It-Yourself Concurrency

Actually, our app isn't as fast as we might like. Try scrolling the table. The scrolling is still choppy. This has been the case since way back in *Custom Table Cells*, on page 93, where we started fetching the avatar images from their URLs. So let's think about what's causing the problem and whether we can fix it.

When the table asks us for a cell—in tableView(cellForRowAtIndexPath:)—we can easily set all the labels with strings from the ParsedTweet, but what we have for the avatar image is an NSURL. So we stop and load the data for that URL, make a new UIImage from it, and assign that to our custom cell's UIImageView. This has to happen for each cell. Moreover, we can only work on one cell at a time. As a new cell comes into view, we have to wait to download the image data, and only when we have it can we continue on to the next cell. It makes swiping quickly through the table impossible.

So, we're blocking the UIKit queue on a slow network access. "Hey, wait a minute," we say, "isn't that exactly what concurrency is supposed to fix? And isn't it exactly why the Social framework does the Twitter API call on a different queue?" Exactly. And that means to fix our problem, we should do what Apple does: *get our network stuff off the main queue.*

> **They Don't Call It "Blocking" the Main Queue for Nothing**
>
> Lest anyone think the issue of keeping long-running tasks off the main queue is an academic problem…well, do we have a story for you.
>
> Years ago, one of the authors of this book was working at a company with a product that worked with video. For a demo, we had to show that the application could copy this video to an analog video tape recorder (VTR). Our solution was to connect the output of the video card to the VTR, and to use an RS-232 cable to send "record" and "stop" commands to the VTR. It seemed easy: to copy the video, we start the VTR recording and play the video from the PC, and then stop the VTR when the video's done. Easy peasy.
>
> *Except that* the guy who wrote this didn't know how threads work in Java, which is what the application was written in. And desktop Java works almost exactly like UIKit: there's a main thread with an endless loop that looks for events like keypresses and mouse clicks, sends them to any code that handles the event, and repaints the window.
>
> So when the user clicked the Record button, the code to play the video and start recording on the VTR was called…on the main thread. And that code effectively said "Wait here until the video is done," which meant that the window didn't update and no further events were processed until the video was done playing.
>
> *Some of these videos were 15 minutes long.* The application couldn't do any repainting or event-handling during this time, so if you covered up the window and then foregrounded it, it wouldn't

repaint. On Windows, dragging the mouse over the window would leave a trail of unerased mouse crud. Clicking a button did nothing. It was a disaster.

And this is pretty much where your author got to learn about threads, and had to completely rewrite this part of the program so that all of the video stuff happened on another thread, freeing up the main thread to immediately get back to work processing events and repainting, and then having the video thread put UI work back on the main thread only when ready.

And if you're still not convinced? Try plopping an NSThread.sleepUntilDate(NSDate(timeIntervalSinceNow:900.0)) as the first line of one of the button handlers. This will block the main queue for 900 seconds, or 15 minutes, during which time the button won't return to its untapped state, rotation events will be ignored, and the user will basically be blocked out of the app. *That's* what we're trying to avoid!

Moving Work Off the Main Queue

When tableView(cellForRowAtIndexPath:) needs an avatar, it does a slow NSURL load, makes an image from it, and sets it on the UIImageView. Only the last of these steps needs to be on the main queue, and the first shouldn't be. So we need a recipe to move work *off* the main queue.

dispatch_async() comes to our rescue again. Recall that it takes two parameters: the queue to put work on, and a closure with the tasks we want performed. What we need now is a different value for that first parameter, one that isn't the main queue, but just some other queue. For this, there's the GCD function dispatch_get_global_queue(), which takes a constant that indicates the priority of the system-provided queue we want. We're not picky, so we can use QOS_CLASS_DEFAULT to let GCD pick an ordinary background queue for us.

If you're an iOS 7 programmer, you might be wondering about that queue name. Well, iOS 8 introduces new "quality of service" constants for GCD queue priorities, which are meant to better express programmer intent. Unfortunately, they're not currently searchable in the Xcode documentation viewer, and are only visible in a C header file. The following table shows the new constants, and their older equivalents, which we'd have to use for code running on iOS 7 or earlier.

iOS 8 QOS Constant	iOS 7 Equivalent
QOS_CLASS_USER_INITIATED	DISPATCH_QUEUE_PRIORITY_HIGH
QOS_CLASS_DEFAULT	DISPATCH_QUEUE_PRIORITY_DEFAULT
QOS_CLASS_UTILITY	DISPATCH_QUEUE_PRIORITY_LOW
QOS_CLASS_BACKGROUND	DISPATCH_QUEUE_PRIORITY_BACKGROUND

Anyway, now we have the pieces we need. In tableView(cellForRowAtIndexPath:), find the if parsedTweet.userAvatarURL != nil block that sets the image, and replace it with the following version:

Concurrency/PragmaticTweets-7-2/PragmaticTweets/ViewController.swift

```
dispatch_async(dispatch_get_global_queue(
  QOS_CLASS_DEFAULT, 0),
  {
    if let imageData = NSData (contentsOfURL:
      parsedTweet.userAvatarURL!) {
    let avatarImage = UIImage(data: imageData)
    dispatch_async(dispatch_get_main_queue(),
    {
      cell.avatarImageView.image = avatarImage
    })
  }
})
```

Lines 1–12 are one big dispatch_async() call. The difference here is that we want to get work *off* the main queue, so on lines 1–2, we use the GCD function dispatch_get_global_queue() with the constant QOS_CLASS_DEFAULT to let GCD pick an ordinary background queue for us. That background queue gets the closure that runs from lines 3–12. This closure contains the "get a UIImage from an NSURL" logic from before, and then sets that image on the UIImageView. But since updating the image view has to happen on the main queue, we use a second dispatch_async() (lines 7–10) to wrap the UIKit work with a closure and put it back on the main queue.

And it's great! Now our table scrolls nice and fast, not blocking on the image loading at all!

Carrier 📶   9:04 PM   ▰

 Janie Clayton-Hasz
RT @lymond: I guess the reason Apple is f-stopping Aperture is that it didn't hav...
Fri Jun 27 19:26:41 +0000 2014

 Janie Clayton-Hasz
RT @wiscoDude: I'm looking for a .NET developer in Madison. 40 hrs/week @ $7...
Fri Jun 27 19:26:19 +0000 2014

 Chris Adamson
Road Trip? RT @Anime Interest: New Indoor #Anime & #Manga Theme Park...
Fri Jun 27 19:07:09 +0000 2014

 Janie Clayton-Hasz
RT @blackpixel: We've got exciting things in the pipeline and are looking for folks to...

There's just one more problem. Look at the figure. Every single one of the images is wrong: Chris is Janie, Janie is Chris, and *iOS Recipes* co-author Matt Drance is Janie, too.

Race Conditions

What's happened? A *race condition*, actually. When a cell goes offscreen and is queued for reuse, it will eventually get dequeued and filled with new data. *But the closure that fills in the image doesn't know that.* In this case, there was some cell for one of Matt's tweets that went off screen, dequeued, and repopulated with one of Janie's tweets (for the first row in the figure), but then the closure finished and filled in the image with Matt's picture. This doesn't happen often—we had to request 200 tweets, plus simulate poor network conditions to get the screenshot—but it *is* a bug, and if there's any way to make it happen in development, it's for sure going to hit someone in the real world.

The fix is to figure out when a closure has taken too long. How do we know that? Well, if the problem is that the cell has already filled in the contents from a different tweet, we can look to see if the parsedTweet that the closure started with has the same data that's displayed by the cell now. So here's the new contents for the if parsedTweet.userAvatarURL != nil block:

Concurrency/PragmaticTweets-7-2/PragmaticTweets/ViewController.swift

```
Line 1  cell.avatarImageView.image = nil
        dispatch_async(dispatch_get_global_queue(
          QOS_CLASS_DEFAULT, 0),
          {
5           if let imageData = NSData (contentsOfURL:
              parsedTweet.userAvatarURL!) {
            let avatarImage = UIImage(data: imageData)
            dispatch_async(dispatch_get_main_queue(),
              {
10              if cell.userNameLabel.text == parsedTweet.userName {
                  cell.avatarImageView.image = avatarImage
                } else {
                  println ("oops, wrong cell, never mind")
                }
15            })
            }
        })
```

We start by clearing out the possibly wrong image, on line 1. The big change is inside the closure that runs on the main queue (lines 8–15): it looks to see if the text already set on the name label matches the userName of the ParsedTweet that the closure captured at the moment the closure was created. If it does, then this image belongs with this cell. If not, then the cell the closure was downloading an image for has already been reused and no longer matches, so the closure can just bail.

The else block is optional of course, but it's interesting to play with our network conditions and see how often the log message pops up in good conditions versus bad (for a way to reproduce this, see the sidebar on page 125). Suffice to say that if we hadn't fixed this, our Edge and 3G users would be *really unhappy*.

Now the race condition is fixed. If the image data comes in too late to use, we just don't use it. And we've once again been reminded of the promise and the hazards of working asynchronously. The figure shows our snappy and accurate app:

So we have a recipe for getting work onto and off of the main thread: just call dispatch_async(), with the work to be done as a closure. For the queue, we use dispatch_get_main_queue() to put work on the main queue, or dispatch_get_global_queue() to get a system queue that can get our work off the main queue. Either way, we're exploiting concurrency, the ability of the system to do many things at once, and now we're smarter about how to let the main queue keep doing its event-dispatching and repainting thing, while we do ours.

Wrap-Up

In this chapter, we furthered our command of how to determine not just "what" to run, but "when" and "how." We built on the last chapter's introduction of closures as an object wrapper for code, and used Grand Central Dispatch to put our closures onto the main thread when they need to access UIKit classes and methods, and get them off the main queue when they need to get out of its way. Between the many built-in APIs that are designed for asynchronicity and concurrency, and our own ability to make things concurrent with GCD, we've got great tools to keep our app snappy.

We've now got a pretty full screen with this table of tweets, but we still want to do a lot more with our app. The only way to do that is going to be to start having several screenfuls of information and navigate between them.

Joe asks:

Can I Slow Down the Simulator Long Enough to See the Cells Get the Wrong Image?

If your Internet connection is really good, you may load the image data too fast to see the wrong-cells bug. This shows off one disadvantage of working with the simulator: its performance is unrealistically good, particularly for networking tasks. A Mac Pro with Gigabit Ethernet is going to get a web service response a lot more quickly than an iPhone with one bar of 3G coverage out in the woods somewhere.

Fortunately, a Mac can simulate lousy network conditions for this kind of testing. From the Xcode menu, select Open Developer Tool→More Developer Tools to be taken to Apple's Xcode downloads page. After asking for a developer ID and password, the page shows optional downloads for Xcode. Look for the latest version of the Hardware IO Tools For Xcode, download it, and double-click the Network Link Conditioner.prefPane to install it.

This adds a pane to the Mac's System Preferences called Network Link Conditioner, which adjusts the performance of the Mac's current networking device (Ethernet, AirPort, etc.) to resemble real-world conditions an iOS device might face, from Wi-Fi with good connectivity to the outdated Edge network experiencing packet loss.

Keep in mind, however, that the Network Link Conditioner degrades *all* network traffic on the Mac, not just the iOS Simulator application. So if we forget to turn it off when we're done testing, it will make everything we do seem like we're getting one bar in the middle of nowhere.

CHAPTER 8

Growing Our Application

So far, our app interface has been restricted to a single view. We've swapped different functionality into and out of this view, but ultimately the small space of an iPhone screen limits what we can do in a single view. In this chapter, we're going to broaden our world by adding the ability to move among multiple view controllers, each of which will provide a unique interface and functionality for different concerns of our app. To do this, we'll learn about how iOS uses navigation controllers to help the user move between these different view controllers. This will open up our app to an almost unlimited potential for functionality; if we want to add a new screen, we just need to write a new view controller and have a way to get to it.

Working with Multiple View Controllers

With our switch to a table view as the main interface for our Twitter app, we're starting to resemble and work like the many other Twitter apps on iOS. However, our functionality is limited: all we can do is load and display the tweets. In fact, we've actually *lost* the "Send Tweet" functionality, because the full screen table view doesn't afford a good place for its button. So what are we going to do?

Usually, iOS tables *do something* when the user clicks on a table row. And most of the time, that something is to show the details of the thing that was clicked on, with a new interface appropriate to the detail view.

What's happening is that iOS is presenting a different view controller, one that is designed specifically for the task at hand. So for our app, that means we want to go from the view controller that shows all the tweets to one that shows just the specifics of one tweet. From here, we could go to another view controller: for example, we could click on the tweeter's profile image to go to a view controller that shows details about him or her. Each view controller is built for one task—showing all the tweets, showing the details of one tweet, showing the details of the Twitter user—which allows us to divvy out functionality to different classes within our codebase.

To start adding new view controllers to our application, we'll want to make a few changes to our source code. We need the ability to arbitrarily grow our application by adding new classes and new storyboard scenes, and we need to start thinking about where we are going to put new code, and where we have opportunities for code reuse. All in all, it's a good time to tackle some much needed refactoring.

Refactoring in Xcode

Refactoring is the disciplined practice of making small changes to a codebase that alters its internal structure without changing its perceived behavior. Xcode offers a handful of refactoring tools; the rest we'll do by ourselves.

Where do we start? Well, we've sketched out our idea for using multiple view controllers, and once we've gone ahead and done that, the default name of our current ViewController is going to be a liability, since we might well ask, "*Which* view controller?" Let's rename it to clear up any future confusion.

Renaming

What should we call it? Looking at its functionality, we could call this something like TweetListViewController. However, in navigation-based apps, we typically refer to the first view controller as the *root view controller*, so let's use RootViewController as our new name.

We might be tempted to just change the name of the file in the Finder or Xcode's File Navigator, but this would cause all kinds of breakage, since other files in the project would still be looking for ViewController files. And finding all those references, particularly in the storyboard, is a tedious and error-prone process. Instead, we'll have Xcode do the name change for us.

Switch to ViewController.swift, find the class ViewController : UITableViewController at the top of the file, and select the ViewController name. Bring up the Refactor menu, either from the Edit menu or from the pop-up menu (via a control-click or right-click). The Refactor menu includes options to rename a selection, create a superclass, extract code into its own method, and a few others. What we want to do is to rename, so select Rename.

Oh no! An error message! Apparently, Xcode isn't yet able to refactor Swift code. We expect Apple to support this eventually, so keep in mind that the

Refactor menu item is there. But for now, we'll have to do it by hand, just like we said we didn't want to. Ugh!

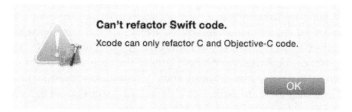

With the class name ViewController still selected, change the name in the class declaration to RootViewController. For consistency, we want the filename to match its contents, so in the File Navigator on the left (⌘1), select ViewController.swift, click again to edit the line, and change its name to RootViewController.swift

So far, that's two steps that a working Refactor menu item would have saved us, but there's one more. The storyboard still thinks that its one scene has a view controller of class ViewController. But that class no longer exists, so if we run now, our table is empty and the debug pane shows the error message Unknown class ViewController in Interface Builder file.

To fix this, go to the storyboard, select the View Controller in the scene list, and visit the Identity Inspector (⌥⌘3) in the utility pane on the right. The first section here is Custom Class, which we used before when we were telling the storyboard to use our custom table cell class. Now we want to reconnect it with our custom view controller class, so change the value of the Class field to RootViewController. Save, run, and the app works again.

The lack of a working Refactor menu item for Swift is a hassle, but at least we have a recipe: rename the class in its source file, rename the source file, and then use the Identity Inspector to rename any occurrences of it in the storyboard.

Organizing Xcode Projects with Groups

So we can rename our classes, and that's great. But if all we could do to keep our files straight was to use naming conventions, the contents of the File Navigator would still become hard to read, once we have dozens or even hundreds of classes.

One way to manage our code is to create groups. These are the folder icons in the File Navigator, several of which were created for us by the Xcode template when we started the project. We can move files into groups to organize them and strategically show and hide them, to make our project easier to

Snapshots

The first time we perform a refactoring—when it works, that is—we're asked immediately before applying the changes if we want to enable automatic *snapshots* of our project before making this change. Snapshots let us save the entire state of the project and all its contents, so if we make sweeping changes that don't end up working out, we can access the snapshots of previous states of the project (via the Organizer window) and roll back to a previous working state. It's similar to reverting back to earlier versions of files with Time Machine, but it's controlled entirely within Xcode and lets us label each snapshot so we know what it represents.

This is a simple enough means of keeping ourselves out of trouble, but it's limited: it only works for one user on one computer. For now, disable snapshots when asked, and we'll adopt a more comprehensive solution in Chapter 15, *Publishing to the App Store*, on page 241.

manage. Note that these aren't real folders on the filesystem; they're just an organizational tool within Xcode.

A common convention in iOS development is to create a group for a view controller and any custom classes used only by that view controller. For us, that would be the newly renamed RootViewController and the ParsedTweetCell. Let's do that. Click on the PragmaticTweets folder, to indicate that's the group we want as the parent of our new group, and select File→New→Group. This adds a group folder

with the name New Group. Rename it to Root VC and then drag the RootView-Controller.swift and ParsedTweetCell.swift files into it. Then do the same thing to create a group called Twitter Classes, and add ParsedTweet.swift to it. The folders in the File Navigator should now look like the figure.

The group's files are indented slightly and can be hidden entirely by turning the disclosure triangle on the side of the group. As we create new view controllers, we'll put them in their own groups, and we can expand just the groups we're interested in at a given time, so we don't see a bunch of files that we're not working on at the moment.

Extracting Method Code

When we're ready to write these other view controllers to show tweet details and user information, we're going to need to make new calls to the Twitter API. And considering all the work we did to get our first call working—talking to the ACAccountStore and getting an account and using it to make a request and so on—we really don't want to repeat all that, right? But right now, that code is all in RootViewController. To make it more general purpose, we're going to need to *extract* it, and then generalize it.

To do this, let's think about how to make a more generic Twitter API caller. The current reloadTweets() method uses the ACAccountStore to construct an SLRequest, then calls its performRequestWithHandler(), which then calls back to our handleTwitterData() in the completion handler closure. The things that are specific to RootViewController are the URL and the parameters sent to the SLRequest (in this case, they specify the home_timeline.json call and its parameters), and the response handling, which is all in another method (handleTwitterData()). Put another way, everything in reloadTweets() other than the URL and the parameters is something we would do for *any* Twitter request, and is therefore reusable.

So what we can do to refactor is to move this code to a general-purpose version that can be called with any URL and parameters, and replace reloadTweets() with a one-line call to this new method, passing in the current URL and parameters. Everything we do in the response is already factored out into handleTwitterData(), so we don't need to change anything there.

The big difference is that the generic Twitter request method should be in a new class so classes other than RootViewController can call it. This class will go in the Twitter Classes group, since it will work with the ParsedTweet class we've already created.

Select the Twitter Classes group and select File→New→File to create a new class file. Choose the iOS →Source→Cocoa Touch Class template, and name the new class TwitterAPIRequest, a subclass of NSObject, with Language set to Swift.

This is the class where we'll move all that code that gets the ACAccount and sends off the SLRequest, stuff we don't want to repeat in lots of places in our app. But of course, that's only one half of what we do with the Twitter API...

Building Our Own Delegate

Let's think ahead. Most of our Twitter requests are going to be pretty much the same thing: get a Twitter ACAccount, send off a URL with some parameters. The only thing that's different is the URL and the parameters, and that's pretty easy. But the other thing our RootViewController does is all the stuff in handleTwitterData(), where it currently goes through the array of tweets to make a table model.

When we're ready to make a view controller to show the details of a tweet, or a user, or search results, or some other kind of response, that's going to be completely different code. So the response-handling code can't live in Twitter-APIRequest. In fact, for the app we have now, we want to leave that stuff in RootViewController so it can populate the table. But we also want TwitterAPIRequest to be able to send its response to lots of different kinds of classes.

What we're going to do here is what so many of the iOS frameworks do: we're going to have a *delegate* that handles parsing the Twitter response data. Indeed, here we can see how the delegation pattern gets its name: our general-purpose Twitter request-maker doesn't know what to do with the response it gets for some arbitrary Twitter API, so it *delegates* that responsibility to another object.

To set up a class to work with a delegate, we typically create a protocol defining all the delegate methods. Select the Twitter Classes group and select File→New→File again. This time we don't want a full-blown Cocoa Touch Class, so we have to choose the generic Swift File:

Name the protocol TwitterAPIRequestDelegate and save it. This creates a .swift file that's empty but for a copyright comment and an import Foundation statement.

Since protocols are just declarations of methods, with no method body, all we have to do is provide that declaration. Here's what we need to enter here:

Growing/PragmaticTweets-8-1/PragmaticTweets/TwitterAPIRequestDelegate.swift

```
Line 1  protocol TwitterAPIRequestDelegate {
    2    func handleTwitterData (data: NSData!,
    3      urlResponse: NSHTTPURLResponse!,
    4      error: NSError!,
    5      fromRequest: TwitterAPIRequest!)
    6  }
```

The protocol declaration starts on line 1 by simply providing a name for the protocol. This is followed by the method definition for handleTwitterData(), whose parameter list is exactly the same as the version we currently have in RootViewController, except that it adds a fourth parameter. This last parameter, fromRequest, identifies the object that's making the delegate callback. If some part of our yet-to-be written code needed to send off several TwitterAPIRequests at once, its implementation of handleTwitterData() could use this value to tell which was which. We saw this earlier in how the UITableViewDataSource and UITableViewDelegate protocol methods typically include a parameter to say which table is calling back.

Making the Twitter Code More General-Purpose

Now that the delegate protocol is declared, we have the pieces in place for our genericized Twitter calls: callers will provide the TwitterAPIRequest with a URL and parameters for their request, and a delegate implementing TwitterAPIRequest-Delegate to handle the response. The delegate is often the caller itself.

So, at the top of TwitterAPIRequest.swift, we'll start by importing the Social and Accounts frameworks, since we'll be using classes from both of them.

Growing/PragmaticTweets-8-1/PragmaticTweets/TwitterAPIRequest.swift
```
import Social
import Accounts
```

Now, inside the curly braces of class TwitterAPIRequest: NSObject, here's how we start declaring our generic Twitter-calling method:

Growing/PragmaticTweets-8-1/PragmaticTweets/TwitterAPIRequest.swift
```
func sendTwitterRequest (requestURL : NSURL!,
  params : [String:String],
  delegate : TwitterAPIRequestDelegate?) {
```

This method declaration takes the three parameters we discussed earlier: the Twitter URL and parameters for the request, and a delegate to handle the response. Notice the third argument is an optional of type TwitterAPIRequestDele-gate, the delegate we just declared. That means any object provided for this argument has to implement the handleTwitterData() method that we just defined in the TwitterAPIRequestDelegate protocol.

Now we're ready to write the implementation. It's a lot of code, but it should look *very* familiar:

Growing/PragmaticTweets-8-1/PragmaticTweets/TwitterAPIRequest.swift
```
    let accountStore = ACAccountStore()
    let twitterAccountType =
      accountStore.accountTypeWithAccountTypeIdentifier(
```

```
      ACAccountTypeIdentifierTwitter)
  accountStore.requestAccessToAccountsWithType(twitterAccountType,
    options: nil,
    completion: {
      (granted: Bool, error: NSError!) -> Void in
      if (!granted) {
        println ("account access not granted")
      } else {
        let twitterAccounts =
          accountStore.accountsWithAccountType(twitterAccountType)
        if twitterAccounts.count == 0 {
          println ("no twitter accounts configured")
          return
        } else {
          let request = SLRequest(forServiceType: SLServiceTypeTwitter,
            requestMethod:SLRequestMethod.GET,
            URL:requestURL,
            parameters:params)
          request.account = twitterAccounts.first as ACAccount
          request.performRequestWithHandler ( {
            (data: NSData!, urlResponse: NSHTTPURLResponse!,
             error: NSError!) -> Void in
            delegate!.handleTwitterData(data,
              urlResponse: urlResponse,
              error: error,
              fromRequest: self)
          })
        }
      }
  })
}
```

That's a lot of code. We can write it fresh, or just copy and paste the contents from reloadTweets() in RootViewController, with the following changes:

- Remove the line that creates the twitterParams local variable.

- Remove the line that creates the twitterAPIURL local variable.

- In the SLRequest initializer, replace the twitterAPIURL and twitterParams local variables with the requestURL and params arguments.

- In the handleTwitterData() call, change the target from self to delegate!, and add the fourth parameter, fromRequest: self.

Now we have a generic Twitter API request-maker that can be used by any and all view controllers that will want to make Twitter requests. To try it out, we'll finish our refactoring by having RootViewController use this class instead of its current code.

Back in RootViewController.swift, declare that the class implements the delegate protocol by appending TwitterAPIRequestDelegate to the class declaration:

Growing/PragmaticTweets-8-1/PragmaticTweets/RootViewController.swift

```
public class RootViewController: UITableViewController,
                               TwitterAPIRequestDelegate {
```

When we do this, we start seeing an error icon in the left column, because we don't actually implement the TwitterAPIRequestDelegate protocol. We do have a handleTwitterData() method, but it takes three arguments, and our delegate expects four. So update the method signature to include that extra argument:

Growing/PragmaticTweets-8-1/PragmaticTweets/RootViewController.swift

```
func handleTwitterData (data: NSData!,
  urlResponse: NSHTTPURLResponse!,
  error: NSError!,
  fromRequest: TwitterAPIRequest!) {
```

Now we can rewrite a *much* simpler reloadTweets() to take just the arguments relevant to what this view controller needs, namely the user's home timeline:

Growing/PragmaticTweets-8-1/PragmaticTweets/RootViewController.swift

```
func reloadTweets() {
  let twitterParams : Dictionary = ["count":"100"]
  let twitterAPIURL = NSURL(string:
    "https://api.twitter.com/1.1/statuses/home_timeline.json")
  let request = TwitterAPIRequest()
  request.sendTwitterRequest(twitterAPIURL,
    params: twitterParams,
    delegate: self)
}
```

Run it and...nothing's changed! And that's exactly what we want! The point of refactoring is to change the code while maintaining the same behavior, and that's just what we've done—only now, it will be easier to grow the project, since much of the Twitter-specific code (and everything relating to the Accounts framework) is no longer in this view controller class, and what's left is directly related to the specifics of this view controller's Twitter request, and the specifics of the handling the response. The latter is still in handleTwitterData(), unchanged but for the addition of a currently unused parameter.

Now that we've completed this refactoring, any other view controllers we write that need to call the Twitter API can use code much like what's now in reload-Tweets() in that they'll just need to provide a URL and a parameters dictionary, and parse the response in the delegate callback. The details will be specific to the Twitter API they're calling (tweet details, user info), but that's exactly what we'd want anyway. So let's start building out those new view controllers.

Using Another TwitterAPIRequest

To prove all this refactoring has been worth it, let's see how much easier it'll be to add Twitter calls to our existing classes or those we may yet create.

Just for kicks—and with the understanding we'll undo this silly code in a few minutes when we're done with it—take a look at AppDelegate.swift. This class has to do with how our app interacts with the rest of the system, something we'll talk about more in Chapter 13, *Launching, Backgrounding, and Extensions*, on page 207. For now, notice there is a method called applicationWillEnter-Foreground(). This is called when the app is brought back to life from the background. Let's do a Twitter call every time this happens.

To do so, we will be using a TwitterAPIRequest, and making our caller a TwitterAPIRe-questDelegate to handle the response. So change the AppDelegate declaration as follows:

Growing/PragmaticTweets-8-1/PragmaticTweets/AppDelegate.swift

```
class AppDelegate: UIResponder, UIApplicationDelegate,
                   TwitterAPIRequestDelegate {
```

This just adds TwitterAPIRequestDelegate to the list of protocols the class must implement, in addition to the UIApplicationDelegate that was already there.

Now we need a simple Twitter API to call. A simple one is users/suggestions, which will send us some suggested topics, based on who we follow. Thanks to our TwitterAPIRequest class, asking for this is really simple; just rewrite applicationWil-lEnterForeground() as follows:

Growing/PragmaticTweets-8-1/PragmaticTweets/AppDelegate.swift

```
func applicationWillEnterForeground(application: UIApplication) {
  let request = TwitterAPIRequest ()
  request.sendTwitterRequest(NSURL (
    string: "https://api.twitter.com/1.1/users/suggestions.json"),
    params: [ : ],
    delegate: self)
}
```

This is only a couple lines, mostly the stuff we care about: the URL to call and the parameters (this request doesn't need any, so we send an empty dictionary). Notice that we didn't have to import the Accounts or Social framework: all that drudgery is stashed away in TwitterAPIRequest, closures and all. Separation of concerns, FTW!

Now we need to provide a handleTwitterData() method, to implement the Twitter-APIRequestDelegate protocol. The AppDelegate doesn't have a UI of its own, so let's just log the JSON to the debug pane:

Growing/PragmaticTweets-8-1/PragmaticTweets/AppDelegate.swift

```
func handleTwitterData(data: NSData!,
  urlResponse: NSHTTPURLResponse!,
  error: NSError!,
  fromRequest: TwitterAPIRequest!) {
    let jsonObject : AnyObject? =
    NSJSONSerialization.JSONObjectWithData(data,
      options: NSJSONReadingOptions(0),
      error: nil)
    println("suggestions JSON: \(jsonObject)")
}
```

Now, run the app. Our table appears as usual. Our new code only runs when the app returns to active duty from the foreground, so use the simulator's Hardware→Home (⇧⌘H) to background the app, then bring it to the foreground by tapping its icon, or select it from the running apps list by double-tapping home (that is, ⇧⌘H twice, quickly). The request will go out and populate our debug pane:

```
suggestions JSON: Optional(<__NSCFArray 0x7fd5ab92e2e0>(
{
    name = Music;
    size = 101;
    slug = music;
},
{
    name = Sports;
    size = 74;
    slug = sports;
},
```

So, with about 10 lines of new code, we can fire off and handle a new Twitter API request. And that's how we're going to build out the functionality of our application, creating new view controllers and letting them reuse this general-purpose Twitter class we've created for ourselves. Of course, this was a somewhat silly exercise—feel free to delete all these changes in AppDelegate.swift—but it does prove out our general-purpose TwitterAPIRequest pretty nicely.

Wrap-Up

In this chapter, we learned techniques that are helpful as projects get bigger. We started by organizing our files into groups, which we can expand, put away, and nest within one another, so we can look at just the files we need at any one time.

Then we looked at Xcode's support for refactoring, which is currently unavailable for Swift but is likely to support it in the near future. Instead, we did our own refactoring to change class names. Then we took on a bigger project: taking the Twitter code in RootViewController and making it a general-purpose class that can be reused by other classes we'll be creating later. We looked at how iOS uses the delegate pattern to hand off responsibility for special-purpose code: the TwitterAPIRequest knows to send requests, but what to do with the response is entirely up to delegates.

Now that we've genericized our Twitter code, we're ready to move beyond the single view and give the user the ability to navigate between scenes, each able to take advantage of the work we've done so far.

CHAPTER 9

Navigating Between View Controllers

Thanks to our refactoring work in the previous chapter, we're now ready to add lots of new view controllers and their corresponding views, each with its own ability to make, receive, and parse Twitter API requests. Thing is, where do they go? We can't just plop another view controller scene onto the storyboard, because the storyboard would have no way to get to it. What we need is a way to navigate between view controllers.

In this chapter, we're going to add view controllers that can show things like tweet and user details, and use three different ways of navigating between multiple view controllers. These are the common idioms we use for moving around in an app on the iPhone and iPad, and they let us choose whether to use the entire screen, split things on different parts of the screen, or even have it both ways, depending on how much screen space we have to work with.

Navigation Controllers

The most common way to work with multiple view controllers is to use a *navigation controller*, which is a view controller that manages a stack of child view controllers. This UINavigationController will become the new point of entry to the storyboard and will have our current RootViewController as the first thing it shows. From there, we'll add more view controllers, and the navigation controller will keep track of which one we're looking at and how to go back to earlier ones in the stack.

We won't have to write a new class for this, as the UINavigationController is meant to be used as is and is seldom subclassed.

Actually, we don't need to write code at all to use a navigation controller; we can do everything in the storyboard. In fact, the best thing about the storyboard is how it visualizes complex navigation schemes. Ours will be pretty simple, but it's nice to know we can grow.

Switch to the storyboard and then locate the Navigation Controller icon in the Object library; it looks like a yellow circle with a blue back arrow in it.

Drag this into the storyboard. During the drag, it will appear as two views connected by an arrow. Drop it close to the existing view controller, but above it. Once you've dropped, the storyboard will have three scenes, and three view controllers with their attached views: our original root view controller, a navigation controller, and a table view controller, as shown in the following figure. Note that we've zoomed out to get all three scenes on screen at once, although all we can do at this zoom level is move scenes around, not edit their views.

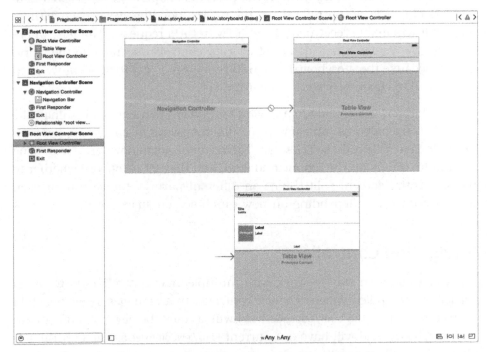

Run the app now and...nothing's different! That's because there's no way in the storyboard to reach the navigation controller or its child view controller. We can change that by selecting the navigation controller—either in the scene list or from the yellow ball in the bar under its view—and bringing up its Attributes Inspector (⌥⌘4). Find the Is Initial View Controller checkbox and select it. In the storyboard graph, the arrow that went into our root view controller now goes into the navigation controller.

Run again and...now our tweets are gone, replaced by a table with the title Root View Controller. What we're seeing is that the app now enters via the navigation controller, which in turn shows its first (root) child controller, which is the empty table view controller that Xcode gave us when we dragged in the navigation controller. But we don't want this controller: all our custom table cell work is back in our old view controller.

What we need to do is to tell the navigation controller to use our old view controller as its root view controller. Notice that in the scene list, the last entry in the Navigation Controller scene is Relationship "Root View Controller". That needs to change. Control-click on the navigation controller, or bring up its Connections Inspector (⌥⌘6). Under Triggered Segues, there's a connection called Root View Controller. Starting from the connection's circle, begin a drag (which will stretch out a blue line) and drop on our old view controller, as shown in the following figure:

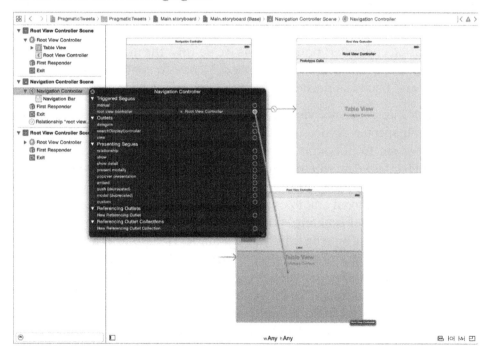

Run again and our app is pretty much back to normal, showing all our tweets as before. The only change is that there's now a big blank space at the top of the screen. Still, progress!

The Navigation Bar

The space at the top of the screen is the *navigation bar*, which appears atop any view controller managed by a UINavigationController. The navigation bar has room for three UI elements, from left to right:

1. A left-side *bar button item*. For anything but the root view controller, this is typically a Back button, and a default back button will be provided if we don't set a different bar button item of our own.

2. A title, either as a string or as a custom view.

3. A right-side bar button item.

We can easily customize all these things in the storyboard. First, as a bit of cleanup, we can get rid of that empty table controller that Xcode gave us, the one that was attached to the navigation controller. Select its view controller and press ⌫; the entire scene disappears. We can also grab the title bar atop our root view controller and move it around the storyboard to get it closer to the navigation controller; notice that as we do this, the arrow connecting the two (representing the navigation controller's "root view controller" relationship) stretches and bends as needed to keep the two connected.

Zoom back into a full size view of the Root View Controller and bring up its Attributes Inspector. Notice that the top bar says Inferred. This is what it's always been set to; the storyboard figures out whether or not to show the navigation bar based on whether the view controller has a navigation controller as a parent, which it now does. Double-click in the center of the navigation bar and it'll turn into an editable text field. Type Tweets and press ↵ to finish editing. Notice that this changes the name of the scene to Tweets Scene, and the view controller icon (the little yellow ball) to Tweets. Run again and our tweets now have a nice title bar. Keep in mind that we haven't added a UILabel or UITextField. What we've done here is to tell the navigation bar what title to use for this view controller. To prove this point, notice in the scene list that what we're editing here is the properties of a "navigation item" within the Root View Controller scene, not a label or any other sort of view.

The two bar button items in the navigation bar also give us an opportunity to add functionality to our app. In fact, they give us a very nice way to bring back our New Tweet feature! In the Object library, scroll down to the smaller Item icon; this is the bar button item, shown in the figure. The UIBarButton is very different from the UIButton we've used before; in fact, it's not even a subclass of UIView! It's an object that contains just enough state to be drawn in a bar and to be able to call a method when tapped.

Drag the bar button item to the right side of the top bar in the Root View Controller scene. A highlight to accept the drop will appear, and after the drop, the bar button item will appear as Item in the bar. We can edit its text in place, but there's a better option. Select the bar button item and bring up the Attributes Inspector. The second attribute listed is Identifier, with a default value of Custom. Custom bar button items are those that have custom labels. However, there are about 20 other choices, representing common actions like Search, Refresh, and Trash. From this list, choose Add. This turns the bar button item into a plus (+) symbol, which is a reasonably intuitive way to tell users that this is how they'll compose a tweet, and more practical in limited space than text like Compose Tweet would be. The next figure shows our finished navigation bar:

Now that we've customized the button's appearance, we need to give it some functionality. Fortunately, our functionality already exists: it's the handleTweet-ButtonTapped() method we wrote way back in *Connecting User Interface to Code*, on page 23. So we just need to wire up a connection. Control-click on the add button to bring up the heads-up display (HUD) showing its connections, and notice that instead of the UIButton's various events (Touch Up Inside, etc.), there is just a Triggered Segues action and a Sent Actions selector. What we want now is to just call a selector, so drag from selector over to the Root View Controller icon (the yellow ball that now says Tweets). When we drop, a pop-up will show us the selectors we can connect to.

Unfortunately, the one we want, handleTweetButtonTapped(), isn't in the list. The reason for this is in the code. handleTweetButtonTapped() currently takes a UIButton as an argument, and a bar button item isn't actually a button. So, in RootViewController.swift, edit that method definition to take AnyObject instead.

Navigation/PragmaticTweets-9-1/PragmaticTweets/RootViewController.swift
```
@IBAction func handleTweetButtonTapped(sender: AnyObject) {
```

Now, back in the storyboard, select the "+" bar button item, control-drag from selector to the view controller icon, and after dropping, choose handleTweetButtonTapped(). Note that there's a faster way to do this: rather than bring up the pop-up, just control-drag from the bar button item to the view controller, which figures out that you want to connect the selector, since the other kinds of connections don't make sense here.

At any rate, run the project again and tap the add button. The tweet compose view controller returns, although at this point the default "I just finished the first project" text seems totally out of date. We've gotten a *lot* further since then! With the addition of the navigation bar, our app much more closely resembles the other major Twitter apps on iOS.

Navigating Between View Controllers

Now that we have our root view controller managed by a navigation controller, we're ready to start navigating. Where shall we go? Since our root view shows a table of tweets, let's allow the user to select one of those tweets to inspect in detail. To do this, we'll add a new view controller scene to the storyboard, indicate how we navigate to it, and write a custom UIViewController subclass to provide the behavior for the new scene.

We can begin in the storyboard. From the Object library, choose the generic View Controller icon, which looks like the rectangular UIView icon inside a yellow circle, as seen in the next figure:

Drag the icon (which turns into a view with usual title bar underneath) into the storyboard, dropping it to the right of the existing root view controller. Once dropped, it appears as a completely empty view, and when not selected, the title bar above the view simply says View Controller. This view controller has no visible contents and cannot be reached from any other view controller, but we can change that easily enough.

From the Root View Controller scene on the left, select CustomTweetCell, which is the one we customized with the styled labels and the icon. Control-drag from there to the new view controller (either its entry in the scene list or its icon, or its view out on the storyboard; any of these will work). This gesture indicates that you want to create a *segue* from the cell to the new view controller when the cell is tapped. Optionally, instead of control-dragging, we can bring up the connections pop-up with a control-click and drag the Triggered Segues: Selection connection over to the new view controller.

Whichever gesture we use, upon ending the drag, a pop-up menu asks us to clarify what we want the connection to do, as seen in the figure. For a selection segue, we have five main choices: Show, Show Detail, Present Modally, Popover Presentation, or Custom. Choose Show.

Once we do this, two interesting things happen to our new view controller. First, it gets a simulated navigation bar, just like when we connected the root view controller to the navigation controller. That's because Interface Builder knows this view controller is managed by a navigation controller, so a navigation bar will be provided at runtime. However, we can't double-click in this one to set its title. The reason is that to customize the appearance of a non-root view controller, the scene needs to have a navigation item, which tells the navigation controller what's different about this scene, usually meaning a title and a right bar button item.

Drag a Navigation Item icon from the Object library to the new scene. You should now be able to double-click in the navigation bar and change its name to Tweet.

The other thing that changed when we dragged the segue between the two scenes is that there's now an arrow connecting the root view controller to our new view controller. In the middle of the arrow is a circular icon that represents the segue, which is the object managing the transition between the two view controllers. We'll have more to say about using segues a little later.

For now, let's run the app and see what we have. Once the tweets table gets populated, tap one of them. The tweets view will slide out to the left while the new view slides in from the right. Although it's empty, we can easily get our bearings thanks to the navigation bar, which shows our Tweet title. The navigation controller also provides a back button on the left, which by default uses the title of the previous view controller: Tweets. Not bad, getting navigation for free without having written any code for it!

Using the Storyboard Segue

When we tap a cell in the list of tweets, we navigate to the new view controller, which we'll customize to show the details for the selected tweet. But hold on, how do we know which tweet was selected? And how will we communicate that to the other view controller?

This is where the segue can help us. Prior to performing a transition between view controllers, the current view controller gets a callback on the method prepareForSegue(), passing in details of the transition in a UIStoryboardSegue object. As inherited from UIViewController, this method does nothing, but we can override it to take some interesting action, based both on our current state and details of the segue.

The UIStoryboardSegue object provides properties for the sourceViewController, destinationViewController, and an identifier, which is a string that we can use to distinguish between different segues in the storyboard. It's a good habit to name any segue we intend to use in code, so click on the segue's circle icon between the two view controllers and display the Attributes Inspector. The only attributes we can edit are the Identifier string and the segue type (which is whatever we set in the HUD when we created the segue: Show, Show Detail, Present Modally, etc.). For the identifier, enter showTweetDetailsSegue.

Now visit RootViewController.swift. Write a new method to override prepareForSegue(), as follows:

Navigation/PragmaticTweets-9-2/PragmaticTweets/RootViewController.swift
```
override public func prepareForSegue(segue: UIStoryboardSegue,
                                     sender: AnyObject?) {
  if segue.identifier == "showTweetDetailsSegue" {
    let row = tableView!.indexPathForSelectedRow()!.row
    let parsedTweet = parsedTweets [row] as ParsedTweet
    println ("tapped on: \(parsedTweet.tweetText!)")
  }
}
```

When called, this looks at the segue argument to see if it matches the identifier we put in the storyboard: showTweetDetailsSegue. If it does, it gets the selected row from the table, looks up the corresponding tweet, and logs its text to the console. Run the app and tap a row to verify this is working; if not, check the spelling of the segue identifier in the storyboard and the code to make sure they match *exactly*.

Sharing Data Between View Controllers

Now that we can get the selected tweet, we need a way to communicate between the view controllers. Actually, our tweet detail view controller may want more information than we have in the ParsedTweet, or things that the home_timeline API doesn't even provide, so we'll need a way to pass the tweet's unique identifier to the second view controller, and then let that view controller get whatever details it needs via a new Twitter API call.

So, add a tweetIdString to ParsedTweet.swift:

Navigation/PragmaticTweets-9-2/PragmaticTweets/ParsedTweet.swift
```
var tweetIdString : String?
```

In the Twitter API response, the tweet's unique ID string is identified with the key id_str, so that's what we need to get from the response dictionary and set on the ParsedTweet. Put this assignment in RootViewController's handleTwitterData(), where we do the rest of our JSON unpacking:

Navigation/PragmaticTweets-9-2/PragmaticTweets/RootViewController.swift
```
parsedTweet.tweetIdString = tweetDict["id_str"] as? NSString
```

Now we're ready to send the tweet ID to the second view controller, and let it get more detailed tweet information.

Sending Data to the Second View Controller

Now we need to put some code behind that second view controller, which we can do with a custom class. It's good practice to put each view controller class and any helper classes in their own group, so in the File Navigator, create a new group called Tweet Detail VC. Then select this group and select File→New→File to create a new Cocoa Touch Class file. Call it TweetDetailViewController, and make sure it's a subclass of UIViewController and the language is Swift.

Property Setters

This class will have one public property, a tweetIDString. When we set this property, we want the view controller to immediately take that ID and fetch the details of the tweet from Twitter. To do that, we can use one of Swift's nifty features: *property setters*. The idea here is the property declaration can include some code that is called immediately whenever the value of the property is set. We do this by appending curly braces to the property declaration, and inside them, a didSet with the curly-braced code we want to run. Let's stub it out like this:

Navigation/PragmaticTweets-9-2/PragmaticTweets/TweetDetailViewController.swift

```
var tweetIdString : String? {
  didSet {
    reloadTweetDetails()
  }
}
```

This will cause the reloadTweetDetails() method to run anytime the tweetIdString is set. Of course, that method doesn't exist yet, so quickly stub out an empty implementation so we don't get build errors.

Navigation/PragmaticTweets-9-2/PragmaticTweets/TweetDetailViewController.swift

```
func reloadTweetDetails() {
}
```

Joe asks:
Is There Also a willSet?

Yep! And it works just like didSet, except of course it executes just before the property is set, not after. We can even use both, if we need to.

Also, if you remember all the way back in *Declaring Properties*, on page 39, we talked about a difference between "stored properties," which are backed by a variable, and "computed properties." There's a get keyword, which is how we'd implement a computed property: its value is implicit from other properties, and the value is something we'd compute and return in the get block.

Sending Data via a Segue

The storyboard doesn't know that the second view controller is supposed to use this class. Fix that by selecting the second view controller, the tweet detail scene, in the storyboard and bringing up the Identity Inspector (⌥⌘3). Under Custom Class, change the class from UIViewController to TweetDetailViewController (it should autocomplete as you type).

Now the pieces are all in place to deliver the tweetIdString from the first view controller to the second when the transition happens. Go back to RootViewController.swift, and rewrite the prepareForSegue:sender:() method as follows:

Navigation/PragmaticTweets-9-2/PragmaticTweets/RootViewController.swift

```
Line 1  override public func prepareForSegue(segue: UIStoryboardSegue,
                                    sender: AnyObject?) {
          if segue.identifier == "showTweetDetailsSegue" {
            if let tweetDetailVC = segue.destinationViewController
     5          as? TweetDetailViewController {
                let row = tableView!.indexPathForSelectedRow()!.row
                let parsedTweet = parsedTweets [row] as ParsedTweet
                tweetDetailVC.tweetIdString = parsedTweet.tweetIdString
            }
    10      }
        }
```

The big change here is lines 4–5, where we ask the segue for its destinationView-
Controller, and attempt to cast it to a TweetDetailViewController. If this works, then
we can assign the tweetDetailVC's tweetIdString on line 8, which will kick off the
setter method we wrote before.

Designing the Second View Controller

Now let's give the second view controller some UI elements to fill in. Add the
following UI elements and their constraints:

- A button at the upper left, with fixed width and height of 60 by 60, the
  top edge pinned 8 points from the top layout guide, and the leading edge
  pinned 0 points from the margin. Use the Attributes Inspector to change
  its type to Custom, which will allow us to change its image.

- A label called Real Name top-aligned to the button. We do this by selecting
  both the button and the label, bringing up the alignment constraints from
  the Align popover, and in the Add New Alignment Constraints section,
  choose Top Edges. Then use the pin constraints to pin the leading space
  8 points from the button, and stretched all the way across so its trailing
  edge is 0 points from the margin. Change the font to System Bold at 17
  point size.

- A label called User Name just below the Real Name label, leading space
  8 points from the button, with a top edge 8 points down from the label
  above it (a fixed distance to the superview will also work), and trailing
  space of 0 to the right margin. Change the font to make it smaller than
  the default, like System font at 15 point size.

- A label called Tweet Text, leading edge and trailing edges 0 points in from
  the side margins, 8 points down from the button, and set to 0 lines so it
  can grow as needed to accommodate the tweet text.

- An image view, top edge 8 points down from the Tweet Text label, leading and trailing edges 0 points from the margins, bottom edge 20 points in. Use the Attributes Inspector to set its mode to Aspect Fit, which will scale the image to fill one or both dimensions, without cropping or stretching (but without necessarily filling the entire space).

When finished, the layout should look something like this:

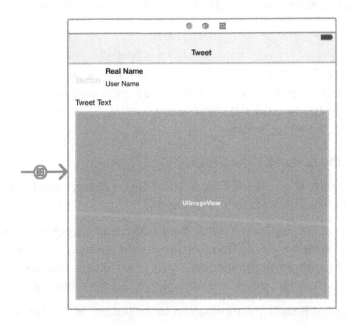

Switch to the Assistant Editor, and make sure that TweetDetailViewController.swift is visible in the right pane (use the jump bar to bring up the right file if necessary). Control-drag from each of these UI components in the view to create outlets in the class file, using the names userImageButton, userRealNameLabel, userScreenNameLabel, tweetTextLabel, and tweetImageView. The resulting outlets should look like this:

Navigation/PragmaticTweets-9-2/PragmaticTweets/TweetDetailViewController.swift
```
@IBOutlet weak var userImageButton: UIButton!
@IBOutlet weak var userRealNameLabel: UILabel!
@IBOutlet weak var userScreenNameLabel: UILabel!
@IBOutlet weak var tweetTextLabel: UILabel!
@IBOutlet weak var tweetImageView: UIImageView!
```

Coding the Second View Controller

Now we need to add the code to make our second view controller get to work. We can wait until our view controller's viewWillAppear() method is called so that if the tweetIdString has been set, it can immediately update the UI.

Navigation/PragmaticTweets-9-2/PragmaticTweets/TweetDetailViewController.swift
```swift
override func viewWillAppear(animated: Bool) {
  super.viewWillAppear(animated)
  reloadTweetDetails()
}
```

Notice that since we're overriding the viewWillAppear() inherited from UIViewController, we have to put an explicit override in the method declaration, and call the superclass's implementation as part of our own.

Now we're ready to use the Twitter classes we refactored in the previous chapter. We're going to use a TwitterAPIRequest to ask for the details, and parse the response. To be the delegate that handles the response, we have to declare that we implement the protocol, so update the class's declaration like this:

Navigation/PragmaticTweets-9-2/PragmaticTweets/TweetDetailViewController.swift
```swift
class TweetDetailViewController: UIViewController, TwitterAPIRequestDelegate {
```

The Twitter API provides the statuses/show.json call to get details about a single tweet, and takes a single parameter, id, with the unique ID of the tweet, so that's what we'll call in our reloadTweetDetails().

Navigation/PragmaticTweets-9-2/PragmaticTweets/TweetDetailViewController.swift
```swift
func reloadTweetDetails() {
  if tweetIdString == nil {
    return
  }
  let twitterRequest = TwitterAPIRequest()
  let twitterParams = ["id" : tweetIdString!]
  let twitterAPIURL = NSURL (string:
    "https://api.twitter.com/1.1/statuses/show.json")
  twitterRequest.sendTwitterRequest(twitterAPIURL,
    params: twitterParams,
    delegate: self)
}
```

This is similar to the code we refactored in RootViewController's reloadTweets() in the last chapter: we create a TwitterAPIRequest, set its URL and parameters, and fire off the request, declaring the current class to be the delegate, meaning its handleTwitterData() method will be called with the response.

A trivial implementation of the callback method could just convert the data parameter into an NSJSONSerialization object, and log it out to see what Twitter sends back to us. To save you that step: the response provides the tweet text, along with a user dictionary that contains a name, screen_name, and much, *much* more. Let's pull out the easy stuff first.

Navigation/PragmaticTweets-9-2/PragmaticTweets/TweetDetailViewController.swift
```swift
func handleTwitterData (data: NSData!,
  urlResponse: NSHTTPURLResponse!,
  error: NSError!,
  fromRequest: TwitterAPIRequest!) {

    if let dataValue = data {
      var parseError : NSError? = nil
      let jsonObject : AnyObject? =
      NSJSONSerialization.JSONObjectWithData(dataValue,
        options: NSJSONReadingOptions(0),
        error: &parseError)
      if parseError != nil {
        return
      }
      if let tweetDict = jsonObject as? [String:AnyObject] {
        dispatch_async(dispatch_get_main_queue(),
          {
            println ("\(tweetDict)")
            let userDict = tweetDict["user"] as NSDictionary
            self.userRealNameLabel.text = userDict["name"] as? NSString
            self.userScreenNameLabel.text = userDict["screen_name"]
                                            as? NSString
            self.tweetTextLabel.text = tweetDict["text"]  as? NSString
            let userImageURL = NSURL (string:
              userDict ["profile_image_url"] as NSString!)
            self.userImageButton.setTitle(nil, forState: .Normal)
            if userImageURL != nil {
              if let imageData = NSData(contentsOfURL: userImageURL!) {
                self.userImageButton.setImage(
                  UIImage(data: imageData),
                forState: UIControlState.Normal)
              }
            }
        })
      }
    } else {
      println ("handleTwitterData received no data")
    }
}
```

The handling of the jsonResponse and using a closure to update the UI on the main queue is identical to what we did in the RootViewController; the only difference is which values we pull out of the tweetDict and then use to update our user interface. It's also different in that we are using a button for the user's icon, something we'll take advantage of in a little bit.

Once the response is received, the various labels and the image button are all updated, including the tweet text, which thanks to autolayout can grow or shrink to as many lines are needed to contain all the text. Try it now and verify that everything's OK.

Adding an Image to the Detail View

So far, we aren't making much use of the extra space in our second view controller, and not showing much more information than could fit in a carefully designed table cell. Let's fill in the image view that we added in the storyboard.

If the selected tweet has an image that was uploaded with Twitter's own image-hosting service (not a third-party service like TwitPic or img.ly), the tweetDict will contain an entities dictionary with extra attachments. Within this, there may be a media array, each describing one attachment as a dictionary. Assuming this is the case, we can take the first element of this array, which will be a dictionary, and look for a media_url.

We can dig into the tweetDict for any image attachments as part of the closure we just wrote. Immediately prior to the }) line that ends the closure, add the following logic:

```
Navigation/PragmaticTweets-9-2/PragmaticTweets/TweetDetailViewController.swift
if let entities = tweetDict["entities"] as? NSDictionary {
  if let media = entities ["media"] as? NSArray {
    if let mediaString = media[0]["media_url"] as? String {
      if let mediaURL = NSURL(string: mediaString) {
        if let mediaData = NSData (contentsOfURL: mediaURL) {
          self.tweetImageView.image = UIImage(data: mediaData)
        }
      }
    }
  }
}
```

This is an unfortunately punitive level of indentation, but it does work as intended. Run the app, look through some tweets, and you should eventually be able to populate the detail view with an image, as in the following figure:

So, now we have a more interesting Twitter app, one that lets us pick a tweet and show it in detail, including whatever information we'd care to pull out of the response, such as presenting location information on a map. More importantly, we have a way forward for expanding the capabilities of the app: as we need new features or new ways to enter or present data, we can navigate to new view controllers, building them out in our storyboard and custom classes.

Modal Navigation

In fact, we'll close out the chapter with a different approach for presenting view controllers, and how it ties into one of the neatest things about navigating through storyboards.

In the tweet detail controller, we used a button rather than an image view to present the user's icon, and this is where we're going to use that: we'll allow the user to tap the icon to go to a third view controller, one that presents details about the user.

Modal Segues

Add another view controller to the storyboard, to the right of the tweet detail view controller (again, it may be necessary to zoom out to organize the views nicely). Scroll so that both the tweet detail view controller and the new view controller are visible at the same time, and control-drag from the user image button to the new view controller; this can also be done by control-dragging through these entries in the scene tree on the left. When we end the drag and release, Interface Builder infers that we want to make a segue to the new view controller, triggered by a tap on the button, and shows a pop-up asking what kind of segue to create. This time, choose Present Modally.

The storyboard will add an arrow connecting the second and third view controllers, with a circle-shaped segue icon in the middle, as seen in the following figure. Notice that this icon is different from the icon for the push segue we used earlier. And there's another thing to notice: *the new view controller doesn't show a navigation bar.* That's because modal navigation is different. Showing another view controller modally doesn't require a navigation controller like a "show" presentation does, so we're always free to create this kind of transition in a storyboard. This is handy because we often need to do something modally, meaning we need to stop the user to either show them something or get some input from them before we continue.

On the other hand, no navigation bar means no back button, and we'll have to deal with that eventually.

While we're thinking about the segue, click its icon and bring up the Attributes Inspector, so we can give it an identifier string: showUserDetailsSegue.

Laying Out the User Detail View Controller

For now, let's build some utility into this third view controller. This will be where we show a user's details, so add the following elements, from top to bottom, so they look like the image below:

- An image view, the top edge pinned 0 points from the margin, width and height pinned to 100, horizontally centered in container.

- A label called User Name, text center-aligned, System Bold 24.0 point, the top edge pinned 8 points below the image view, leading and trailing constraints 0 points from the margin.

- A label called Screen Name, text center-aligned, the top edge pinned 8 points below the username label, leading and trailing constraints 0 points from the margin.

- A label called Location, text center-aligned, the top edge pinned 8 points below the screen name label, leading and trailing constraints 0 points from the margin.

- A label called Description, text center-aligned, set to 0 lines so it can wrap as needed, the top edge pinned 8 points below the location label, leading and trailing constraints 0 points from the margin.

- A button titled Done, the top edge pinned 8 points below the description label, horizontally aligned in the container.

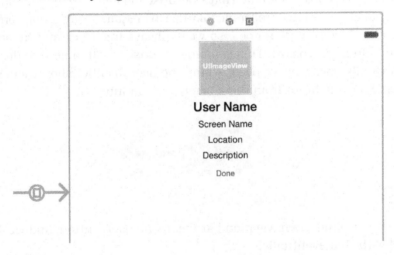

Now we want to tie this into code, so we'll need a custom view controller, like we did before with the tweet details scene. In the File Navigator, create a group called User Detail VC. Within that group, create a new file, using the iOS Cocoa Touch Class template, calling it UserDetailViewController and making it a subclass of UIViewController, written in Swift.

Back in the storyboard, select the view controller icon for this scene (from the scene list on the left or the view's lower title bar), and use the Identity

Inspector (⌥⌘3) to set the class to UserDetailViewController. That will allow us to bring up the Assistant Editor (making sure that UserDetailViewController.swift is in the right pane) to control-drag outlets for the image view and all the labels. When done, the properties should look like this:

Navigation/PragmaticTweets-9-3/PragmaticTweets/UserDetailViewController.swift

```
@IBOutlet weak var userImageView: UIImageView!
@IBOutlet weak var userRealNameLabel: UILabel!
@IBOutlet weak var userScreenNameLabel: UILabel!
@IBOutlet weak var userLocationLabel: UILabel!
@IBOutlet weak var userDescriptionLabel: UILabel!
```

Coding the User Detail View Controller

Our code for this third view controller is going to be a lot like the second: we'll expose a public property, and let it use that to refresh itself from the Twitter API every time it needs data. Twitter lets us get the user details from just a screen name, so let's make that a public property in the UserDetailViewController.swift file:

Navigation/PragmaticTweets-9-3/PragmaticTweets/UserDetailViewController.swift

```
var screenName : String?
```

As before, we'll fire off a TwitterAPIRequest and expect the class to parse the result, which means it will be the delegate for the Twitter request. So we need to update the class declaration to indicate we implement that delegate protocol:

Navigation/PragmaticTweets-9-3/PragmaticTweets/UserDetailViewController.swift

```
class UserDetailViewController: UIViewController, TwitterAPIRequestDelegate {
```

Since we want to update the view whenever it appears, we'll make our Twitter call in viewWillAppear(). To get the user details, we'll use Twitter's users/show.json request, which takes just a screen_name parameter. So here's the method to write:

Navigation/PragmaticTweets-9-3/PragmaticTweets/UserDetailViewController.swift

```
override func viewWillAppear(animated: Bool)  {
  super.viewWillAppear(animated)
  if screenName == nil {
    return
  }
  let twitterRequest = TwitterAPIRequest()
  let twitterParams = ["screen_name" : screenName!]
  let twitterAPIURL = NSURL (string: "https://api.twitter.com/1.1/users/show.json")
  twitterRequest.sendTwitterRequest(twitterAPIURL,
    params: twitterParams,
    delegate: self)
}
```

When we get a response, we'll get the delegate callback as handleTwitterData(), which we can write as follows:

Navigation/PragmaticTweets-9-3/PragmaticTweets/UserDetailViewController.swift

```
func handleTwitterData (data: NSData!,
  urlResponse: NSHTTPURLResponse!,
  error: NSError!,
  fromRequest: TwitterAPIRequest!) {

    if let dataValue = data {
      var parseError : NSError? = nil
      let jsonObject : AnyObject? =
      NSJSONSerialization.JSONObjectWithData(dataValue,
        options: NSJSONReadingOptions(0),
        error: &parseError)
      if parseError != nil {
        return
      }
      if let tweetDict = jsonObject as? [String:AnyObject] {
        dispatch_async(dispatch_get_main_queue(),
          {
            self.userRealNameLabel.text = tweetDict["name"] as? NSString
            self.userScreenNameLabel.text = tweetDict["screen_name"]
                                          as? NSString
            self.userLocationLabel.text = tweetDict["location"]
                                          as? NSString
            self.userDescriptionLabel.text = tweetDict["description"]
                                          as? NSString
            if let userImageURL = NSURL (string:
              tweetDict ["profile_image_url"] as NSString) {
                if let userImageData = NSData (contentsOfURL: userImageURL) {
                  self.userImageView.image = UIImage(data:userImageData)
                }
            }
          }
        })
      }
    }
}
```

This is our third time unpacking a Twitter response, so it should be looking pretty familiar: use NSJSONSerialization to convert the data to an NSDictionary, then use known keys in the response to pull out interesting values and set them in the UI, using dispatch_async() to do all this on the main queue, as required by UIKit.

The last thing we need to do is to set the screenName property. That's something the second view controller (tweet detail) will do as it begins the segue to the third (user detail). Switch to TweetDetailViewController.swift and add an implementation of prepareForSegue:sender:().

```
Navigation/PragmaticTweets-9-3/PragmaticTweets/TweetDetailViewController.swift
override func prepareForSegue(segue: UIStoryboardSegue, sender: AnyObject?) {
  if (segue.identifier == "showUserDetailsSegue") {
    if let userDetailVC = segue.destinationViewController
      as? UserDetailViewController {
        userDetailVC.screenName = userScreenNameLabel.text
    }
  }
}
```

Run this version of the app, choose a tweet to view in detail, and then click the user icon. This will perform a modal transition to the user detail view controller, showing the user in all his or her glory.

Chris Adamson

invalidname

Grand Rapids, MI, USA

I write, stream, and code stuff. I also raise children and sometimes clean things

Done

This looks great, but there's just one little problem: *we're trapped*. There's no back button, and the Done button does nothing. Now what do we do?

Exit Segues

There are a few ways we could implement the back button, but the most generally useful is the *exit segue*. With an exit segue, we can go backward in a navigation, regardless of whether we came by way of push or modal segues.

What's tricky about exit segues is that they don't appear on the storyboard the same way push or modal segues do. Instead, their existence is implicit. We can only perform an exit segue if a previous view controller has exposed a method for us to come back to. These methods, commonly called *unwind methods*, have to follow a certain signature—they take a UIStoryboardSegue parameter and have return type IBAction—but they don't have to have any code—they just have to exist.

We want our user detail view controller to unwind to the tweet detail view controller, so write the following method in TweetDetailViewController.swift:

```
Navigation/PragmaticTweets-9-4/PragmaticTweets/TweetDetailViewController.swift
@IBAction func unwindToTweetDetailVC (segue: UIStoryboardSegue?) {
}
```

An unwind method needs to have the @IBAction annotation (so we can make connections to it in the storyboard), needs to take a UIStoryboardSegue as a parameter, and should return nothing. This particular unwindToTweetDetailVC() implementation does nothing, but if we did need to collect data from the other view controller, this would be a great place to do so. In a sense, the unwind method is a counterpart to the prepareForSegue:sender:() method, in that the prepare method can send data to a view controller that we're transitioning to, and the unwind method can get data from it when it's done.

In the storyboard, click on the user detail view controller's Done button and control-drag up to the orange box on the right of the title bar above the view, which shows the tooltip Exit as we hover over it, as shown in the figure. When we complete the drop, a popover appears showing all the unwind methods we can connect to.

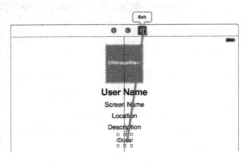

Now run the app, drill down to the user details, and tap Done. The modal transition unwinds and we're back at the tweet details view controller. All this with no code...well, no code that does anything, anyway. We could put a println() in the unwindToTweetDetailViewController() to see that it's being called.

Perhaps more interestingly, we can unwind to *any* earlier view controller. For example, if we go to RootViewController, write an unwindToRootViewController() there, and connect to an exit segue that uses that method instead, our Done button would take us all the way back to the root view controller, skipping over the tweet detail view controller entirely. This can be immensely helpful in complex storyboards where our navigation controllers get four or five view controllers deep, and we find the user may want a nice "start over" or "go home" button; exit segues make this really easy.

Programmatic Segues

It's possible to perform segues programmatically, which can be useful if we have a long-running action that should perform a segue when it's completed, like a login screen dismissing itself when a remote server sends us a response that the password has been accepted.

To programmatically go forward, a view controller can call the performSegueWith-Identifier() method. The identifier parameter it takes is the same string we've been using in prepareForSegue(), reminding us why we always want to put identifier strings on segues in the storyboard.

Programmatically performing exit segues is a little trickier, since they don't initially appear in the storyboard in a way that we can give them identifiers. But we can force the issue by control-dragging from the view controller icon to the exit segue icon, as shown here. This adds an Unwind Segue From entry to the view controller's children scene list, which we can then select and edit its attributes to give it an identifier. And then we can call performSegueWithIdentifier() to perform the unwind programmatically.

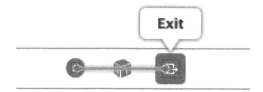

Wrap-Up

This has been a very long chapter, in which we've radically reworked our app into one that is far more capable and extensible than when we started. We've gone from being tied to one screen to having as many as we care to create.

To do this, we reworked the storyboard from a single-view design to a navigation metaphor, putting a navigation controller at the beginning of the storyboard and letting it manage the user's progress through our root view controller and a new tweet detail view controller, giving us forward/back navigation pretty much for free. We saw how to use storyboard segues to deliver information between view controllers, which allowed our root view controller to tell the tweet detail view controller just which tweet the user tapped on. Then we tried out a modal transition to show the user detail view controller, and we saw how exit segues let us return to any previous view controller and deliver data back to them in the unwind method.

This is how many popular apps work: navigating forward and backward through view controllers, each specific to some part of the app's overall functionality. From here, we can add any new features we might think of.

In the next chapter, we're going to look at another way of managing multiple view controllers, one that's particularly well suited to the iPad.

CHAPTER 10

Taking Advantage of Large Screens

We've got a pretty nifty Twitter app at this point, one that lets us scroll through tweets, navigate into a detailed view of a tweet, and then drill down to details about the account that sent it. It's pretty nice on an iPhone.

But, come to think of it, we haven't tried running it on an iPad. And we did make it a universal app in the beginning. So let's see what that looks like. Use the scheme selector in Xcode's toolbar to change to a model of iPad—we often use iPad 2, because as a non-Retina device it fits on the Mac screen—and run the app. In landscape, it looks like this:

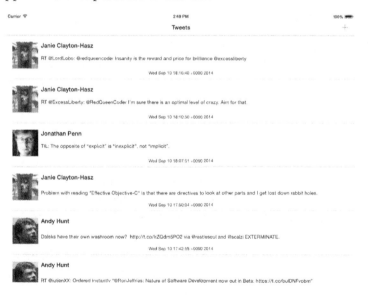

It's...*OK*. Kind of. It's not like any of the views are in the wrong place or anything. And it works fine. It just doesn't take any advantage of all the extra room on the screen. In fact, it looks a lot like the Android screenshots that speakers at Apple events will show off to demonstrate how stretching a phone UI to a tablet screen doesn't work.

So, let's not do that. In this chapter, we're going to take advantage of some unique options that let us use the iPad screen to a better effect, while still working the way we want on iPhone. We'll adapt to larger screens—starting with the iPad and then the iPhone 6 Plus—so that our app can have the best of both worlds.

Autolayout and the Many-Screen-Sizes Problem

Actually, this chapter isn't really where we start dealing with bigger screens. By using autolayout, we've been dealing with differing screen sizes all along. Instead of nailing our UI components to specific coordinates and sizes, we've used constraints like "center this button horizontally," "put this text view 8 points below this other one, wherever it is," and "let this label use whatever space is available inside the superview's margins." Thinking that way, and using these kinds of relative layout instructions, works on screens of different sizes and shapes.

Apple calls this an *adaptive* user interface, one that adapts not only to the physical factor of the device, but also to user preferences, like larger fonts for vision-impaired users.

Split Views on iPad

When the iPad was first introduced, Apple changed the name of the operating system from iPhone OS to iOS, and added some iPad-specific features to the SDK. The most distinctive is probably the *split view*. This is a UI metaphor that combines a narrow view on the left side of the screen with a wide view on the right. In portrait orientation, the left view usually can be shown or hidden, whereas in landscape view the left view is always present.

Several built-in apps on iOS use the split view. Mail shows message senders and subjects in the left view and the message content on the right. Settings has the master list of settings categories on the left and the UI for the selected topic on the right. The split view lends itself well to this sort of a "master-detail" metaphor: the main list of items is in a table on the left, and selections in this table populate the contents of a detail view on the right.

Conveniently, this is also how our Twitter app works. We have a list of tweets, and when we tap one of them, we bring up details on it in a new view. For starters, let's adapt our app to use the split view like this.

Adding a Split View to the Storyboard

To adopt the split view, we need to go to the storyboard and zoom out for a view of our current view controllers. Right now, they're in a left-to-right flow, starting with the navigation controller, and proceeding through the root view controller, the tweet detail view controller, and the user detail view controller. Go to the Object library, find the Split View Controller icon (shown in the figure), and drag it to the storyboard. The drag will put four scenes on the storyboard, so do the drop someplace where there's lots of room to work with.

Post-drop, the default split view goes off in a couple of different directions, as seen in the following figure. On the left, the split view controller scene has one connection that goes up and right to a navigation controller, and from there to a table view controller. The split view controller also has another connection that goes down and right, to a plain and empty view controller.

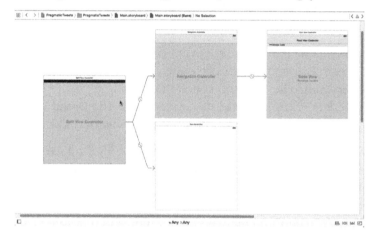

With the default arrangement of scenes, the navigation controller exists largely to provide a navigation bar for the master table view, since the table will often want to have add and edit buttons. Meanwhile, the default detail view is empty, since its contents will totally depend on the content presented by the table and which row is selected.

We already have suitable view controllers to play both of these roles, so rather than customizing the default scenes, we will delete them and replace them with our own. Our RootViewController, the scene currently labeled Tweets, will replace the default one, and our TweetDetailViewController will become the detail scene. Here's how we're going to do that:

- Start by deleting the split view's default table view controller, the one at the upper right that says Root View Controller. We do this by selecting the scene, or its view controller icon in the scene list, and pressing the delete key (⌫).

- The split view is going to control the relationship between the Tweets view controller and the various detail view controllers, so we need to let it move around the storyboard by breaking its existing connections. First, control-click our old initial navigation controller to bring up its connections HUD, and click the X to break the connection to the root view controller. Next, select the segue—the circle in the arrow between the Tweets scene and the Tweet Details scene—and delete it as well.

- Now that it's free, we can connect our Tweets table to the master portion of the split view. Drag the Tweets scene up to the right of the split view's navigation controller. Control-click on the navigation controller and find the connection called Root View Controller. Drag from this connection over to the Tweets scene to make the connection.

- Now for the detail part of the split view controller. Delete the empty default detail scene that came with the split view controller. Drag our original navigation controller into the space that was just vacated. Control-click the split view controller to see its connections. The Detail View Controller connection is now empty; drag this to the Navigation Controller scene.

- But where does this navigation controller go? After all, we broke its connection to the Tweets scene that it was originally connected to. Instead, control-click the navigation controller to bring up its connections HUD, and connect the root view controller to the Tweet Detail View Controller scene. Now the bottom half—the "detail" flow—of our split view controller goes from Navigation Controller to Tweet Detail to User Detail.

- Finally, select the split view controller, bring up its Attributes Inspector (⌥⌘4), and select the Is Initial View Controller checkbox so that the split view will get to do its thing when the app comes up.

Wow! That's a lot of clicky-draggy! Well, if nothing else, this should allay any fears about deleting and reconnecting storyboard scenes. And if things ever go truly bad, there's always the Undo command. At any rate, the storyboard should now look like the following figure, with the upper branch of the split view going to a navigation controller and our Tweets table, and the lower branch going to the Tweet Detail scene, and then on to User Detail.

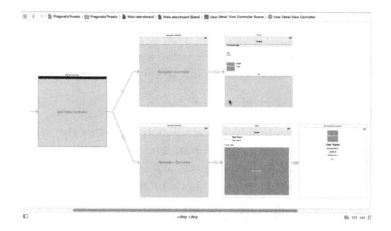

Go ahead and run the app like this, with the scheme selector still set to some flavor of iPad. In portrait, all we'll see is the unpopulated detail view with its empty labels for the username and tweet text. However, a left-to-right drag gesture will reveal the master view, the list of tweets, on the left. Rotating the simulator to landscape (⌘← or ⌘→) will cause the master list to always be visible, as seen in the following figure:

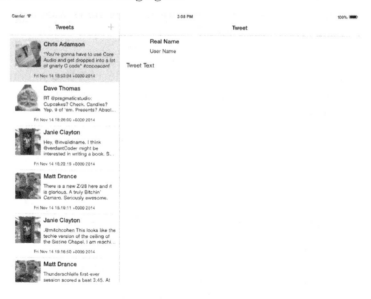

So far, so good! The master view appears when it needs to in landscape and can be brought up in portrait, and all the work we did to populate the list of tweets is still working as before.

There's just one thing: *tapping on the rows no longer does anything.* Previously, we had created a segue to connect the table to the Tweet Detail scene, which gave us the navigation between scenes. But we deleted that segue, and now there's no way to send data between the scenes. So what do we do now?

Connecting Scenes in a Split View Controller

When we built our navigation in the storyboard, creating the segue from the table to the detail scene took care of handling taps on the table for us, and telling us (in prepareForSegue()) which destinationViewController was coming in, which is how we told the second view controller which tweet to show in detail. With that gone, we will have to handle things on our own.

First we go to RootViewController.swift, where we'll write an implementation of tableView(didSelectRowAtIndexPath:). The trick is going to be getting information to the TweetDetailViewController, which we don't have a reference to: it's not a property, and we don't get told about it via a prepareForSegue() method anymore.

The only thing these two view controllers have in common anymore is that they're both connected to the same UISplitViewController. As it turns out, that's exactly the key we need. The UIViewController class has an optional property, splitViewController, defined as "the nearest ancestor in the view controller hierarchy that is a split view controller."

Now let's think about what we can do with that. The UISplitViewController has an array property, viewControllers, that represents the child view controllers it manages. So there should be two: the navigation controller that's in front of our RootViewController, and the TweetDetailViewController.

BigScreens/PragmaticTweets-10-1/PragmaticTweets/RootViewController.swift
```
Line 1   override public func tableView(tableView: UITableView,
   -        didSelectRowAtIndexPath
   -        indexPath: NSIndexPath)  {
   -          let parsedTweet = parsedTweets[indexPath.row]
   5          if self.splitViewController != nil {
   -            if (self.splitViewController!.viewControllers.count > 1) {
   -              if let tweetDetailNav = self.splitViewController!.viewControllers[1]
   -                  as? UINavigationController {
   -                if let tweetDetailVC = tweetDetailNav.viewControllers[0]
   10                     as? TweetDetailViewController {
   -                  tweetDetailVC.tweetIdString = parsedTweet.tweetIdString
   -                }
   -              }
   -            }
   15         }
   -         tableView.deselectRowAtIndexPath(indexPath, animated: false)
   -  }
```

This short method starts on line 4 by getting the ParsedTweet from our model that corresponds to the clicked row, just like in the navigation segue case.

The next few lines are a defensive nest of if statements, by necessity. Line 5 tests to see if the splitViewController property is non-nil, since we would only want to perform this logic if we're a child of a split view. If so, line 6 checks to see that there are at least two child view controllers, since we will need to work with the second one. Lines 7–8 check that the first VC in the detail flow—the bottom half of the split in the storyboard—is a navigation controller. If so, lines 9–10 attempt to cast the navigation's root view controller to a TweetDetail-ViewController, to make sure we're talking to the kind of view controller we think we are.

If all of this works out, then line 11 assigns the tweetIdString property. As a handy side effect, this kicks off the reloadTweetDetails() called by the didSet() property setter that we wrote way back in *Property Setters*, on page 147. In fact, this is the reason we needed to write that setter: in the navigation case, we could always count on viewWillAppear() to call reloadTweetData(), but in the split view scenario, the detail view will appear at launch and just stay there, so we need to make sure that setting tweetIdString will update the display.

Finally, line 16 deselects the tapped row so it doesn't stay highlighted.

Run again and our selecting a tweet populates the detail view as expected. With all the space afforded by the iPad, tweets that have images make particularly good use of the screen, as seen in the following figure.

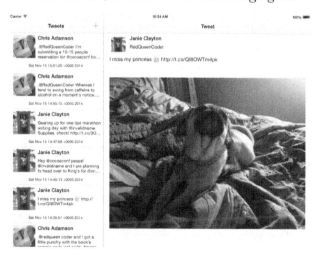

Split Views on the iPhone

So it's great that we have our app making better use of the space on the iPad, but that begs the question of what's happening on the iPhone. Does it have a side-by-side split view too? How will that fit on a dinky iPhone 4s? We'd better check what's going on, so use the scheme selector to switch to one of the smaller iPhone models (the 4s, 5, or 5s) and run the app again.

What happens is pretty unexpected, as seen in the following figure:

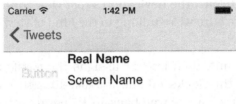

Somehow, our changes have caused us to start on a full-screen detail view instead of the master view with the list of tweets. Also, there's a navigation bar over the detail view, even though there wasn't one on top of the right pane of the split view on the iPad.

What's going on is that the split view controller realizes there's not enough space on the screen for both view controllers, so it has crunched down into a navigation-like metaphor for showing the two parts of the split on separate pages. This is a new feature for iOS 8, and it lets us use a split view controller for both iPad and iPhone. In earlier versions of iOS, we had to have completely separate storyboards for iPhone and iPad. So this is a big win for building Universal apps—those that run on iPhone and iPad—if only it did the right thing out of the box.

Notice that the back button at the top left says Tweets (the title of the master view, which it gets from a navigation item), and we can tap it to go back to the list of tweets. However, if we tap one of the tweets, it doesn't populate the detail view and take us to it. So we have two things to fix: we want to start on the master view controller (the list of tweets) instead of the detail, and we want tapping a table row to fill in the detail like it did in the old navigation app, and in the iPad version of the split view.

Handling Collapsing Split Views

The first step to dealing with the user starting on the wrong scene is knowing that our code is even in this scenario and that we need to do something different. Actually, we can gain the ability to address the problem by becoming the split view controller's delegate. The delegate gets told about changes like rotation, which cause it to rework how it presents its contents. It gets these callbacks at startup too, including one that says it's running in the compact space of an iPhone.

Start in RootViewController.swift by appending UISplitViewControllerDelegate to the comma-separated list of protocols in the class declaration. This will allow our RootViewController to become the split view controller's delegate.

We want to become the delegate as soon as possible, so viewDidLoad() is a good place to do so. At the bottom of that method, add the following code:

BigScreens/PragmaticTweets-10-2/PragmaticTweets/RootViewController.swift

```
if splitViewController != nil {
  splitViewController!.delegate = self
}
```

All this does is to check if there's a splitViewController parent, just like we checked when we handled the table row tap. If there is, we become its delegate.

So now we can get the split view's delegate callbacks. We need to figure out which of its methods will tell us when we're running on the small space of an iPhone. It turns out the method we need is splitViewController(collapseSecondaryView-Controller:ontoPrimaryViewController:). This message is the split view telling the delegate that it doesn't have enough room for both view controllers, but it gives the delegate a chance to adapt the second view controller into its user interface (perhaps by shrinking it or adding it to some other part of the UI), before the split view controller gives up and removes the second view controller.

Actually, removing the second view controller, the detail scene, is exactly what we want. If we just return true, the split view controller will give up on the detail view controller, leaving us with just the master view controller, which is the list of tweets. So implement the method like this:

BigScreens/PragmaticTweets-10-2/PragmaticTweets/RootViewController.swift

```
func splitViewController(_splitViewController: UISplitViewController!,
  collapseSecondaryViewController secondaryViewController: UIViewController!,
  ontoPrimaryViewController primaryViewController: UIViewController!)
    -> Bool {
  return true
}
```

Run the app on one of the iPhone models now, and we come up on the list of tweets.

Restoring Discarded View Controllers

Well, that's great, except that tapping on a row still doesn't do anything. And the reason for that is in our tap-handling logic in tableView(didSelectRowAtIndexPath:). When we implemented that before, we made sure the split view controller had two child view controllers, so we could take the second one (the TweetDetailView-Controller) and populate it.

But we can't do that now, because *there is no second view controller*. We just told the split view controller that it was OK to discard the second view controller. So that's just great.

Maybe we'll just have to remake that view controller ourselves! Fortunately, it's pretty easy to do so with storyboards. There's a UIStoryboard class that offers just three methods, two of which are for creating scenes from within the storyboard. The one we need is instantiateViewControllerWithIdentifier(), which takes a string and gives us back a UIViewController, with its view and all its subviews laid out exactly like we created them in the storyboard.

For this to work, we need to give the Tweet Detail scene a unique ID string. In the storyboard, select the Tweet Detail View Controller, and bring up its Identity Inspector (⌥⌘3). In the Storyboard ID field, enter TweetDetailVC, as shown in the following figure:

Perform a clean build (Product→Clean, or ⇧⌘K), since changes to storyboards aren't always picked up by Xcode's build process, and we want to make sure this scene is findable by that string.

Now we can re-create this view controller when we need it. The place we're going to do so is in RootViewController's tableView(didSelectRowAtIndexPath:). We want to handle the case where the split view controller has only one child view controller, so find the closing brace that matches if (self.splitViewController!.viewControllers.count > 1) {, and replace its closing brace with the following else block.

```
Line 1  } else {
     2    if let detailVC =
     3      storyboard!.instantiateViewControllerWithIdentifier("TweetDetailVC")
     4        as? TweetDetailViewController {
     5        detailVC.tweetIdString = parsedTweet.tweetIdString
     6        splitViewController!.showDetailViewController(detailVC, sender: self)
     7      }
     8  }
```

On lines 2–4, we ask the storyboard to try to find the scene whose view controller has the ID TweetDetailVC, and cast it to a TweetDetailViewController. If that works, then we've got our detail view controller, and its whole view hierarchy, just as laid out in the storyboard. In turn, that means we can get it to load its contents like we always have, by setting its tweetIdString (on line 5). Then we just have to navigate to it. UISplitViewController gives us that ability with the showDetailViewController() method, on line 6.

And that's it! Run the app on a simulated iPhone, and it works just like the navigation version did from the previous chapter, perfectly well suited to the small space of the iPhone. Back on the iPad, we get a side-by-side split that makes better use of all the screen real estate. Best of both worlds, and in iOS 8, we get it all with one storyboard and this little bit of tricky code.

Size Classes and the iPhone 6

So it's great that the split view gives us one behavior for the iPad and another for the iPhone.

Except, well, that new iPhone 6 is *really* big. Maybe not iPad big, but it at least makes you wonder whether it's really appropriate to lump all iPhones together. After all, iOS 8 runs on everything from the 4s (with its 320x480, 3.5-inch screen) to the iPhone 6 Plus (414x736, 5.5-inch screen). Even within the iPhone range, there may be times we want to go to a side-by-side mode with our split view.

To do so, we need to understand how iOS 8 represents sizes.

Size Classes

In iOS 8, screens, view controllers, and views all have a collection of sizing information called a *trait collection*. These traits are collected by the UITraitCollection class, and include things like the points-to-pixels scaling factor (2.0 for Retina devices, 3.0 for the iPhone 6 Plus, 1.0 for the old iPad 2), the device idiom (phone or pad), and a very general way to represent the available space in each dimension.

The available space is represented as a *size class*, and has two values: compact and regular. Those should sound familiar, because they're the values of the sizing bar at the bottom of the storyboard pane, which we saw way back in *Storyboards*, on page 15. Let's think back to the grid that appeared in the pop-up, and the descriptions it provided: regular width and height were described as an iPad, whereas compact width and regular height represented an iPhone in portrait orientation.

Traits are inherited from the screen, to the one window that's always on the screen, through view controllers, and views, down to each individual view, like a button or table. Along the way, they can be changed. So an iPad screen will have regular width size class in either orientation, but the left side of a split view will have compact width, since the layout of the split view constrains how much space it can use.

The split view's decision about whether to use a side-by-side or a two-screen layout is based on the width size class it inherits. If it thinks it's in a compact space, it will use the navigation-style two-screen approach; if it inherits regular width, it will use a side-by-side presentation.

So, if we wanted to make the split view go side by side on an iPhone 6, we would just have to convince it that it has regular width to work with, not compact. Let's do that.

Container Controllers

We can't just tell the split view controller that it has regular width: it has to inherit this from a parent view or view controller. We can do that by creating a *container controller*, a view controller that contains other view controllers. This parent will own the split view controller and will be in a position to give it a trait collection that says it has regular width, if we decide we want to go side by side.

To get started, go to the storyboard, look through the Object library (^⌥⌘3) and find the plain View Controller icon, a yellow ball with a dashed box inside it. Drag this icon to the left of the split view controller.

 The way we get this view controller to "own" the split view controller is pretty weird. We need to use a *container view*, instead of the usual UIView that comes with a view controller. So, in the scene list, find the view that's a child of this new view controller and delete it. This will also delete the top and bottom layout guide objects from the scene. Now, in the Object library, find the Container View icon, shown in the figure as a gray box inside a white box inside a gray box. Drag it onto the new view controller icon or its box in the storyboard; it will become the sole child of the view controller.

This also adds a new view controller scene to the storyboard, connected by a segue. What's interesting is that this isn't a segue that transitions between scenes; it's an embed segue that tells the container scene which view controller to show first. So it's great that Xcode gave us a default view controller to embed, except we don't want that one; we want to embed the split view controller.

So, control-click on the container view to show its connections HUD. The first one will show that viewDidLoad() has an embed segue connected to that blank view controller. Drag from the circle in this connection to the split view controller. This will allow us to make a segue connection. At the end of the drag, choose Embed as the segue type. We should always name our segues, so click the segue icon between the two scenes, bring up its Attributes Inspector (⌥⌘4), and give it the storyboard identifier embedSplitViewSegue.

Now the empty view controller that the container view supplied for us has no connections at all, so we can delete it.

Control-click on the container view to show its updated connections. For Triggered Segues, it will show viewDidLoad() via an embed segue to the Split View Controller. This is the weird part: this segue isn't performed as part of a navigation like in the last chapter; it happens when the view loads, at which point the container view controller will get its one and only look at the child view controller that it's going to contain.

This scene is going to be the beginning of our app, so choose the view controller, go to the Attributes Inspector (⌥⌘4), and select the Is Initial View Controller box. This won't visually change anything, since control will flow immediately to the split view controller child. But it will ensure that this view controller loads first, which we need. The beginning of the storyboard should now look like the figure on page 176.

Now we're at the point where we need to write some code, to grab the reference to the split view controller and be able to change its trait collection. In the File Navigator, select the Pragmatic Tweets group and use New Group to create the group Size Class Override. Within this group, choose New File to create a new Cocoa Touch Class, with the name SizeClassOverrideViewController, a subclass of UIViewController written in Swift. Finally, in the storyboard, select the view controller with the container view, bring up its Identity Inspector (⌥⌘3), and change the class to SizeClassOverrideViewController. Now the container view controller will be our custom class.

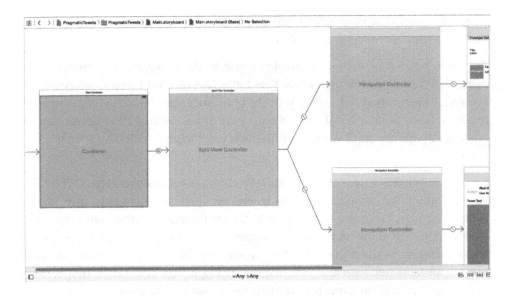

What we need to do with this code is grab a reference to the split view controller, and send it our preferred size class traits. In SizeClassOverrideViewController.swift, start by creating a property to refer to the UISplitViewController.

BigScreens/PragmaticTweets-10-3/PragmaticTweets/SizeClassOverrideViewController.swift

```
var embeddedSplitVC : UISplitViewController?
```

As implied by the name of the embed segue, our one look at the split view controller happens when the view loads. This will make a call to prepareForSegue()—just like when we're navigating between scenes—so we override that method to grab the reference to the destinationViewController.

BigScreens/PragmaticTweets-10-3/PragmaticTweets/SizeClassOverrideViewController.swift

```
override func prepareForSegue(segue: UIStoryboardSegue, sender: AnyObject?) {
  if segue.identifier == "embedSplitViewSegue" {
    embeddedSplitVC = segue.destinationViewController as? UISplitViewController
  }
}
```

Now we're in a position to start changing the split view's sense of how much room it has to work with!

Overriding Trait Collections

Now let's think about what we want to tell the split view controller, and when. It will use a side-by-side view when it thinks its width size class is regular and not compact. We could probably swing the side-by-side view on an iPhone 6, but not a 4s. Let's look at our sizes.

Model	Dimensions (points)	Scale factor
iPhone 4s	320×480	2.0
iPhone 5 / 5s	320×568	2.0
iPhone 6	375×667	2.0
iPhone 6 Plus	414×736	3.0
iPad 2	768×1024	1.0
iPad Retina/iPad Air	768×1024	2.0

So, assuming that we don't want to try to go side by side on the 4s, and we definitely want to do so on the big iPhone 6 models, let's pick a value in the middle. We'll just say that any width bigger than 480 is enough for us to try side by side.

When the device is rotated, view controllers get a callback to the method viewWillTransitionToSize(). That's the perfect place to pull our trickery. We'll override that method, check the size we're transitioning to, and if it's wide enough for us, we'll override the split view controller's trait collection. Here's how we do that.

BigScreens/PragmaticTweets-10-3/PragmaticTweets/SizeClassOverrideViewController.swift

```
Line 1  override func viewWillTransitionToSize(size: CGSize,
     -    withTransitionCoordinator coordinator: UIViewControllerTransitionCoordinator) {
     -      if size.width > 480.0 {
     -        let overrideTraits = UITraitCollection (
     5          horizontalSizeClass: UIUserInterfaceSizeClass.Regular)
     -        setOverrideTraitCollection(overrideTraits,
     -          forChildViewController: embeddedSplitVC!)
     -      } else {
     -        setOverrideTraitCollection(nil,
    10          forChildViewController: embeddedSplitVC!)
     -      }
     -  }
```

We look at the incoming width on line 3. If it's greater than 480.0, lines 4–5 create a new UITraitCollection. The initializers for this class take either one of the four traits—horizontalSizeClass, verticalSizeClass, userInterfaceIdiom, or scaleFactor—or an array of already initialized trait collections to merge together. All we care about is setting the horizontalSizeClass to the enum value UIUserInterfaceSizeClass.Regular.

Then all we have to do is pass this to our embeddedSplitVC. A parent view controller can override a child's trait collection with setOverrideTraitCollection(), which is what we do on lines 6–7. This is only possible from a parent view controller—other VCs can't go changing each other's trait collections willy-nilly—which is why we had to go through the whole rigmarole of setting up our custom container controller.

Finally, if our width isn't big enough for the split view controller go into side-by-side mode, we use setOverrideTraitCollection() with nil, on lines 9–10, which lets it inherit its traits as before.

With our sneaky override of the size class now complete, run the app again on different models in the Simulator (keeping in mind you'll have to sign into Twitter on each one if you haven't already, as they store their system settings separately from each other). On a sufficiently large device, the split view controller will now go into side-by-side mode when rotated to landscape, as seen in the following figure:

Wrap-Up

In this chapter, we stopped looking at our app through iPhone goggles. We thought about how it used the space available on an iPad, and switched to a split view to make better use of all the screen real estate. We discovered that this gives us a navigation-like experience for iPhone sizes when the side-by-side view doesn't really make sense, although we did have to do a little work to make it work like we wanted it to. And in between the extremes of the little iPhone 4s and the iPad, there are now several iPhone models at intermediate sizes, so we saw how to inspect our size classes and even change them.

So, we've done some work on how users see our app. Now it's time to enhance how they interact with it. In the next chapter, we'll look at how to create and handle touch gestures on our own, so our app won't just look great, it will literally feel great, too.

CHAPTER 11

Recognizing Gestures

Touch is the defining trait of user interfaces on the iPhone and iPad. It's what makes working with the data seem so direct: flicking a table to scroll it, pinching a photo to resize it, or drawing freehand with our fingers. iOS builds in sensible touch controls for all of its provided views, and we can build upon those further by creating our own.

Gesture Recognizers

The first versions of the iPhone SDK gave us only low-level raw touch data via the UIView methods touchesBegan(), touchesMoved(), touchesEnded(), and touchesCancelled(). These delivered sets of UITouch events, and from the raw geometry and timing of these events, we could track events like swipes, using logic like "if the touch moved at least 50 points up, and not more than 20 points to either side, in less than 0.5 seconds, then treat it as an upward swipe."

As one might expect, this was a huge pain in the butt to implement and led to variations in user experience as different developers interpreted the touch data differently, based on what "felt right" to them.

Fortunately, the situation was cleaned up in later versions of iOS thanks to *gesture recognizers*. With these classes, iOS determines for us what counts as a swipe or a double-tap, and calls into our code only when it detects that a matching gesture has occurred.

The top-level UIGestureRecognizer class represents things like a gesture's location in a view, its current state (began, changed, ended, etc.), and a list of target objects to be notified as the recognizer's state changes. Subclasses provide the tracking of distinct gestures like taps, pinches, rotations, and swipes, and these subclasses also contain properties representing traits specific to the gesture: how many taps, how much pinching, and so on.

Segue Gestures

One handy trick for our Twitter app would be to give the user a better view of a given tweeter's avatar. From the user detail screen we built in the last chapter, we could go to a new screen that shows the image in a larger view, and allow our user to pinch-zoom and move around the avatar in detail.

To do this, we'll need a new "user image detail" scene in the storyboard. Find the View Controller icon in the Object library, and drag it into the storyboard, to the right of the User Detail View Controller scene that is currently the end of our storyboard. To this new scene, add the following:

- An image view, with width and height pinned to 280 points, vertically and horizontally aligned in its container

- A button, with the title Done, pinned 20 points up from the bottom of the container, horizontally aligned in the container

We'll put some logic into that scene later, but for now, we just need to create a way to get to it from the user detail scene. We could do that by replacing the detail scene's image view with a button and then adding a segue on the button tap. But to show how flexible gesture recognizers, we'll do functionally the same thing by giving the existing image view the ability to handle taps, thereby turning it into a de facto image button.

 Scroll through the Object library and find the gesture recognizer icons. They're displayed as blue circles against dark gray backgrounds, some with swooshes that represent movement. Find the tap gesture recognizer, which is represented as a single static circle, shown in the figure.

Drag this icon onto the UIImageView that's above the User Name label in the User Detail View Controller scene. This won't cause an immediate change to the image view, but the gesture recognizer will become a top-level member of the scene, a sibling to the view controller and the various segues, in the list on the left. Select it from this list and view it with the Attributes Inspector (⌥⌘4). As shown in the figure, the gesture recognizer allows you to

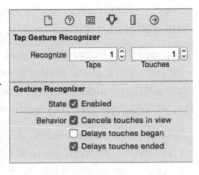

configure the number of sequential taps (single-, double-, triple-, etc.) and the number of touches (how many fingers touching the screen) required to trigger the recognizer.

Connecting Gesture Recognizers

One thing we don't see here is how the gesture recognizer is related to the image view. For that, go to the Connections Inspector (⌥⌘6). There we see that the Referencing Outlet Collections have a property called gestureRecognizers that is connected to the Image View (if it just says View, you probably dropped it on the full view and not the image view; delete the recognizer from the scene and try again).

So it's not that the recognizer refers to the view; instead, the view knows that the recognizer is one of its potentially many gestureRecognizers. Now let's address the question of the what the recognizer does when it's tapped. In the Connections Inspector, we see a few interesting properties: a triggered segue action, a delegate outlet, and a sent action selector. The delegate doesn't help us here: the UIGestureRecognizerDelegate is meant to let our code adjudicate when two gesture recognizers want to handle the same gesture. What's useful for us are the selector, which calls a method when the gesture begins, ends, or updates, and the segue action, which takes us to a new scene.

What we want is the segue, so draw a connection line by dragging from the circle next to action in the Connections Inspector to anywhere in the new image detail scene. It would also work to do a control-drag from the gesture recognizer in the user detail scene over to the image detail scene; Xcode will figure out that a connection between scenes can only be a segue (and not some other kind of connection). At the end of the drag, a pop-up asks what kind of segue

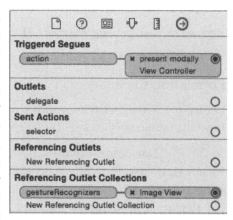

we want; coming from a modal scene, the only choice that will work is another Present Modally segue. Our gesture recognizer's connections should now look like the figure.

We can try running now, choosing a tweet, and drilling down to user details, but clicking the image won't perform this segue yet. To see why, select the image in the user detail scene, and bring up the Attributes Inspector (⌥⌘4). Notice that User Interaction Enabled is unchecked, since image views by default don't handle user input. But this means that it won't process touch events, which in turn means our gesture recognizer will never fire. Simple fix here: just check the User Interaction Enabled box.

Run the app now and we can drill all the way to our new scene, which at this point only shows a Done button, since we haven't populated the image view yet. Moreover, the Done button doesn't work, and we're trapped on this scene. Let's fix that before we move on. The fix is to use an unwind segue. Back in UserDetailViewController.swift, add an empty implementation for unwindToUserDetailVC():

`Gestures/PragmaticTweets-11-1/PragmaticTweets/UserDetailViewController.swift`
```
@IBAction func unwindToUserDetailVC (segue : UIStoryboardSegue) {
}
```

Now, we can go to the image detail scene in the storyboard, and control-drag from the Done button to the orange Exit Segue button. At the end of the drag, we have two methods we can unwind to: choose the unwindToUserDetailVC() method we just created. Run again, and we can go back from the image detail scene.

So what we've accomplished at this point is to bring tap handling to a UIImageView, a class that ordinarily supports no user interaction whatsoever. And we did it without really writing any code—we just created the gesture recognizer in the storyboard, connected it to a new segue, and gave ourselves a no-op method to unwind to.

But we're just getting started. There's a lot more we can do to the default image view.

Populating the Image

Before we start gesturing around with the image view, it'll help to actually have an image we can see. So let's deal with that now.

In the File Navigator, create a new group called User Image Detail VC, and within that, use New File to create a new class UserImageDetailViewController, a subclass of UIViewController. At the top of this new UserImageDetailViewController.swift file, declare a property for the user image URL:

`Gestures/PragmaticTweets-11-2/PragmaticTweets/UserImageDetailViewController.swift`
```
var userImageURL : NSURL?
```

We'll set that property every time we follow the segue to the new scene, so we have some work to do in the storyboard. First, select the image detail scene's view controller icon (either from the frame below the scene or in the scene's object list), go to the Identity Inspector (⌥⌘3), and change the class to UserImageDetailViewController. Since we will need to know when we're taking the segue to this scene, select the segue, bring up the Attributes Inspector (⌘⌥4), and set the identifier to showUserImageDetailSegue.

Now we're going to be able to set the image URL when we segue to the new scene. We do this back in UserDetailViewController.swift. Next, we need to save the URL of the image. Right now, the user detail scene just creates a UIImage to populate this class's image view, but there's a good reason it should save off the URL: it will let us get a higher-quality image. Currently, it uses the key profile_image_url to get an image URL from the Twitter response. The value is a URL string like https://pbs.twimg.com/profile_images/290486223/pp_for_twitter_normal.png. As it turns out, that _normal is used by Twitter to indicate an icon at a standardized 48×48 size. That's fine for the user detail view controller, but it will be very blocky in the 280×280 image view in the next scene. Fortunately, if we just strip the _normal, we can get the image in the original size uploaded by the Twitter user, and that will look nicer in the next scene. So start by giving the UserDetailViewController this new property:

`Gestures/PragmaticTweets-11-2/PragmaticTweets/UserDetailViewController.swift`

```
var userImageURL : NSURL?
```

Then, down in handleTwitterData(), inside the closure, change the last few lines (after the self.userDescriptionLabel.text = tweetDict["description"] as? NSString line) so they use this property to set the userImageView.image, rather than a local userImageURL variable.

`Gestures/PragmaticTweets-11-2/PragmaticTweets/UserDetailViewController.swift`

```
self.userImageURL = NSURL (string:
  tweetDict ["profile_image_url"] as NSString!)
if self.userImageURL != nil {
  if let userImageData = NSData(contentsOfURL: self.userImageURL!) {
  self.userImageView.image = UIImage(data: userImageData)
  }
}
```

Now we're ready to send the good version of the user image URL to the UserImageDetailViewController by writing a prepareForSegue:() method:

`Gestures/PragmaticTweets-11-2/PragmaticTweets/UserDetailViewController.swift`

```
Line 1  override func prepareForSegue(segue: UIStoryboardSegue, sender: AnyObject?) {
     -    if segue.identifier == "showUserImageDetailSegue" {
     -      if let imageDetailVC = segue.destinationViewController
     -        as? UserImageDetailViewController {
     5          var urlString = userImageURL!.absoluteString
     -          urlString = urlString!.stringByReplacingOccurrencesOfString (
     -            "_normal",
     -            withString: "")
     -          imageDetailVC.userImageURL = NSURL(string: urlString!)
    10       }
     -    }
     -  }
```

We begin on line 2 by checking that we're doing the segue to the user image detail view controller. If so, we can cast the destinationViewController on lines 3–4. We can then get an NSString version of the URL (line 5), and strip out the _normal substring (lines 6–8). Finally, we make a new NSURL for the full-size image and send it to the user image detail view controller on line 9.

Once the segue is performed, the UserImageDetailViewController will have the URL for the full-size image. Now all we need to do is to populate the image view in that scene. Start by going to the storyboard, going to the last scene (the User-ImageDetailViewController), and selecting the 280×280 image view. Bring up the Assistant Editor (the "linked rings" toolbar button, or ⌥⌘↩), with UserImageDetailViewController.swift in the right pane, and control-drag from the image view in the storyboard to somewhere inside the class (perhaps right after the userImageURL we created), to create an outlet that we'll name userImageView.

Gestures/PragmaticTweets-11-2/PragmaticTweets/UserImageDetailViewController.swift

```
@IBOutlet weak var userImageView: UIImageView!
```

Now that we can see the image view in code, go back to the standard editor, visit UserImageDetailViewController.swift, and add a viewWillAppear() method:

Gestures/PragmaticTweets-11-2/PragmaticTweets/UserImageDetailViewController.swift

```
override func viewWillAppear(animated: Bool)  {
  super.viewWillAppear(animated)
  if userImageURL != nil {
    if let imageData = NSData (contentsOfURL: userImageURL!) {
      userImageView.image = UIImage(
      data:imageData)
    }
  }
}
```

Run the app now, and we can navigate all the way to the image detail scene, which will show the higher-quality user image and not the 48×48 icon. In the following figure, we've drilled down for a look at Janie's Twitter avatar, shown in the figure on page 185.

That's a nice, normal-looking image for now. But we're about to start letting our fingers have some fun with it.

Pinching and Panning

How can we play with images on iOS? The whole point of a touch interface is to provide the feeling of interacting directly with our data, so we should be thinking of moving the image around with a drag, zooming in and out of it with pinch gestures, and so forth.

Carrier 🛜   2:35 PM   🔋

Done

Let's take a look at what gesture recognizers give us. Here's a table summarizing the concrete subclasses of UIGestureRecognizer and the important properties and/or methods exposed by each:

Class	Important Properties and Methods
UILongPressGestureRecognizer	minimumPressDuration, allowableMovement
UIPanGestureRecognizer	translationInView:, velocityInView:
UIPinchGestureRecognizer	scale, velocity
UIRotationGestureRecognizer	rotation, velocity
UIScreenEdgePanGestureRecognizer	edges
UISwipeGestureRecognizer	direction
UITapGestureRecognizer	numberOfTapsRequired, numberOfTouchesRequired

As we look at the names of the gesture recognizers, we can start to get some ideas: UIPanGestureRecognizer handles dragging a finger around, so we can use that to move the image around. The UIPinchGestureRecognizer seems like it would be a natural for pinch-to-zoom functionality. So it looks easy enough to recognize the gestures we want. Question now is: what do we do with it? How is a scale or translationInView() going to help us change the appearance of the image view?

Affine Transformations

The properties and methods provided by the gesture recognizers work well with a trait common to all graphic objects in iOS: *affine transformations*. A transformation, speaking generally, changes how we draw something. More technically, transformations indicate how points in one coordinate system map to another. Affine transforms are special, because they maintain parallel lines between the two coordinate systems.

A specific example of how we already use affine transforms may be helpful here. Think of how when you print out a document, you can save paper by using the printer dialog to print two pages of the document on one sheet of physical paper, putting two portrait-oriented pages side by side on one land-scape page. To do that, each page of your document goes through three transformations:

- The page is rotated 90°, so that it prints "sideways."

- The page is shrunk down (*scaled*) by about 50% (well, for a US letter page anyway...legal or A4 would have slightly different math).

- The page is moved (*translated*) so that odd pages are left-aligned against the edge of the portrait page, and even pages are left-aligned approximately along the center fold of the page.

Each of these can be represented as an affine transform. Moreover, all of them can go in a single transform by simply applying each transform to the one that came before it.

For our purposes, every UIView has a transform of type CGAffineTransform. This is a struct, not a class, and consists of just six CGFloats: a, b, c, and d, tx, and ty. These six values represent any combination of rotation, scaling, skewing, and translation (movement) operations. Technically, they represent six members of the matrix in the following equation.

$$[x'\ y'\ 1] = [x\ y\ 1] \times \begin{bmatrix} a & b & 0 \\ c & d & 0 \\ t_x & t_y & 1 \end{bmatrix}$$

What this equation provides is the transformed values for any point, x' and y', given their original values (x and y) and the contents of the affine transform matrix. This works out to a pair of simple equations:

$x' = ax * cy + t_x$

$y' = bx * dy + t_y$

Notice that the t_x and t_y values stand alone as terms in the equations. These are the "transform" values. If a, b, c, and d are all 1.0, then t_x and t_y can be used directly along the x- and y-axes.

On the other hand, if we only work with a, b, c, and d, we can easily scale an object while maintaining its aspect ratio: if we set a and d to 2.0, then every coordinate value will double, and this transform will represent doubling the size of an object. Or we can use sines and cosines to represent rotation. Or we can use all the terms to combine scaling, rotation, and translation.

Transforms and Layers

The CALayer objects that provide the actual drawing of our views have a different way of representing transforms, the CATransform3D. As its name implies, this transform works in three dimensions, with a z-axis that comes out of the screen toward the viewer. Any time we want to do transforms that work with a sense of depth, like views that flip over or are viewable from the side, we need to work at the CALayer level.

Fortunately, we don't have to use the members of CGAffineTransform directly here. In fact, we almost never do. Core Graphics provides a set of convenience functions to create affine transforms for rotation, scaling, and translation operations, either as absolute values or as modifications of existing affine transforms. So if we ever found ourselves writing the printer driver that had to do side-by-side printing as described earlier, we could create one affine transform to the rotation, use that to create a transform to do the scaling (of the rotated page), and then use that to make the translation (of the rotated and scaled page).

Transforming the Image View

Now that we see what affine transforms offer us, the properties and methods exposed by the gesture recognizers start to make more sense. The pinch gesture recognizer provides a scale that we could use to make a scale transform, and the pan recognizer offers translationInView() that will be perfect for making a translation.

To make use of these transforms, we have a few options. UIView has a transform property, so we can set that directly. The underlying CALayer that provides the view's appearance also has a transform property, although that one is of type CATransform3D and works in three dimensions. A more advanced option would be to write our own subclass of UIView or CALayer that draws its own contents; the Core Graphics library used for drawing allows us to set an affine transform on our drawing operations, and is the only way to use multiple transforms.

To keep it simple for now, we'll just reset the UIImageView's transform property, which it inherits from UIView.

The Pan Transform

 Let's start with a pan transform to move the image around. In the storyboard, go to the user image view detail scene, the one with the 280×280 image and the Done button. In the Object library, find the Pan Gesture Recognizer icon, which looks like a blue circle leaving a streak below it. Drag and drop the pan recognizer on to the image view.

Now we need to give the recognizer a method it can call. Select the pan gesture recognizer in the scene's object list, and switch to Assistant Editor (⌥⌘↩), making sure UserImageDetailViewController.swift is in the right pane. Control-drag from the gesture recognizer (either in the scene's object list or from the bar atop the scene), to any free space inside the class, perhaps down by the closing curly brace. At the end of the drop, a pop-up asks for what kind of connection to make—be sure to change from Outlet to Action—and for a name for the action method. Let's call it handlePanGesture(). Also, before clicking Connect, change Type from the default AnyObject to UIPanGestureRecognizer.

This connection will call handlePanGesture() when a pan gesture starts, updates, or ends on the image view. At least it *would*, if image views processed touch events by default. Just as with the image in the previous view controller, we have to explicitly enable user interaction with this image view to make it respond to touch events. Switch back to the storyboard's standard editor, select the image view, bring up its Attributes Inspector, and select the User Interaction Enabled checkbox.

Switch back to the standard editor and bring up UserImageDetailViewController.swift so we can write this method that we just connected. This is where we're going to ask the gesture recognizer how far it's moved, and use that to update the image view's affine transform.

For this to work, we need to understand what the gesture recognizer tells us. If we look up translationInView() in the documentation for UIPanGestureRecognizer, we find it returns "a point identifying the new location of a view in the coordinate system of its designated superview." There's also an important note in the discussion of the method:

> The x and y values report the total translation over time. They are not delta values from the last time that the translation was reported. Apply the translation value to the state of the view when the gesture is first recognized—do not concatenate the value each time the handler is called.

What this is telling us is that as we get new callbacks as handlePanGesture() is repeatedly called during the drag, the value reported back to us is relative to the image view's initial transform, not the last value we set it to. That means we should plan on saving the image view's transform the first time we get called. Define that as a property up in the top of the @class:

Gestures/PragmaticTweets-11-2/PragmaticTweets/UserImageDetailViewController.swift
```
var preGestureTransform : CGAffineTransform?
```

Now we can assign that property the first time we're called back by the gesture recognizer. When we're called back, we can ask the gesture recognizer for its state, which can be started, changed, ended, cancelled, or a few other administrative and error states. When the value is UIGestureRecognizerState.Began, we'll save off the initial transform of the image view. Begin the handlePanGesture:() like this:

Gestures/PragmaticTweets-11-2/PragmaticTweets/UserImageDetailViewController.swift
```
@IBAction func handlePanGesture(sender: UIPanGestureRecognizer) {
  if sender.state == .Began {
    preGestureTransform = userImageView.transform
  }
```

When a pan gesture begins, this if block saves the image view's transform to our preGestureTransform property, since all subsequent event coordinates will be relative to this initial transform. Now we're ready to handle moving the view around. So continue handlePanGesture() with a second if, as follows:

Gestures/PragmaticTweets-11-2/PragmaticTweets/UserImageDetailViewController.swift
```
Line 1  if sender.state == .Began ||
   2      sender.state == .Changed {
   3        let translation = sender.translationInView(self.userImageView)
   4        let translatedTransform = CGAffineTransformTranslate(
   5          preGestureTransform!, translation.x, translation.y)
   6        userImageView.transform = translatedTransform
   7  }
```

We get the translationInView() on line 3. This is a CGPoint whose x and y members represent how far we have moved along each axis from where the pan began. With that information, we can use the CGAffineTransformTranslate() function to create a new transform that represents that distance from the original preGestureTransform (lines 4–5). Then, on line 6, we just set that as the new transform property of the image view.

Does this work? Try it. Drill down to an user image detail and try dragging the picture around. You should have total freedom to put it wherever you like, even under the Done button or partially offscreen, as seen in the following figure. Pretty cool, but we should clean up after ourselves before we go further.

The Identity Transform

So it's great that we can drag the image wherever we like…but that does mean we can drag it completely off the screen. Problem!

Let's give ourselves a "panic button": if the user double-taps the image, it'll go back to its default position.

In the storyboard, add a new tap gesture recognizer to the image view. Select the tap gesture recognizer icon from the scene's object list or the title bar atop the scene, bring up the Attributes Inspector, and set the number of taps to 2. This means it will take a double-tap for the recognizer to fire.

Next, switch to Assistant Editor, and control-drag from the tap gesture recognizer into UserImageDetailViewController.swift to create a new action method. When the pop-up appears at the end of the drag, call the method handleDoubleTapGesture(), and switch the type from AnyObject to UITapGestureRecognizer.

So how do we write this method? We want to go back to the image view's original transform, before any of our changes. By default, UIViews have an *identity transform*, which means no scaling, rotation, or translation. This is a CGAffineTransform where a and d are 1.0, and b, c, t_x and t_y are all 0.0. Run that through the earlier formulas and we find that makes x' equal x and y' equal y. This "do nothing" is provided to us as the constant CGAffineTransformIdentity.

Gestures/PragmaticTweets-11-2/PragmaticTweets/UserImageDetailViewController.swift

```swift
@IBAction func handleDoubleTapGesture(sender: UITapGestureRecognizer) {
  userImageView.transform = CGAffineTransformIdentity
}
```

Restoring the identity transform on a UIView is a one-line call. Run the app, drag the image around, and double-tap to send it back to where it started. Easy peasy!

The Scale Transform

The other common gesture we should add to our image viewer is a pinch-to-zoom feature. Again, this naturally links the scale property of the gesture recognizer—in this case a UIPinchGestureRecognizer—to the ability of affine transforms to perform scaling operations.

Back in the storyboard, go to the Object library and locate the pinch gesture recognizer icon. As before, drag it on to the image view to add it to the scene. Switch to the Assistant Editor with UserImageDetailViewController.swift in the right pane, select the icon in the scene or the title bar, and control-drag to create a new action method. Name the action handlePinchGesture() and change the parameter type to UIPinchGestureRecognizer.

What does the pinch gesture's scale give us? According to the docs, it's "the scale factor relative to the points of the two touches in screen coordinates." And, as was the case with the pan recognizer, this value is relative to the beginning of the gesture, not to the last time we were called. So, once again, we need to make use of the preGestureTransform to hold on to our initial value.

Gestures/PragmaticTweets-11-2/PragmaticTweets/UserImageDetailViewController.swift

```swift
@IBAction func handlePinchGesture(sender: UIPinchGestureRecognizer) {
  if sender.state == .Began {
    preGestureTransform = userImageView.transform
  }
  if sender.state == .Began ||
    sender.state == .Changed {
      let scaledTransform = CGAffineTransformScale(
        preGestureTransform!, sender.scale, sender.scale)
      userImageView.transform = scaledTransform
  }
}
```

As with the pan recognizer, we use the start state to save off the image view's initial transform, on lines 2–4. Then on lines 5–6, we deal with the scale value of a started or changed event. On lines 7–8, we use CGAffineTransformScale() to create a new CGAffineTransform by taking the original preGestureTransform and applying the scale value to both the x and y factors of the scaling transform. And then on line 9, we set this as the new value of the image view's transform.

Run the app and give it a whirl. To simulate a pinch gesture in the Simulator, hold down the option key on the keyboard, which will show the pinch points as two circles that move with the mouse or trackpad. By adding the shift key, we can move the pinch points without registering as a pinch. In the following figure, we've panned to the right and pinch-zoomed in to pick out two *Neon Genesis Evangelion* cosplayers coming off the escalator behind Janie (yes, her Twitter avatar is from an anime convention, how did you guess?).

To better understand the math behind the transform, try changing the x- and y-scaling values sent to CGAffineTransform-Scale(). For example, if we set the last argument, sy, to the constant value 1.0, then the pinch will become a horizontal stretching operation, because the y value will always be the same after the transform (since it's being multiplied by 1). Another fun trick is to multiply the scaling value by -1.0, which causes the image to flip around the axis, making it an upside-down mirror image.

Subview Clipping

Thanks to the natural pairing of the gesture recognizers and the affine transforms, we've added the dragging and pinch-zooming functionality that will be familiar to our users from many other apps they use. However, views that are allowed to just sprawl all over the screen aren't something we usually see on iOS. It may be fun, but it feels wrong, and we hardly want to let the user make a mess of our user interface.

Let's rein in the madness a little bit. We'll put the image view into another view, and have it clipped off at that view's edges. That will put an end to sliding the image offscreen or under the Done button.

In the storyboard, select the image view and delete it (with the Backspace key or the Edit→Cut menu item). Notice that the three gesture recognizers survive this, because they are top-level objects in the scene, and not children of any view or view controller.

From the Object library, find the plain view (the popover will show its class as UIView), and drag it to the middle of the scene's main view. Use the autolayout popovers to pin its width and height to 280 and to horizontally and vertically align it in the container. Then go to its Attributes Inspector and check the Clip Subviews box. What this does is to constrain ("clip") drawing to the bounds of the view, so if the contained image view goes beyond those boundaries, it will just get cut off.

Next, drop an image view into this subview. It should allow itself to fill the parent subview; one way to make this work for sure is to drag the image view onto the subview's entry in the scene list, rather than onto the storyboard layout. Like its parent, create autolayout constraints pin its size to 280×280 and horizontally and vertically align it in its containers.

Now we need to fix our connections. Select the view controller from the scene members list and bring up the Connections Inspector (⌥⌘6). The userImageView is no longer connected, because we deleted the object it was connected to. Drag from that connection's circle to the new image view to make a new connection.

The gesture recognizers also have no incoming connections anymore, so they won't be called. To fix that, we're going to connect them to the 280×280 plain view, rather than directly to the image view. Select the subview, and repeatedly drag from its gestureRecognizers entry in the Connections Inspector to each of the gesture recognizers, ultimately creating three connections.

Done

Try running the app and drill down to the image detail view. When we drag around, any part of the image that goes beyond the bounds of the 280×280 view is simply cut off, as shown in the following figure. We can also perform our gestures anywhere in the view, not just on the image view, and have them recognized. That means we can push the image entirely outside the bounds of the container view, but we can also bring it back with a double-tap anywhere in that view.

Wrap-Up

In this chapter, we took hold—literally—of the touch gestures that are the hallmark of iOS user interfaces. By giving the user the ability to manipulate an image by dragging it around with one finger and pinch-zooming it with two, we immediately create a sense of close contact with the image. Gesture recognizers make it easy to pick up the most common touch gestures and have them call back to our code when gestures are detected. And because both the recognizers and the onscreen views are concerned with how much movement or scaling is indicated by a gesture, it works well to connect the two by means of affine transforms, which cleanly represent translation, rotation, scaling, and combinations thereof.

Armed with this knowledge, we can bring new touch handling features to scenes throughout our app. It will also be useful if we ever need to create our own custom views, since a view is basically a combination of appearance and interactivity, meaning that a custom view just needs to handle custom drawing and custom event-handling. And we just saw how to do the second of those things.

CHAPTER 12

Working with Photos

One of the main things people use a client app for is to take pictures and share them with their friends. No good Twitter app would be complete without this functionality.

The good news for you is that Apple has realized how important this functionality is to its users and has given us a brand spanking new Photos framework for iOS 8. Now you have more options and control over the camera than you have ever had before.

PhotoKit is a pair of new frameworks introduced in iOS 8: *Photos* and *Photos UI*. Photos is the framework that allows us to access photos and videos from the photo library. Photos UI is a paired framework that allows us to create photo-editing app extensions. This allows you to store all of your neat photo-editing effects on your photos in your photo library instead of having them trapped in the application you created them with. If you create a really cool photo in one application, you can now access it with another. This wasn't possible before.

It is now possible to do anything from simply sharing a photo in a tweet—which is what we will be doing in this chapter—to creating a fully comprehensive photo-editing application on the level of Adobe Photoshop.

It has never been easier to customize your photos on the iPhone. We are just going to scratch the surface of all the awesome things that Apple gives you to express yourself and capture life's moments.

Photo Assets and PHAsset Class

Photos and videos are, at their base level, model objects. Think back to our old friend, the Model-View-Controller, introduced back in *Model-View-Controller*, on page 81. A well-designed model object should be a reusable piece of information that can be accessed from many different controller objects without any dependencies tying it to one specific application or project.

Model objects contain data, and they provide access to and implement logic on data. Photos and videos are just sets of data that we store on our phone that can be accessed and modified by many different applications. Our photo model objects are also read-only and thread safe, so no worrying about another application coming in and changing our photos out from under us.

Every photo and video we use is also considered an asset. Individual assets belong to collections. These are the building blocks of how our photographs are organized; it's important to remember this structure when working with PhotoKit.

The *PHAsset* class is the foundation of everything we will be doing this chapter. PHAsset encompasses not just photos but videos as well. This class stores the asset's media type, creation date, location, and whether it has been tagged as a favorite. All of these properties give you a tremendous amount of control over filtering out which specific photos you would like to use.

For example, say you take a family vacation to Disney World every year. You want to find a specific picture in your photo library, but you aren't sure which trip it was that you took the picture on. You can filter the photos by location and whether they're tagged as a favorite to narrow down which photo it might be. If you know which trip it was on, you can filter them down further by creation date.

Fetching Our Assets

We know that we want to find a photo from our library and bring it into our project. Like similar functions in iOS, this is referred to as "fetching." The class we use to do this is *PHFetchResult*, which has a suite of class methods to fetch our photos from the photo library.

Adding a Camera Button

First we set up our project to allow our user to access this functionality. We have some room in the top-left corner of our root view controller, so let's set up our functionality there.

Go to the Object library and choose a new Bar Button item to add to the storyboard. Locate the Tweets scene, the one with the table view, and add the button to the top left. Over in the Attributes Inspector, you will have the option from the drop-down menu to set the button to a camera icon.

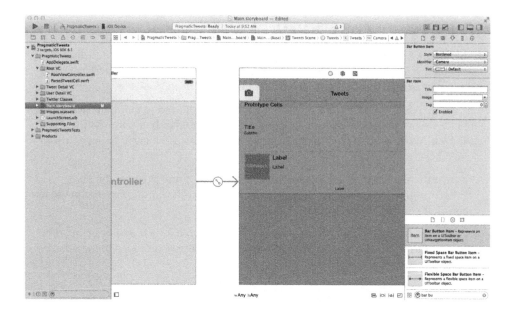

Open the Assistant Editor and connect the button to an IB outlet in the RootViewController.swift to create a method that handles the button click.

Photos/PragmaticTweets-12-1/PragmaticTweets/RootViewController.swift
```
@IBAction func handlePhotoButtonTapped (sender: UIBarButtonItem) {

}
```

One last thing we need to do in the root view controller before we move on is to import the Photos framework. Scroll to the top of the file and add the following:

Photos/PragmaticTweets-12-1/PragmaticTweets/RootViewController.swift
```
import Photos
```

Finding and Filtering Our Photos

As we mentioned earlier, there are many options for how we want to fetch our assets. We can filter them by type, collection, and whatever other filters/predicates we choose.

We just want to share photos with our Twitter followers, so let's go ahead and set up our fetch request to go and get access to our photos.

Think back to our Model-View-Controller. Our PHAsset fulfills our Model requirement. The View Controller will fulfill the "C" in "MVC."

> ## Hey, Where Are All My Photos?!
>
> The iPhone Simulator in Xcode is a wonderful piece of software, but unfortunately it does have a few limitations. There are certain functions you can only perform using the hardware. Getting access to the camera is one of them.
>
> If you are using the Simulator for this chapter, you will need to manually add some photos to your photo library. One functionality the Simulator has is the ability to surf the Web. When you open your Safari app, you can Google images to save to your photo library.
>
> To save the photos to your photo library, simply press and hold on the image you wish to download. You will see a pop-up asking you if you want to save the photo to your photo library. Piece of cake, which is a lie.
>
> And if you already have image files on your Mac, it's even easier: just drag and drop them to the iOS Simulator app while it's running, and they'll be added to the Simulator's photo library automatically.

In this example project, we are only going to retrieve the most recent photo taken. There are many other things we can do with this functionality beyond that, but this is just a simple introduction to the framework.

Navigate back to the handlePhotoButtonTapped method, and add the following code:

`Photos/PragmaticTweets-12-1/PragmaticTweets/RootViewController.swift`

```
Line 1  var fetchOptions = PHFetchOptions()
    -   PHPhotoLibrary.requestAuthorization {
    -     (authorized: PHAuthorizationStatus) -> Void in
    -     if authorized == .Authorized {
    5       fetchOptions.sortDescriptors =
    -         [NSSortDescriptor(key: "creationDate", ascending: false)]
    -       let fetchResult = PHAsset.fetchAssetsWithMediaType (
    -         PHAssetMediaType.Image,
    -         options: fetchOptions)
   10       if let firstPhoto = fetchResult.firstObject  as? PHAsset {
    -         self.createTweetForAsset(firstPhoto)
    -       }
    -     }
    -   }
```

Let's step through this code piece by piece:

1. On line 1 we need to create an instance of PHFetchOptions. We want to narrow down our search to only our most recent photo; therefore, we must figure out a way to tell the method exactly which photo we want it to return.

2. Lines 2–14 request access to the photo library from the user. The photo library requires that the user specifically authorize our Pragmatic Tweets

app to access the photo library. If the user does not authorize this, the photos functionality will not work. Users should be able to go to their settings to authorize it later if they accidentally denied access.

This is a naturally asynchronous action; like requesting access to the Twitter account, we don't know how long it will take the user to respond to our request. So requestAuthorization() takes a closure that will be called when the PHAuthorizationStatus is determined. Our closure runs from lines 3–13.

3. When we're ready to fetch the assets, we will be able to request results be sorted in a given order. The fetchAssetsWithMediaType() method takes an array of NSSortDescriptors, which we prepare on lines 5–6. Since we want to retrieve our most recent photo, we need to make sure our photos are ordered chronologically. The creationDate descriptor starts with the earliest date first, so we need to specify that we want descending order. We found the creationDate descriptor in the documentation for PHFetchOptions. You can explore there to see how else you can sort your photos.

4. We make our call to fetchAssetsWthMediaType() on lines 7–9, passing in the PHAssetMediaType to look for (Images in our case), and the fetchOptions, which include our sort descriptors.

5. Finally, we check the result on lines 10–12 to make sure that there is, in fact, a most recent photo in the library. If there is, we are going to create a tweet from that photo. This calls a createTweetForAsset() method that we will be creating shortly.

Up next, we will need to implement our convenience method to generate a tweet that includes our photo. Add the following code underneath our handlePhotoButtonTapped() method:

Photos/PragmaticTweets-12-1/PragmaticTweets/RootViewController.swift

```
Line 1  func createTweetForAsset (asset: PHAsset) {
   -      var requestOptions = PHImageRequestOptions()
   -      requestOptions.synchronous = true

   5    PHImageManager.defaultManager().requestImageForAsset(asset,
   -        targetSize: CGSizeMake(640, 480),
   -        contentMode: PHImageContentMode.AspectFit,
   -        options: requestOptions) {
   -          (image:UIImage!, info: [NSObject : AnyObject]!) -> Void in
   10         let tweetVC = SLComposeViewController (forServiceType:
   -            SLServiceTypeTwitter)
   -          let message = NSLocalizedString(
   -            "Here's a photo I tweeted. #pragsios8",
   -            comment:"")
```

```
15        tweetVC.setInitialText(message)
          tweetVC.addImage(image)

          dispatch_async(dispatch_get_main_queue(), {
            self.presentViewController(tweetVC, animated: true, completion: nil)
20        })
      }
    }
```

1. We start on line 2 by creating a PHImageRequestOptions instance. This will be used in a few lines by requestImageForAsset(), which takes this options object as a parameter. On line 3, we set the synchronous option to true. We want to make sure that our tweet does not get sent without its photo attached, so we are specifically telling the application to wait until it has the photo.

2. The requestImageForAssset() method will give us a UIImage for our photo library PHAsset, and takes a few parameters to specify the image we get back. On line 6, we set the size of our photo to tweet. We could just say we want the photo to be the base size of the photo in our library, but the image might be 4,000 pixels wide, which would take a really long time to upload and probably be overkill for a simple tweet.

3. The contentMode parameter lets us tell the Photos framework what to do if the photo's aspect ratio doesn't match the size we just provided. On line 7, we use AspectFit to specify that we want to scale our photo to stay proportional and fit its largest dimension into the returned image. If we specified AspectFill, it would fit the entire size but possibly sacrifice pixels to do so.

4. requestImageForAsset() is another asynchronous method, so it lets us use a closure (lines 9–21) to provide the code that will run when the image is done being prepared. In it, we prepare an SLComposeViewController and autopopulate its default text. This is just like what we did so many chapters ago when we prepared our first tweet!

5. An SLComposeViewController can also take an image argument, and that's what we've done all this work to prepare. On line 16, we finally get to set the image on the compose view controller.

6. Finally, we can present the SLComposeViewController, so the user can review the photo and the default text, and send the tweet. Lines 18–20 wrap this with a dispatch_async() that puts it on main queue, since we have no idea what queue is running the closure that is providing us with the image.

7. We are now calling our tweet view controller. We are passing our customized tweet into the method and sending it out into the world.

Run the app, tap the photo button, and see the most recent photo attached to the tweet composer. Send the tweet and after a reload, you'll be able to see it in your timeline.

Core Image

Now that we have our photos posting properly to Twitter, wouldn't it be fun to jazz them up a little? There are all kinds of apps out on the market to apply filters to your photos, and it would be really cool if we could do that, too. Well, guess what, we can!

Core Image is a framework that was introduced in iOS 5, but it existed in Mac OS X before that. Core Image contains over a hundred photo filters for you to use and incorporate into your projects. Each successive iteration of iOS has introduced more image filter options, and with iOS 8 comes the ability to write your own image filters.

Here's a photo I tweeted. #pragsios8 http://t.co/BqWdXZ3Pyk

Important Core Image Classes

Core Image is made up of a couple of classes that create the basis of the functionality of the framework. These classes are like the Lego blocks you use to build your Core Image applications.

The first class we are going to explore is the *CIContext* class. Most of the frameworks in iOS that do drawing utilize contexts. If you were to move on from here and work with Core Animation or OpenGL, you would encounter their own flavors of context. A context is basically just the thing that the drawing is being performed on. Since we want to draw a filter on a photo, we need to specify that as its context.

The next class we are going to talk about is *CIImage*. CIImage does not contain any image data. Rather it contains a set of instructions to be sent to the

CIContext about how you plan to modify the components you are applying to an image.

The last class you need to know about for Core Image is the *CIFilter* class. CIFilter is a dictionary that holds all of the attributes for each filter you use. For example, if you had a filter for RGBA, your CIFilter instance would hold the values for each of these attributes.

Any time we want to add a filter to an image, we will have to go through the following steps:

1. Create a CIImage object. We can do this several different ways. We can instantiate our CIImage by URL reference, by loading image data directly, or receiving our image data from a Core Video pixel buffer.

2. Create a CIContext to output your CIImage to. CIContext objects are buffers and should be reused, so you don't need to create a context for every single thing you are doing.

3. Create a CIFilter instance to apply to your image. This is the step where you will set all of the properties, the number of which will vary based on which filter you are using.

4. Receive the filter output. This is the end of the processing pipeline where you will take possession of your shiny new filtered image.

Spiffy! We have a brand-new image. Wait, what do we do with it? An image isn't like a car coming off the assembly line. We can't touch, hold, or feel it. How do we retain this image after it pops off the conveyor belt?

There are several ways of doing this, but since we already know that we are not working on a video or exporting this to an OpenGL project, the best way for us to take possession of our filtered image is to use [CIContext createCGImage:fromRect:]. We could also use [UIImage imageWithCIImage], which is slightly easier, but it performs badly. It's important to consider the most efficient way of doing something, not just the easiest way.

Filters and Filter Documentation

So far we have been talking about all of these awesome filters that exist on iOS, but we haven't actually seen any of them yet. It's time to dig into what some of these filters are and what they do.

There are well over a hundred filters, but they are broken down into a few categories. Here are some of the more useful ones:

- Blurs: These are the famous (or infamous, depending which way you look at it) effects that were utilized in the iOS 7 design aesthetic but were not implemented easily until iOS 8. Oops.

- Color Adjustments and Effects: These filters allow you to adjust your colors in a controlled way to either correct your projects or let you do complex effects with color.

- Compositing: If you have not played with compositing blend modes in either programming or in Photoshop, you are in for some fun. These are powerful filters that allow you to do some complex effects. One of the authors used these blend modes to add color and complex shading to a black-and-white manga scan by adding a layer to hold the color and having an underlying layer contain the black-and-white drawings, which was really cool.

A complete list of these filters is available in the Core Image Filter Reference in the Xcode documentation. If you are interested in seeing the code associated with how these effects were created, check out *GPUImage*.[1] GPUImage is an open source framework for image processing that contains many similar filters to the ones used in Core Image. The difference is that you can look at the shaders written to get an idea of how that awesome effect you are using was put together so that you can learn how to modify it and roll your own—a new functionality in iOS 8. Writing shaders is beyond the scope of this book, but if you are interested in writing shaders, this is an invaluable resource.

Adding a Filter to our Photos

All right, enough talk. Let's go ahead and add our filter to our project.

We need to import the framework we are using. Go to the top of the root view controller and import the Core Image framework:

Photos/PragmaticTweets-12-2/PragmaticTweets/RootViewController.swift
```
import CoreImage
```

We need to modify our closure within createTweetForAsset(). Add the following just before the SLComposeViewController is created:

Photos/PragmaticTweets-12-2/PragmaticTweets/RootViewController.swift
```
Line 1  var ciImage = CIImage(image: image)
    2   ciImage = ciImage.imageByApplyingFilter("CIPixellate",
    3     withInputParameters:
    4     ["inputScale" : 15,
    5     ])
```

---

1. https://github.com/BradLarson/GPUImage/

```
6 let ciContext = CIContext(options:nil)
7 let cgImage = ciContext.createCGImage (ciImage, fromRect: ciImage.extent())
8 let tweetImage = UIImage (CGImage: cgImage)
```

1. On line 1, we create our CIImage object. We'll be using this to gather the pieces to apply our filter to our photo.

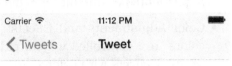

2. Lines 2–5 create and apply our filter. For this example, we chose the easy-to-use (and easy-to-see!) CIPixellate, but there are over a hundred filters to choose from. If you want to apply a different filter, feel free to do so; just look it up in the Core Image Programming Guide, and replace its string name and its required parameters in the imageByApplyingFilter() call.

Here's a photo I tweeted. #pragsios8 http://t.co/6wydqCel9w

3. On line 6, we need to create a CIContext. Without a context, we won't be able to draw anything to our screen because our CIImage doesn't actually contain any pixels. It is a set of instructions to be passed to our CIContext, and if we don't have one, our work will go nowhere.

4. A CIContext can't create a UIImage directly, but it can provide its lower-level bitmap equivalent, the CGImage, on line 7. From that, line 8 can easily create a UIImage, tweetImage.

Finally, we mustn't forget to have the SLComposeViewController use our new tweetImage. Update the call to addImage() like this:

Photos/PragmaticTweets-12-2/PragmaticTweets/RootViewController.swift
```
tweetVC.addImage(tweetImage)
```

Run your application and try posting another photo. The photo you see should have the pixelation filter applied to it.

Wrap-Up

We have all the classic components for a wedding: something old (Core Image), something new (PhotoKit), something borrowed (GPUImage), and something blue (color modification filters), and now our Twitter client can tweet a photo! But we have just scratched the surface of what you can do with these technologies. We hope you will continue to explore the possibilities with these deep and comprehensive frameworks.

One functionality we haven't gone over yet is how to turn your photo-editing application into an extension. We will be tackling the new iOS 8 extensions in the next chapter.

CHAPTER 13

Launching, Backgrounding, and Extensions

We've been working to make our Twitter app better and better, gradually building out its capabilities and learning new skills along the way. Our users are going to be happy with how they can see their timeline, drill down into details, and send new tweets.

However, ours is just one of many apps on the user's device. It will come and go as needed, with the typical user spending only a minute or less in our app, or any other. That's the nature of apps on mobile devices: App A does Thing A, App B does Thing B, and never the twain shall meet. But as iOS has evolved over the years, it has accumulated more and more ways in which apps can work together to increase their mutual usefulness. Apps have gained the ability to launch one another and exchange data and documents, albeit under significant restrictions. In iOS 8, it's even possible to offer part of our application for direct use inside other applications.

In this chapter, we're going to take advantage of these opportunities, and extend the functionality of our app into other apps the user might be using. In the process, we'll also get a feel for the life cycle by which apps are launched, killed, and launched anew.

The App Life Cycle

If someone asked us to point to the first line of our app, what would we say? Unlike old C programs—or even the Objective-C that we used prior to iOS 8—there's no command-line friendly main() function that kicks off our execution. If we think back to where started, we had just two classes: AppDelegate and ViewController, along with Main.storyboard. Clearly, we're not driving this car; we're a passenger. So let's start by getting a sense of where iOS is taking us when our app starts up and when we get an opportunity to tell the driver where we're going.

For a Swift app, iOS creates a UIApplication object to set up the app's runtime environment: its use of the display, its ability to handle touches and rotation events, and so forth. This object is also how we can interact with the rest of the iOS system, as we'll see shortly. The UIApplication has an array of windows, typically one per screen, and there's only one screen unless we're hooked up with a video output cable or AirPlay. Each window has a rootViewController. And that's where the storyboard comes in: the application creates an instance of the view controller in the storyboard's initial scene, and puts its view into the window.

UIApplication can also have a UIApplicationDelegate object, which is informed of major life-cycle events that affect the app. This is the AppDelegate class that Xcode gave us to start with. When all the app setup is done, the application(didFinish-LaunchingWithOptions:) method gets called. From our point of view, this is where the app "starts," although a bunch of stuff has already been done for us by this point. Some apps will use this callback to set up stuff that needs to be working immediately, or objects that will live for the entire life of the app, like data stores.

Of course, at some point, users will leave our app by pressing the home button, taking a phone call, accepting a notification from another app, and so on. That's not the end for us; they might come back. UIApplicationDelegate tells us about these actions, with methods like applicationDidEnterBackground(), applicationWil-lEnterForeground(), and so on. We used applicationWillEnterForeground() on a lark back in *Using Another TwitterAPIRequest*, on page 136, when we made a quick Twitter call every time our app is foregrounded. There are also the related methods applicationWillResignActive() and applicationDidBecomeActive() that tells us we've been suspended so users can deal with an interruption like an alert from an incoming phone call or SMS message. If they take the call or switch to the Messages app, we'll be backgrounded, but if they choose to ignore it, we'll become active again.

If our app is backgrounded long enough, it will eventually be terminated, so if our app needed to save data for the next time it's launched, going to the background is the right time to do that work. If the user force-quits us in the foreground, the app delegate finds out by way of a different method: application-WillTerminate().

Opening via URLs

The application and its delegate also have methods that relate to how our app interacts with the rest of the system. For example, if we receive a *push notification* from Apple's push notification service—something we'd have to set up on a server, and which is beyond the scope of this book—we would get it in the app delegate callback application(didReceivePushNotification:fetchCompletionHandler:).

One way we can work directly with other applications on the device is found in a rather unusual place: URLs. UIApplication offers the method openURL:(), which will launch other applications and have them deal with the NSURL. Most web page URLs, with schemes http or https, will open Safari. For example, we can background ourselves and send Safari to this book's home page with a one-line call:

```
UIApplication.sharedApplication().openURL(
  NSURL(string: "https://pragprog.com/book/adios2/ios-8-sdk-development"))
```

Not all URLs go to Safari. If the host is www.youtube.com, the YouTube app will open instead, if present. phobos.apple.com iTunes Store URLs will open the iTunes app. And other URL schemes can be used to launch default system apps—for example, mailto:, facetime:, and tel: open the Mail, FaceTime, and Phone apps, respectively. Check out the Apple URL Scheme Reference in the Xcode documentation for the exact syntax and more information.

What's really cool is that third-party applications can also participate in this system. Any app can create a new URL scheme that it handles, and then other apps that open this URL will launch that app. Since our app does so much with Twitter, let's offer up our services to other apps.

Declaring a URL Scheme

We start our URL support by just picking a name. It needs to be plausibly unique, since Apple does *nothing* to police URL schemes. If every Twitter app declares that it will open URLs with the scheme twitter:, who knows which one will launch? Instead, let's go with pragtweets:.

Let's think about what service makes sense to offer other applications. We will receive a full URL from the caller, so we could design an API kind of like REST endpoints, with different URL paths leading to different features within our app. We'll only implement one for now, but we could keep adding to it later by just looking for different strings in the URL.

The user may already have an app to show recent tweets (or see them in Notification Center), so let's choose something unique that we offer. For this example, we'll let a URL take us straight to the user detail screen. If we get a URL of the form pragtweets://host/user?screenname=name, we'll go right to the UserDetailViewController, as if we had drilled down on one of name's tweets.

At the very top of the File Navigator, click on the top-level PragmaticTweets project icon, and when the project settings come up in the Content View, make sure the selected target is the PragmaticTweets app (as opposed to the PragmaticTweetsTests target). This editor lets us configure how the build process and the resulting app work: what versions of iOS we deploy to, whether we have capabilities like iCloud or in-app purchase, which source files get built and how, and so on.

The Info tab has metadata for our app such as its display name, what features must be present on a device for it to work, and what kinds of documents it accepts or produces. At the bottom of this view, there's a URL Types section. Expand the disclosure triangle, and then press the plus (+) button to show the settings for a new URL type, seen in the following figure:

The important entry here is the URL Schemes text field, which takes a comma-separated list of schemes we accept. Enter pragtweets here, without the trailing colon character (:). The identifier should be a reverse-DNS style unique identifier, like com.pragprog.yourhandle.pragmatictweets, and the Role should be None, so that we aren't making any promises about what we do with the URL (the Viewer and Editor values are more appropriate for dealing with documents passed between apps).

Once we run this app once, the system will know to send any URL with the scheme pragtweets: to our app. Now we need to actually do something with this URL when it arrives.

Creating a New Scene

When our app gets opened via a properly formatted URL, we want to go directly to the UserDetailViewController scene, bypassing the two scenes before it (the list of tweets and the tweet detail). This is possible because all we have to give the user detail scene is the screenName we want to view; it will get everything else it needs via its own TwitterAPIRequest.

The iOS URL Scheme Ecosystem

Passing around URLs is commonly used for apps to exchange small amounts of information, particularly when they're developed by totally unrelated parties. You may have seen this when an app asks you to log in with a web identity like Facebook, Google, or LinkedIn, then automatically returns to the app.

Part of the secret sauce here is *x-callback-url*, a de facto standard by which an app calls another with a URL, passing in a URL with its own registered URL scheme, which allows the second app (or possibly a web page loaded in Safari) to return control to the original app when it's done. It's kind of disorienting for the user to see the apps switching back and forth, but given the degree to which iOS apps are isolated from one another, it has held up pretty well in practice.

The x-callback-url specification is hosted at http://x-callback-url.com, where you can also find information about popular iOS apps that support being opened via URLs.

We *could* create a new segue from the split view directly to the user detail scene. This would be totally legal. But there's a problem: the Done button is set to unwind to the tweet detail scene, but in the case where we come straight from the split view scene, there won't be a previous tweet detail scene, and that will produce an error.

We have a couple of options. We could nuke the exit segue and instead set up a button handler that calls UIViewController's dismissModalViewController() method. This would work for both cases, but it assumes we always come in via a modal segue.

The option we'll use is to just create another user detail scene, reachable only from the first scene and used only for this URL handler. It makes our storyboard a little bigger, but it lets us customize too—an acceptable trade-off.

In Main.storyboard, select the yellow ball icon for the User scene, and do a copy-and-paste. (⌘C, then ⌘V). The newly pasted instance will be placed exactly atop the old one. In the layout area, drag this scene by its title bar and notice that it doesn't have any segues associated with it. Move it closer to the beginning of the storyboard (perhaps under the initial view controller), and then use the name field next to its view controller icon in the scene list to give it a unique name to keep things straight (like User Detail from URL Scene).

Control-click on the Size Class Override View Controller at the beginning of the storyboard to see its connections. Under Triggered Segues, drag from the Manual connection ball down to the new user detail scene, as seen in the following figure. Upon dropping, choose the Present Modally segue type.

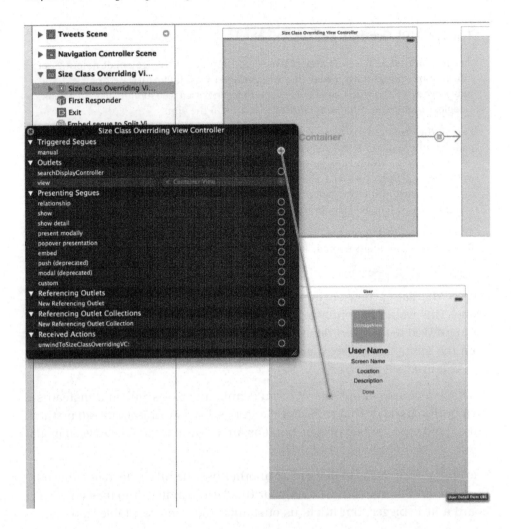

We're going to need to run this segue manually when the URL comes in, which means we'll need an identifier string. Select the segue, bring up the Attributes Inspector, and set the identifier to ShowUserFromURLSegue.

Handling the Open URL Callback

Now we're ready to call this segue when our app is launched from a URL. When that happens, our AppDelegate will receive a callback to the method application(openURL:sourceApplication:annotation:). This method returns a Bool indicating whether it handled the URL successfully, so we should only return true if we can successfully pick out a screenname.

To do that, we're going to rely on the NSURL class. It has several methods that break down a URL into its various parts: scheme(), path(), query(), and so on. We'll take the segue if the path is /user and the query is of the form screen-name=foo.

Lifecycle/PragmaticTweets-13-1/PragmaticTweets/AppDelegate.swift

```
Line 1   func application(application: UIApplication, openURL url: NSURL,
           sourceApplication: String, annotation: AnyObject?) -> Bool {
             var showedUserDetail = false
             if (url.path? == "/user") {
       5         if let query = url.query {
                   let components = query.componentsSeparatedByString("=")
                   if (components.count > 1 &&
                     components[0] == "screenname") {
                       if let sizeClassVC = self.window?.rootViewController
      10                 as? SizeClassOverrideViewController {
                           sizeClassVC.performSegueWithIdentifier("ShowUserFromURLSegue",
                             sender: self)
                           showedUserDetail = true
                     }
      15            }
                 }
             }
             return showedUserDetail
       -   }
```

We start on line 3 with a showedUserDetail Boolean that will become true only if we kick off the segue (way inside the ifs, on line 13). Then on line 4, we look to see if the URL's path is user; this kind of logic would let us expand to handle URLs that open tweets or other kinds of requests.

On line 5, we unwrap the optional query property. If it exists, we can split apart the name and value on line 6 with componentsSeparatedByString(). That lets lines 7–8 verify that there are two components, and the first is screenname. Note that we're kind of cheating because there is only one key-value pair; the more general case of ?key1=value1&key2=value2&... would take a lot more work to pick apart.

If we made it this far, then our URL is good. Lines 9–10 ask for our window's rootViewController as our SizeClassOverrideViewController class, the first scene in the storyboard. If that cast works, then we can tell the view controller to manually perform the ShowUserFromURLSegue segue, on lines 11–12.

At the very end, on line 18 we return a Bool to indicate whether we showedUserDe-tail. This is to uphold the contract established in the docs for the applica-tion(openURL:sourceApplication:annotation), which expects us to return true or false to indicate whether we handled the URL.

We now have enough done to try it out. Run the app, and then in the Simulator, use Hardware→Home (⇧⌘H) to background our app. Open up Safari and enter a URL like pragtweets://localhost/user?screenname=pragprog (the hostname is ignored, so anything will work there). Press Return or click Go and it should show an alert like the following figure, asking if you want to open the page in PragmaticTweets. Click Open.

This opens our app and goes immediately to the user detail scene. None of the fields are filled in yet because we haven't sent the values to that view controller. Let's take care of that.

Our AppDelegate can't see the UserDetailViewController when it kicks off the segue. But the first scene will get a look at it, in prepareForSegue(). That scene will need to know about the screen name to show, so switch to SizeClassOverrideViewController.swift and add a screenNameForOpenURL property:

Lifecycle/PragmaticTweets-13-1/PragmaticTweets/SizeClassOverrideViewController.swift
```
var screenNameForOpenURL : String?
```

This class already has a prepareForSegue() method, to deal with the embedSplitViewSegue at startup, so just add an else if to handle the ShowUserFromURLSegue:

Lifecycle/PragmaticTweets-13-1/PragmaticTweets/SizeClassOverrideViewController.swift
```
override func prepareForSegue(segue: UIStoryboardSegue, sender: AnyObject?) {
  if segue.identifier == "embedSplitViewSegue" {
    embeddedSplitVC = segue.destinationViewController as?
      UISplitViewController
  } else if segue.identifier == "ShowUserFromURLSegue" {
    if let userDetailVC = segue.destinationViewController
      as? UserDetailViewController {
        userDetailVC.screenName = self.screenNameForOpenURL
    }
  }
}
```

Now that this view controller is ready for the segue, go back to AppDelegate.swift and, on a new line right before we performSegueWithIdentifier(), send the screen name to the view controller that needs it.

Lifecycle/PragmaticTweets-13-1/PragmaticTweets/AppDelegate.swift
```
sizeClassVC.screenNameForOpenURL = components[1]
```

Run again, switch to Safari, open the pragtweets: URL, and this will show the user detail scene with the real name, description, and avatar image.

The last thing we have to do is to fix the Done button, which still thinks it can unwind to the tweet detail scene (since that's what was in the scene we copied over). First, in SizeClassOverrideViewController.swift, create an unwind method that we can go back to:

Lifecycle/PragmaticTweets-13-1/PragmaticTweets/SizeClassOverrideViewController.swift
```
@IBAction func unwindToSizeClassOverridingVC (segue: UIStoryboardSegue) {
}
```

Then, back in the storyboard, go to the new User Detail From URL scene and control-click or right-click the Done button to show its connections (or bring up the Connections Inspector, ⌥⌘6). Use the x-button to delete any existing unwind segue, close the connections pop-up, then control-drag from the button to the orange Exit icon in the title bar atop the scene, and when the list of unwind methods appears, choose unwindToSizeClassOverridingVC().

Run again, and open the user detail URL from Safari. Now, not only can we view the user details, but we can also use the Done button to return to the first scene of the app. Now our app is useful not only to our users, but it offers other apps (or web pages in Safari) the ability to send users over to us with just a simple URL.

App Extensions

Using URLs to bring users into our app, and even to a specific feature, is a very handy feature. But it does mean leaving the app the user was in and coming over to ours. Throughout the history of iOS, each app has lived in its own *sandbox*, prohibited from directly interacting with other apps. Each app has its own section of the filesystem and can't see anything outside its folders. Each app runs in its own process and cannot share resources like frameworks or dynamic libraries. This can lead to a lot of duplication of effort across apps.

iOS 8 has started to break down the walls between applications by allowing apps to create *app extensions*. From the user's point of view, extensions are packaged with an app and allow it to extend some of its functionality into other apps. From the developer's point of view, the extension is another target in the Xcode project, one that can share code and certain runtime resources.

iOS defines several *extension points*, which are different kinds of functionality that an app extension can provide, and a hook into that functionality via an API or some aspect of the user interface. In iOS 8, the following extension points are provided:

Extension Point	Description
Action	Manipulate content from the host app
Document Provider	Access and manage a filesystem
Keyboard	Provide text input with custom keyboard input method
Photo Editing	Edit a photo or video within the Photos app
Share	Share content with others, like via a social network
Today	Provide "glanceable" content in Notification Center

In most cases, we develop an app extension as a view controller, which allows us to customize the view for our extension as well as put the control logic behind it. Extensions have a shorter life cycle than full apps; they're expected to be small and short-lived, since they come up only briefly in order to provide services to another app that's already running. They're also more limited in what they can do; extensions can't access the camera or microphone, and some have to ask permission to do things like access the network.

The idea of an extension is to offer something that our app can do, that would be useful to other applications. Our app knows a lot about getting data from Twitter, so maybe there's something we can do related to that.

Creating a Keyboard Extension

Have you ever wanted to type an email and use someone's Twitter handle but could not remember it exactly? Maybe you were on a forum and you wanted to praise that book by @RedQueenCoder and...wait, was it really @invalidname? (That can't be right, can it?)

Well, with our extension, we're going to offer a custom keyboard that is a table of all our user's Twitter friends. That way, when users are in this scenario, they can just switch to our keyboard, tap the name of their friend, and have that text inserted directly into the host application.

Start a keyboard extension by clicking on the project icon at the top of the file and choosing File→New→Target. This opens the Target Template sheet shown in the following figure. From the list on the left, choose Application

Extension, and on the right, choose the Custom Keyboard template and click Next. On the following page, name the product PragmaticTweepsKeyboard, and ensure the language is Swift.

Once the new target is created, Xcode will ask if we want to "activate" the PragmaticTweepsKeyboard scheme. This means that the Build (⌘B) and Run (⌘R) commands will build and run the keyboard code, not the main app. That's what we want to do for now. Later, when we're done with the extension and ready to turn our attention back to coding and debugging the main app, we can do that by choosing PragmaticTweets in the scheme selector, next to the stop button on the toolbar.

The template creates a group called PragmaticTweepsKeyboard that contains a single KeyboardViewController.swift file, and a Supporting Files group that has a file called Info.plist. This target is actually runnable as is. Try it. A sheet will slide down asking which app we want to run, listing the default apps on the Simulator, as well as our own Pragmatic Tweets. Safari is a good choice, since it has a text field that's easy to get to.

Once Safari runs, the custom keyboard will now be available, but we have to explicitly ask for it. Switch to the Settings app in the Simulator and navigate to General→Keyboards→ Add New Keyboard. PragmaticTweets will now be listed as one of our choices, as you can see in the figure.

Click on PragmaticTweets to add its keyboard. Switch back to Safari, and click in the address bar to show the default keyboard (if the keyboard doesn't show at all, check the Hardware→Keyboard menu item to make sure the Simulator isn't using your Mac's hardware keyboard). Next to the spacebar, there will be a globe icon; this is the button to switch between keyboards when more than one is available, either through internationalization settings or custom keyboards like ours. Click the globe to cycle through keyboards. Eventually, one of them will be a gray space that just says Next Keyboard. This is our keyboard, and it's providing the one thing all keyboards *must* offer: a button to advance to the next keyboard. It may not be very interesting, but it's a start!

Custom keyboards broken in Xcode 6.1

This example worked great in Xcode 6.0, but if you don't see your custom keyboard in Safari, it may be from a bug introduced in Xcode 6.1. From Apple's Xcode release notes:

> Localization and Keyboard settings, including 3rd party keyboards, are not correctly honored by Safari, Maps, and developer apps in the iOS 8.1 Simulator. [NSLocale currentLocale] returns en_US and only the English and Emoji keyboards are available. (18418630, 18512161)

If the only keyboards you can see are English and Emoji, it means this error is still there. While the keyboard won't work in Safari, there are some places where it will work, including the Spotlight search bar (drag down from the home screen to expose Spotlight), Contacts, Calendar, and Photos. So try out our custom keyboard in Spotlight, and let's all hope Apple fixes this bug soon.

Creating an App Extension Storyboard

In Xcode, click Stop and switch over to KeyboardViewController.swift. Curiously, Xcode's template for keyboard extensions builds the user interface with code, in viewDidLoad(). It adds the Next Keyboard button, and connects it to a method called advanceToNextInputMode(). That's something it inherits from its superclass, UIInputViewController, and we'll have to remember to implement that ourselves.

Building our UI in code isn't something we've done before, and isn't necessarily a good idea, so let's give ourselves the ability to lay out our keyboard with a storyboard instead.

We don't add our UI as a scene to Main.storyboard, since that's part of the main app and won't be available to our extension. Instead, we need a new storyboard. Select the PragmaticTweepsKeyboard group, and choose File→New→

File. When the template chooser comes up, select the iOS User Interface group and the Storyboard template, as shown in the following figure. Name the file PragmaticTweepsKeyboard.storyboard, and in the list of targets in this dialog, make sure that the PragmaticTweepsKeyboard is checked, and PragmaticTweeps is not; this will include the storyboard in the keyboard extension, but not in the main app (which doesn't know anything about it).

The new storyboard is completely empty. Drag in a view controller to create a new scene, and in its Attributes Inspector (⌥⌘3), choose Is Initial View Controller.

This scene looks like any other scene, and that's actually a problem. Our usual storyboard scenes take up a whole screen, but a keyboard should only fill part of the screen. We're going to do some custom sizing to make things fit. At the top of the view controller's Attributes Inspector, change Size to Freeform, and in the Size Inspector (⌥⌘4), change the height to 204. This doesn't lock us into that height; we'll have to set that with our views' autolayout constraints. What this setting does give us is a more realistic sense of our custom keyboard's size.

We'll keep the UI simple but still distinct so users know it's a custom keyboard. Drag a Navigation bar from the Object library (^⌥⌘3) to the top of the view, and use the Pin button to set its top constraint to 0 and its left and right to 0, with the Margins checkbox deselected; this lets us stretch all the way to the side of the screen. Edit the title to say Pragmatic Tweeps, and add a bar button item on the right. The button will be our Next Keyboard button; you can change the text to Next, or paste in the Unicode globe character (U+1F310), if you want to get fancy.

Immediately below the navigation bar, drop in a table, pinning its top constraint to 0 points from the navigation bar, and its leading and trailing constraints to 0 points from the superview with margins off. Also in the Pin pop-up, set its height to 160 points. When added to the 44-point height of the Navigation bar, this equals the 204 points we set for ourselves in the view controller's freestyle size.

Finally, custom keyboards usually use different color schemes to set themselves off from the app content. A simple way to do this is to play with the tint and the title color of the Navigation bar in its Attributes Inspector. In the following figure, we've used the brown-and-yellow color scheme of the http://pragprog.com home page banner:

Now we have to get the keyboard extension to use the storyboard instead of building the UI in code. Under PragmaticTweepsKeyboard→Supporting Files, open Info.plist, which is a special kind of XML file called a *property list*. This file opens with the custom editor seen in the following figure. Use the disclosure triangle to expand the NSExtension group, select it, and use the minus (--) button to remove the NSExtensionPrincipalClass line. This entry described which class provided the keyboard, and implied we would build our UI in code. We need an approach to let us supply a storyboard and have that indicate which class is associated with our keyboard UI.

On the NSExtensionPointIdentifier line, click the plus (+) button to create a new row. This is how we're going to tell the extension to find our storyboard. Replace the highlighted New Item key with NSExtensionMainStoryboard, and for the value, enter PragmaticTweepsKeyboard.

Key	Type	Value
▤ ‹ › ▤ PragmaticTweets › ▤ PragmaticTweepsKeyboard › ▤ Supporting Files › ▤ Info.plist › No Selection		
▼ Information Property List	Dictionary	(11 items)
Localization native development r...	String	en
Bundle display name	String	PragmaticTweepsKeyboard
Executable file	String	$(EXECUTABLE_NAME)
Bundle identifier	String	com.pragprog.yourhandle.PragmaticTweets.$(PRODUCT_NAME:rfc1034identifier)
InfoDictionary version	String	6.0
Bundle name	String	$(PRODUCT_NAME)
Bundle OS Type code	String	XPC!
Bundle versions string, short	String	1.0
Bundle creator OS Type code	String	????
Bundle version	String	1
▼ NSExtension	Dictionary	(3 items)
▶ NSExtensionAttributes	Dictionary	(4 items)
NSExtensionPointIdentifier	String	com.apple.keyboard-service
NSExtensionMainStoryboard	String	PragmaticTweepsKeyboard

Once we've added the keyboard, go back to Safari and cycle through keyboards with the globe key. We'll be able to see our keyboard from its customized navigation bar. It doesn't do anything yet...in fact, we're trapped because the Next Keyboard button doesn't do anything. Still, we're getting close!

Implementing the Custom Keyboard

We have to do three things for our keyboard to work: implement the next keyboard button, fill in the table with the names of our user's Twitter friends, and insert text when a table row is tapped. The first step is the easiest, so we'll do that first.

Implementing the Next Keyboard Button

We might as well make all our storyboard connections at once, since there aren't many to do. Switch to KeyboardViewControllerStoryboard.storyboard, and select the view controller. In its Identity Inspector (⌥⌘3), set its Custom Class to KeyboardViewController. Now we can use the Assistant Editor (⌥⌘↩) to bring up KeyboardViewController.swift in the right pane. Control-drag to create outlets to the tableView and nextKeyboardBarButton. The properties at the top of the class should look like the following (in addition to a nextKeyboardButton hanging around from the original template):

Lifecycle/PragmaticTweets-13-2/PragmaticTweepsKeyboard/KeyboardViewController.swift
```
@IBOutlet weak var nextKeyboardBarButton: UIBarButtonItem!
@IBOutlet weak var tableView: UITableView!
```

Also, control-drag from the bar button item to create an action (not another outlet!) called nextKeyboardBarButtonTapped(). We'll write this in a bit to handle switching keyboards.

Now we can code. In KeyboardViewController.swift, we'll start by clearing out junk we don't want. Delete the methods textWillChange(), textDidChange(), updateViewConstraints(), and all the contents of viewDidLoad() except for the first line, super.viewDidLoad. Also, delete the nextKeyboardButton property that the template gave us (but not the nextKeyboardBarButton property that we just created with the Assistant Editor).

Advancing to the next keyboard turns out to be easy. Our superclass gives us a method for it: advanceToNextInputMode(). So we just call that in our nextKeyboardBarButtonTapped():

Lifecycle/PragmaticTweets-13-2/PragmaticTweepsKeyboard/KeyboardViewController.swift
```
@IBAction func nextKeyboardBarButtonTapped(sender: UIBarButtonItem) {
  advanceToNextInputMode()
}
```

Run the keyboard target, and, once we bring up the keyboard, we should now be able to cycle through all the keyboards, including our own, now that its Next Keyboard button works. Yay, integration!

Implementing the Table View

Our next task is to implement the table view that shows our user's Twitter friends. For this, we need the TwitterAPIRequest and TwitterAPIRequestDelegate classes that we developed for the app a while back. Select these files in the File Navigator and bring up the File Inspector (⌥⌘1). In the Target Membership section, click the checkbox to add each of them to the PragmaticTweepsKeyboard target. This means these files will be built for and deployed with each project.

Our strategy is going to be that viewDidLoad() will call the Twitter API and request the list of friends, which we'll put in an array that will serve as a table model. This means our class needs to implement the TwitterAPIRequestDelegate (to handle the Twitter response), as well as the usual table protocols, UITableViewDataSource and UITableViewDelegate. Add these protocols to the class declaration:

Lifecycle/PragmaticTweets-13-2/PragmaticTweepsKeyboard/KeyboardViewController.swift
```
class KeyboardViewController: UIInputViewController,
UITableViewDataSource, UITableViewDelegate, TwitterAPIRequestDelegate  {
```

Note that this will start kicking up an error until we implement handleTwitterData(), which we'll do momentarily.

We said we'd keep our list of tweeps in an array for the table methods to use, so add that as a property near the top of the class.

Lifecycle/PragmaticTweets-13-2/PragmaticTweepsKeyboard/KeyboardViewController.swift
```
var tweepNames : [String] = []
```

Now we're ready to implement the UITableDataSource methods based on this array. There will be one section, it will have as many rows as the array has members, and each cell will be a default cell whose text is the array member string, prepended with an @ character. So here are the methods to do that:

Lifecycle/PragmaticTweets-13-2/PragmaticTweepsKeyboard/KeyboardViewController.swift
```
func numberOfSectionsInTableView(tableView: UITableView) -> Int {
  return 1
}

func tableView(tableView: UITableView,
  numberOfRowsInSection section: Int) -> Int {
    return tweepNames.count
}
```

```
func tableView(tableView: UITableView,
  cellForRowAtIndexPath
  indexPath: NSIndexPath) -> UITableViewCell {
    let cell = tableView.dequeueReusableCellWithIdentifier("DefaultCell")
      as UITableViewCell
    cell.textLabel!.text = "@\(tweepNames[indexPath.row])"
    return cell
}
```

For that to work, we need to go into the storyboard and do a couple of things. First, select the table, and in its Attributes Inspector, change the number of Prototype Cells to 1. This creates a table cell in the storyboard. Select it and change its identifier to DefaultCell, since that's what tableView(rowForCellAtIndexPath:) expects. Next, right-click or control-click the table (or show its Connections Inspector), and connect the delegate and dataSource properties back to the Keyboard View Controller icon, so our methods actually get called.

Our last task for now is to get the friend names from Twitter. There's an API for that, https://api.twitter.com/1.1/friends/list.json, which returns a richly detailed dictionary for each of our user's friends.

Lifecycle/PragmaticTweets-13-2/PragmaticTweepsKeyboard/KeyboardViewController.swift
```
override func viewDidLoad() {
  super.viewDidLoad()
  let twitterParams : Dictionary = ["count":"100"]
  let twitterAPIURL = NSURL(string:
    "https://api.twitter.com/1.1/friends/list.json")
  let request = TwitterAPIRequest()
  request.sendTwitterRequest(twitterAPIURL,
    params: twitterParams,
    delegate: self)
}
```

This composes a TwitterAPIRequest, just like our others throughout the book, asking for up to 100 responses, and providing this class itself as the delegate to handle the response that comes back.

We get the response back in our handleTwitterData() delegate method, which receives the JSON data and has to parse it.

Lifecycle/PragmaticTweets-13-2/PragmaticTweepsKeyboard/KeyboardViewController.swift
```
Line 1  func handleTwitterData(data: NSData!,
    -     urlResponse: NSHTTPURLResponse!,
    -     error: NSError!,
    -     fromRequest: TwitterAPIRequest!) {
    5       if let dataValue = data {
    -         var parseError : NSError? = nil
    -         let jsonObject : AnyObject? =
```

```
         NSJSONSerialization.JSONObjectWithData(dataValue,
           options: NSJSONReadingOptions(0),
10         error: &parseError)
       if parseError != nil {
         return
       }
       if let jsonDict = jsonObject as? [String:AnyObject] {
15         if let usersArray = jsonDict ["users"] as? NSArray {
           self.tweepNames.removeAll(keepCapacity: true)
           for userObject in usersArray {
             if let userDict = userObject as? [String:AnyObject] {
               let tweepName = userDict["screen_name"] as NSString
20               self.tweepNames.append(tweepName)
             }
           }
         }
         dispatch_async(dispatch_get_main_queue(),
25           {
             self.tableView.reloadData()
         })
       }
     } else {
30       println ("handleTwitterData received no data")
       }
     }
```

The top of this method is like most of our other JSON parsing in the book. What's different is the contents, which the authors puzzled out from logging the raw response: it's a top-level dictionary, with a key users that contains an array of dictionaries, each with the details of one friend. So line 14 tries to get the top-level dictionary, line 15 tries to get the users array, and if that works, we clear out the current tweepNames on line 16.

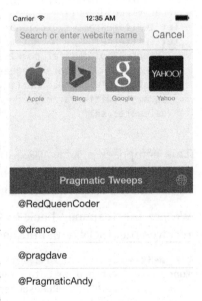

For each dictionary in the users array (line 17), we try to cast to a dictionary (line 18). If that works, we get the screen_name from the dictionary on line 19, and append it to the tweepNames array on line 20. Finally, lines 24–27 put a closure back on the main queue to do a reloadData() on the table.

That was a fair amount of work, but now we have live data in our keyboard. Run the keyboard target again and check out the results. Our keyboard should show a table of tweeps, as in the following figure:

Inserting Text into the Host App

We're almost there! We can bring up our keyboard and see all our tweeps; we just need a tableView(didSelectRowAtIndexPath:) method to insert the text of a given cell into the host app.

The extension classes provided by the Xcode templates provide objects that give us a hook into our host application. These vary by the type of extension. For custom keyboards, the UIInputViewController we subclass has a textDocumentProxy object that is our gateway to the text component that we're typing into. It's defined as a bare NSObject, but it implements three protocols that can help us:

- UITextDocumentProxy—Provides the text before and after the insertion point and lets us move the insertion point

- UIKeyInput—Lets us determine if the document is empty and insert text into it

- UITextInputTraits—Indicates traits like what kind of input is needed (plain text, URL, phone number, etc.), whether autocorrection is on and what kinds of corrections it wants to make, and so forth

The one that will help us the most here is UIKeyInput. We can use that to insert the text of the selected row directly into the text component. So add the following tableView(didSelectRowAtIndexPath:) method:

Lifecycle/PragmaticTweets-13-2/PragmaticTweepsKeyboard/KeyboardViewController.swift
```
func tableView(tableView: UITableView,
  didSelectRowAtIndexPath indexPath: NSIndexPath) {
    if let keyInputProxy = textDocumentProxy as? UIKeyInput {
      let atName = "@\(tweepNames[indexPath.row])"
      keyInputProxy.insertText(atName)
    }

    tableView.deselectRowAtIndexPath(indexPath, animated: true)
}
```

This attempts to cast self.textDocumentProxy to the UIKeyInput protocol, and if it can, it uses the insertText() method to insert the selected row's text, prepended with the customary Twitter @ character.

Try it out. A great place to use it is in the Contacts app, as seen in the following figure, where we've scrolled down to the Twitter field to directly insert Chris' Twitter handle (yes, he really is @invalidname):

Wrap-Up

In this chapter, we've gone beyond the bounds of our original application and opened up our functionality to other apps on the user's device. By defining a custom URL scheme and implementing openURL() in the app delegate, we made it possible for other apps to open our app programmatically, and even pass in data for us to work with, like the screen name of a user for our app to fetch and display details about.

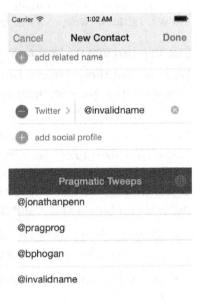

Thanks to iOS 8 extensions, we now have the ability to go the other way: users can stay in an application but use functionality we provide through extension points like custom keyboards. There are lots of other extension points, although for something as common as Twitter, doing a sharing extension hardly makes sense when other apps could just call the Social framework themselves. Offering a custom keyboard of our user's Twitter friends lets us expose our app's functionality in a useful and unique way.

Now that we've got a pretty complete application, our next task is going to be learning how to take a step back to figure out what to do when things go wrong.

CHAPTER 14

Debugging Apps

Congratulations! We have completed all the code for our app. Now we can get started on the real work we will be doing as a developer: debugging.

Bugs happen. Even the most awesome rock-star programmer writes bugs. In truth, developers spend only a fraction of their time writing code. A lot more time is taken up by debugging that code. So one of the single biggest favors we can do for ourselves is to become fast and efficient debuggers.

In this chapter you'll learn about several methods for debugging, starting with the most basic one, println(). We'll cover the various kinds of breakpoints, and then we'll take a nickel tour of LLDB, Xcode's default debugger. You will learn how to print to the console using a breakpoint and how to monitor a variable for changes. Finally, you'll find out how to make your app crash in the place that the problem exists and not several steps afterward.

By the end of this chapter you'll have the skills for dispatching bugs fast so you can move on to bigger and better things.

println(): The First Line of Defense Against Bugs

If you've spent time among other iOS developers or gone on Stack Overflow, you've probably heard someone mention the println() method or its Objective-C predecessor, NSLog(). This the first—and often the last, unfortunately—piece of debugging advice new developers receive. We first saw it way back in *Logging*, on page 26, and have used it occasionally throughout the book, usually as a placeholder to make sure our app reached the new code we were writing.

The gist of println() is that it will print a message to the console that only we will see. It might seem counterintuitive to create output that only we will see, but it is vitally important to have some means of verifying what is happening in our program. println() output also goes to a system log file, so we can collect it from beta testers to illuminate problems with our app.

Let's put ourselves in a situation where we might want to use println() to find our way out. In RootViewController.swift, find the reloadTweets() method, and change the URL it uses, like this:

Debugging/PragmaticTweets-14-1/PragmaticTweets/RootViewController.swift
```
let twitterAPIURL = NSURL(string:
  "https://api.twitter.com/1.1/statuses/foo_bar.json")
```

Of course, there is no Twitter API call at the endpoint https://api.twitter.com/1.1/statuses/foo_bar.json, but this isn't a completely unrealistic scenario either. We might have mistyped the URL, or the web service API might change and remove something we were counting on. At any rate, when we run the app, we come upon an empty table. Pull to refresh, and it's still empty.

If we didn't know the root cause was the bad URL, we'd have to think of reasons this might be happening. We might be parsing the JSON incorrectly. It's possible the table is not connected to the view controller, causing self.tableView.reloadData() to do nothing. Or the delegate might not be connected, so we'd never get callbacks to tableView(rowForCellAtIndexPath:). We can mentally walk along the path our code takes from the refresh to the updated table, as shown in the following figure, in order to figure out where the problem might be, but we can't verify it without running some kind of test.

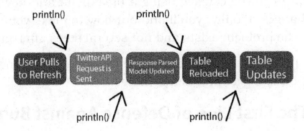

As you can see from the figure, there are at least four points in the operation where something could have gone wrong—maybe more, when we consider that some of these steps have multiple steps within them. We don't need to add a println after the last operation because we already have observed that the table did not update.

By setting up feedback for every step in the process, we can now observe at what point in this chain the message breaks down: the request is sent, and the response is parsed (to some degree), but we never update the table. By throwing down a bunch of println()s, we can at least focus our search on handleTwitterData(), since we reach that method but it fails to update the table.

Breakpoints

At this point, you might be looking at this and thinking, "There is something wrong with this. My Spidey sense detects Code Smell." Trust your Spidey sense. This solution is fraught with potential problems for your project.

Look at all those nasty println statements all over our project. Ideally, we should never include a println command in code that we send to Apple. Although they may help for debugging, println statements are inefficient and slow our app for absolutely no reason. Additionally, any code we add to our project opens up the possibility of breaking something. What's the point of using something that might break our code in order to figure out how to fix it?

Wouldn't it be great if we could still print all our commands to the console without having to sift through all our code looking for those sneaky println statements?

Breakpointing Bad

The answer to our conundrum are *breakpoints*. You have probably inadvertently already created a breakpoint when you clicked on an error to try to see what it said. Now we are going to create breakpoints on purpose.

Breakpoints are a feature in the Xcode development environment that lets us freeze our app at a specific point and figure out what our code is doing. They are like a photograph of all the functions that are happening, what threads are running, and what all our variables are set to at a given moment in time. Understanding breakpoints is the key to many of the debugging techniques available to us in Xcode.

Breakpoints are part of the *Low-Level Debugger*. LLDB is the debugger for Xcode. Many of its functionalities have been built into the user interface, such as the ability to create and edit breakpoints, as we'll see shortly. It also has many other commands that are not included in the user interface and need to be entered via the Xcode terminal. By learning these, we can become efficient debuggers...plus, we can do things that look like magic and we can impress our friends and family.

We have already seen the easiest and most common way people create breakpoints in Xcode. Click in the gutter to the left of our code to create a breakpoint on any line, as seen in the following figure. Create a breakpoint in the first few lines of handleTwitterData(), inside the if let dataValue = data block.

```
65
66      func handleTwitterData (data: NSData!,
67        urlResponse: NSHTTPURLResponse!,
68        error: NSError!,
69        fromRequest: TwitterAPIRequest!) {
70        if let dataValue = data {
71          var parseError : NSError? = nil
72          let jsonObject : AnyObject? =
73            NSJSONSerialization.JSONObjectWithData(dataValue,
74            options: NSJSONReadingOptions(0),
75            error: &parseError)
```

Right now when we create a breakpoint, it is kind of limited. It will just signal the code to pause on this line. That's helpful enough, as it will let us know the app got that far, which is what we were tempted to use println()s for. Fortunately for us, breakpoints can do so much more than that.

Right-click (or control-click) on the breakpoint to reveal the breakpoint menu, as seen in the following figure. As you will see, one of our options is Edit Breakpoint. Let's go ahead and select that and see what we can do with it.

```
89      fromRequest: TwitterAPIRequest!) {
90        if let dataValue = data {
91          let jsonString = NSString (data: da
92                                            = nil
93    Edit Breakpoint...              ? =
94    Disable Breakpoint            jectWithD
95                                   tions(0),
96    Delete Breakpoint
97
98    Reveal in Breakpoint Navigator
99        }
100       if let jsonArray = jsonObject as? A
```

Take a look at the default options for editing breakpoints (as seen in the next figure). Notice that we have the following options:

- Add a condition.
- Ignore the breakpoint a variable number of times.
- Add an action.
- Determine if we want the program to pause or not after the program hits the breakpoint.

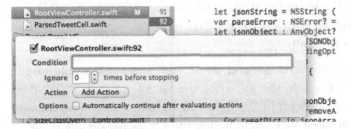

The ability to ignore a breakpoint is particularly useful if we are dealing with a large collection of items. If we were analyzing a collection of ten million keys and values but we only wanted to know what the forty-second value was, we could tell the compiler to ignore the first forty-one values and analyze the one we want to make sure it is "Life, the Universe, and Everything."

Breakpoint Logging

Rather than burdening our code with lots of println() statements, breakpoints offer something easier to remove when we have finished debugging our code. Click the Add Action button. Notice that one of our options is Log Message, as seen in the following figure:

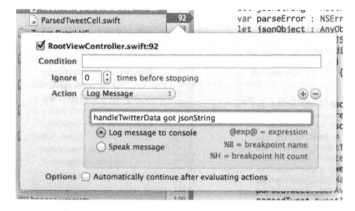

Log Message lets you do exactly that: log a message to Xcode's debug console. Since we are attaching this behavior to a breakpoint, it is easier to go back later and filter out all of our debugging tools. Instead of a lot of messy code, we have some nice, neat breakpoints, as seen in the following diagram. In fact, it gets better: breakpoints are saved only in the local user's Xcode configuration. So, if we send this project to our colleagues, there will be nothing for them to clean up.

The Debugging User Interface

So far, what we've accomplished is pretty much what we got from using a bunch of println()s: we can tell how far our code got before something went wrong. But handleTwitterData() is a long method; are we seriously going to have to put breakpoints all over it and edit each one to add a unique logging message?

At this level of debugging detail, we can do better than that. Go ahead and run the app. The usual startup routine will call reloadTweets(), eventually resulting in a callback to handleTwitterData(), which is where it hits our breakpoint and the Mac automatically switches the foreground application from the iOS Simulator to Xcode. By default, stopping on a breakpoint also causes two debugging-related panes (shown in the following figure) to appear automatically:

- Debug Navigator (⌘6)—Shows the app's usage of CPU time, memory, and other resources. When the app is stopped on a breakpoint, it also shows the state of active threads.

- Debug Area (⇧⌘Y)—As first mentioned in *The Xcode Window*, on page 11, this space at the bottom of the window can show output from println(). When stopped on a breakpoint, it also lets us look at variables and their values. In this figure, the Debug Navigator is on the left and the Debug Area is on the right.

In the bottom right of the Debug area are three important icons: a trashcan and two little boxes. The trashcan clears logged text from println() or breakpoints that log messages. The two boxes show or hide the two panes of the Debug area: the left shows a variables view, and the right shows the log messages.

At the top of the Debug area, there's a toolbar that includes a blue breakpoint icon, along with several other tiny buttons. The breakpoint button turns breakpoints on or off. The next button to the right is a play/pause button, which allows us to continue after hitting a breakpoint.

The next three buttons are the *step buttons*. The first, *Step Over*, allows the app to continue to the next statement in the current method and then stops

Debugging Grand Central Dispatch Issues

Back in *Putting Work on the Main Queue*, on page 118, we noted that there isn't an easy way in code to tell what queue is running our code, but breakpoints make it easy. In the figure on page 232, notice that the Debug Navigator's list of threads and queues shows us the breakpoint is stopped in Thread 4, whose GCD queue is called "SLRequest perform request queue (serial)" (it's truncated in the figure, but while you're stopped on the breakpoint, enlarge the left pane to see for yourself).

Right above that, notice that the thread we're *not* on is called com.apple.main-thread (serial). That's obviously the main thread, meaning that the code we're currently executing is not main, so it cannot touch UIKit methods or properties, unless it puts its work back on the main queue, typically via dispatch_async().

again. Further right, the down and up arrow icons represent *Step In* and *Step Out*, respectively. Step In means that we will enter the statement on this line of code and stop on its first line. Usually, this is only useful if the statement is in code we've written, as the debugger can't show us the source for Apple's framework code (or third parties'). Step Out does the opposite: it lets the app continue until the current method returns, and stops on the first line in the calling method after returning.

Stepping Through Breakpoints

We are going to use the step buttons to solve our problem. Use the Step Over button to advance one line at a time after the breakpoint. A green arrow in the source will show us where we are after each step.

Our progress will go back and forth on the call to JSONObjectWithData() a few times, but it will eventually reach if let jsonArray = jsonObject as? [[String:AnyObject]], and then fail to enter the if block. Instead, we'll reach the bottom of the method.

Progress! We now know we are failing because our JSON response isn't an array like we expect. That, of course, begs the question "what the heck is it then?"

To figure that out, we need to make another trip through this method. Press the Continue button (between the Breakpoints and Step Over buttons) to let the app continue normally. It finishes its work and fails to update the table. In the Simulator, do a pull-to-refresh on the table, which will make a new Twitter request and hit our breakpoint again. Press Step Over until we're sitting on the if statement again.

Use the pane buttons next to the trashcan icon to make sure that both the variables and console panes are showing. The variables view shows us all the variables currently in scope: the parameters that were passed in to handleTwitterData(), local variables we've created, and self. Variables that have public properties have disclosure triangles that we can use to inspect those variables; we could look at the self.parsedTweets array this way.

Since we know we aren't entering the if let on this line, we know that jsonObject isn't an array. But why not? We can see in the variables view that there is an error and a parseError in scope, but both are nil, so there hasn't been a network or JSON parsing problem.

We need details! Fortunately, LLDB is here to help us out. Any of these variables can be inspected in multiple ways. Let's hypothesize that the Twitter API has used its response to tell us about an error. That would be in the urlResponse. Right-click (or control-click) urlResponse, and from the pop-up menu, choose Print Description Of "urlResponse", as shown in the following figure:

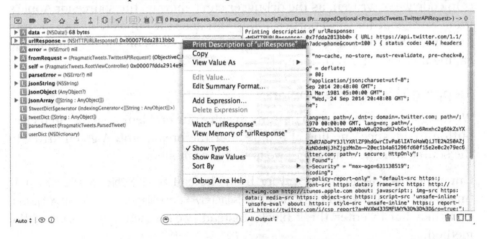

The Debug area will fill in with a log of the object, in this case formatted like a dictionary (only the first few lines are shown here, reformatted to fit the book's layout):

```
Printing description of urlResponse:
<NSHTTPURLResponse: 0x7fb733eb9220> {
  URL: https://api.twitter.com/1.1/statuses/foo_bar.json?adc=phone&count=100 }
  { status code: 404, headers {
    "Cache-Control" =
            "no-cache, no-store, must-revalidate, pre-check=0, post-check=0";
    "Content-Encoding" = deflate;
    "Content-Length" = 80;
    "Content-Type" = "application/json;charset=utf-8";
```

Clear as a bell, we can pick out status code: 404. We asked for an endpoint that doesn't exist, and that leads us back to the underlying problem.

Sometimes, we don't even have to print the description. When possible—which usually means for simple things like numeric values and strings—the variables view will show a simple description in the list itself, and we can mouse over a variable in the source while we're stopped on a breakpoint to see its value.

Exception Breakpoints

Another class of breakpoints happens when dealing with uncaught exceptions. Certain problems, instead of failing or crashing immediately—which would at least let Xcode show us which line of code blew up—will throw an NSException object. The exception bubbles up through calling methods until someone deals with it. If nobody does, we usually end up seeing it on a page of scary-looking machine code with a message like libsystem_kernel.dylib`__pthread_kill:. Lot of good *that* does us.

Pretend that Xcode is a dinosaur. Xcode goes about its merry way grazing on a bunch of leaves until it accidentally eats some poisoned berries. Xcode starts feeling kind of sick but decides to keep walking and consuming leaves, even though it knows it is sick. It finally succumbs to the poison and falls over dead a mile away from the poisoned berries.

As the caretakers of the Xcode dinosaur, we want to make sure we don't keep poisoning it, and it would be helpful to us if the Xcode dinosaur knew not to wander away from the berries so that we can figure out where they are and clear them out.

That is what *exception breakpoints* are for. When we set an exception in the code, we are telling Xcode that if it encounters something that is going to eventually kill it, we want it to stop going and show us where the bad stuff is. In more concrete terms, we want a breakpoint when the exception is raised, not 20 returns later after it hasn't been caught.

Creating an exception breakpoint is easy. We start in the left pane with the Breakpoint Navigator (⌘7), which shows all breakpoints currently set for our project, organized by class and method. Down at the bottom of the screen we have a plus 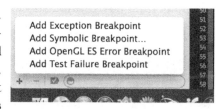 sign. Clicking on the plus button will open a dialog allowing you to create a few new types of breakpoint.

Choose the Add Exception Breakpoint option. This will create a breakpoint that will automatically stop the program at the exact location where an error will occur. It is a good idea to set the exception breakpoint at the beginning of our program to deal with any issues we might encounter while we are coding. We only need one exception breakpoint.

Fortunately, we need exception breakpoints a lot less in Swift than we did in Objective-C and earlier versions of iOS and Xcode. For example, an array index out of bounds mistake—like asking for the eleventh member of a ten-member array—would be an exception in Objective-C and would dump us into the main() method that launched the app. In Swift, array index out of bounds show up as fatal error: Array index out of range, with Xcode pointing to the offending line.

Still, other classes in Foundation may throw exceptions, and exception breakpoints are the key to making sense of them.

Symbolic Breakpoints

If we look at the list of breakpoints we can create with the plus button in the Breakpoint Navigator, we observe that there is an option called Add Symbolic Breakpoint.

A *symbolic breakpoint* is a breakpoint programmed to pause the app whenever a specified method is called. The thing that makes this interesting is that we can set a symbolic breakpoint on *any* method in *any* class, not just the classes we wrote. So we could set a symbolic breakpoint to pause the app whenever viewDidLoad is called. Since viewDidLoad exists in all our UIViewController subclasses, this could be a good way of monitoring behaviors that span the scope of our project.

The following figure updates our hypothetical control flow to use a symbolic breakpoint. If we put a breakpoint on UITableView's reloadData() method, we'd stop on any call to it, whether directly from our code or as a side effect (for example, from navigating between scenes).

Unfortunately, in Xcode 6, the symbol in the Breakpoint Editor pop-up needs to be written in Objective-C syntax, not Swift. So, setting the symbol to

UITableView.reloadData() won't do anything, but -[UITableView reloadData] will pause as we expect. Hopefully, this UI will become Swift-friendly in an upcoming update to Xcode.

We have covered a lot of different ways that we can use breakpoints in our program. At this point, you might be wondering which is the best way. The best way is the one that works for you. We have debugged our program using several kinds of breakpoints, so it is possible to do the same task many different ways. Pick which one you like best or what works best for your specific issues.

Setting Up Your Debugging Environment

When we're in serious debugging mode, it can sometimes help to make sure our debugging tools are ready to deploy immediately. With that in mind, we are going to set up a special debugging tab with an immersive debugging environment. In programming, being organized is vitally important. It will help our efficiency to have a dedicated space where all of our debugging tools are laid out consistently.

Think of your debugging tab like you would your kitchen. When you go to your kitchen to cook, you can get a recipe started right away because you know where all your tools are. If you didn't know where to find your measuring cups and the food processor, it would take a lot longer to get something started.

First thing we'll do is to create a dedicated debugging tab. You can create a new tab by entering ⌘T, just as you would in a web browser, but there is a better way to create a dedicated debugging tab.

Go to Xcode→Preferences or press ⌘ to access the Preferences window. The third tab from the left is Behaviors. This panel controls all of the behaviors an app will have at each and every stage of its life, along with controlling behaviors present in both automated testing and using OpenGL. Since these skills are a little beyond the scope of a beginner book, we won't be going over them, but we just wanted you to know they are there for when you want to take your next steps.

We want to make sure that we can see all of our testing tools while we are running and debugging our application. Find the Running section of the list. Instead of just waiting to hit a breakpoint, we want to see the debugger when the app starts, when it pauses, and when it generates output.

Click Starts and look at the options available to us. You will see an option that says "Show tab named *empty text box* in *drop-down menu*." Click on the checkbox to ensure that it is selected. In the text box, name it something appropriate, like Debugging. Lastly, go into the drop-down menu and select Active Window.

The last thing we need to do before moving on to other parts of the run cycle is to make sure our debugger is showing. If we look at the option two below the Show Tab option, we will see an one that says "Show debugger with *drop-down menu*." Again, click on the checkbox to ensure this option is selected and choose Variables & Console View from the options. Our Behaviors for the Starts menu should look the way it does in the following figure:

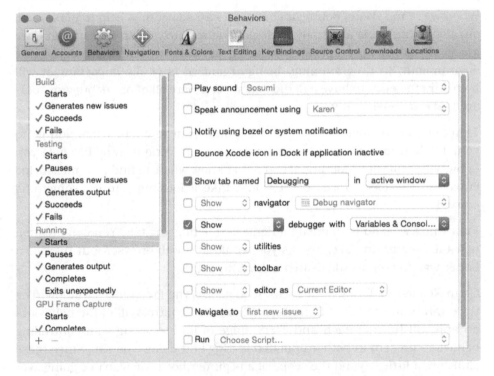

Next, let's move on in the left column to the behaviors we want when we pause our program. We want to show the debugger with Variables & Console View, but now we also want to select the option above that one, which selects a navigator window to show, and we want the Debug Navigator. Make sure your options look the way they do in the following figure:

Lastly, in Generates Output make sure that you have it set to show the debugger with Variables & Console View.

There! Now we have a handy debugging environment that will always be there for us when we need it. Since this is your debugging environment, make sure you go through and look at all the options you think you might want or need. There is nothing that says everyone must have the same options, so feel free to customize this to suit you.

Wrap-Up

In this chapter, we explored some self-defense techniques against bugs. A bug we wrote in five seconds might take five hours to track down and correct. Being able to effectively use the tools provided to us to track down our issues faster means we free up more of our time for doing the fun coding stuff we want to be doing.

Next, we tackle our final challenge. We have our awesome bug-free app. Now we need to do the most important thing of all: publish the app on the App Store so that we can rake in the dough!

CHAPTER 15

Publishing to the App Store

We've come from no code, no tools, and no plan, and now we've got a working, testable Twitter client. That's great! However, it only runs in the Simulator and only then as a result of an Xcode build. The point of writing iOS apps is to run them on iOS devices. Now it's time to take that final step.

As we start thinking of our app in terms of getting it to end users, we're going to want to begin accounting for the app's life cycle and its life beyond the Simulator. How do we get it onto our own devices and into the hands of testers? How do we get it up on the store, and once it is, what happens when people start downloading and using it? What if they turn up bugs or ask for new features?

When we write the last line of code, we're not done—we may just be getting started.

In this chapter, we're going to add some "grown-up" processes to our development: taking care of our source, testing it on the device, getting it on the store, and managing the app's life after it ships.

Protecting Our Code with Source Control

So far, we've made the implicit assumption that our code could live just fine as one collection of source files and resources on one computer, used by one developer. By and large, this isn't realistic; apps are often created by multiple developers working together, and even solo developers often move their projects between desktops and laptops.

To make this more practical, many developers use source control systems (also known as *revision control*). Source control systems exist as both network services and client-side applications, and they allow us to manage multiple versions of the files in our project. This means if we introduce an error in some version of a given source file, we can roll back to an earlier version of the file. Most such systems are also meant to be used by multiple developers, allowing us to get a copy of the code, add to or change it, and send those changes back to other developers.

Xcode offers support for two popular source control systems: Subversion and Git. The two have deep differences in design and philosophy—Subversion is based on a single canonical repository for a codebase, whereas Git's more distributed mindset allows for many differing instances of a project—but Xcode works with a subset of features that both systems implement in similar ways.

Source-Controlling an Existing Project

Let's add the benefits of source control to our project. When we created the PragmaticTweets project, we could have set up a local Git repository for it. Since we didn't then, we will do so now. However, Xcode's Git support doesn't include the ability to create new repositories once a project has been created without one, so we need another application to do that. The most universal approach is to use the /usr/bin/git command-line program from the Terminal.

It's possible that neither Subversion nor Git will be installed on your machine, since they're part of Xcode's *command-line tools*. To install them, go to Xcode's Preferences and select the Downloads tab. If one of the items is Command-Line Tools, click its Install button and wait for the install to finish. This will install git, svn, and many other developer-oriented command-line programs.

Now we're going to add source control to our existing application. This is easier to do in Git because of its distributed nature: we can convert any folder to a Git repository, and if we decide later to share it with other developers, we can let them clone our repository (or connect our repository to a *remote*, meaning an instance of the project hosted on a remote server), then push our changes out to partners and pull others' changes from them. With Subversion, we would have to set up a single, authoritative server first. In practical terms, Git encourages us to adopt source control early, which is one reason Xcode offers to set up a Git repository for new projects when we create them.

Launch the Terminal application from /Applications/Utilities. We need to change our working directory to the PragmaticTweets directory via the cd command. If you're not familiar with the command line, just type cd and a space character, and then drag the PragmaticTweets folder to the Terminal window—this will type out the filesystem path as the next part of the command. So, if PragmaticTweets is on the Desktop, we change directories with cd /Users/yourname/Desktop/Pragmat-icTweets or cd ~/Desktop/PragmaticTweets, which uses the Unix home directory shortcut, ~.

To have Git start source-controlling our code now, we issue three commands: one to create the Git repository, one indicating we have files to add, and one to commit our changes (that is, to add the files). On the command line, it looks like this:

```
⇒ git init
‹ Initialized empty Git repository in
  /Users/cadamson/Desktop/PragmaticTweets/.git/
⇒ git add .
⇒ git commit -m "Created new PragmaticTweets repository"
‹ [master (root-commit) 7d94af6] Created new PragmaticTweets Repository
   31 files changed, 2738 insertions(+)
   create mode 100644 PragmaticTweepsKeyboard/Info.plist
   create mode 100644 PragmaticTweepsKeyboard/KeyboardViewController.swift
   create mode 100644 PragmaticTweepsKeyboard/PragmaticTweepsKeyboard.storyboard
   create mode 100644 PragmaticTweets.xcodeproj/project.pbxproj
  «Many more output lines omitted.»
```

The git init creates the actual Git repository, which is stored in an invisible .git directory. git add . tells Git we want to add all the files from the current directory (.) to the repository. Finally, git commit performs the add, along with providing a log message (via the -m flag) that we can check later. Every time we make a change, we should provide a useful log message saying what we did so that we can understand in the future what changes were made in each commit.

Working with a Source-Controlled Project

So now we've set up the Git repository with initial versions of all the project files. Let's make a change and see what that looks like. Go to any source file and add a comment, and then save the file. As soon as we save, the File Explorer puts an *M* to the right of the filename. The *M* means the file has local modifications. If we add a file to the project, it will show an *A* icon, and if our code comes from a networked repository that has changes waiting for us, we'll see a *U* (for "update"). One icon we don't want to see is the exclamation point ("!"); that means that our local copy of the file and a pending update have both changed the file, which means Xcode will have to merge the changes into one version, something that will require careful editing if the same lines of the file have been updated. We avoid this in team situations by pulling updates and pushing commits frequently.

So we know the file is modified, but if we work across a bunch of files and make lots of changes, it would be nice to know exactly what has changed. We can do this by clicking the third button on the toolbar's editor control, which puts us into the Version editor. This view has three modes, selected by buttons at the bottom; the default is Comparison mode:

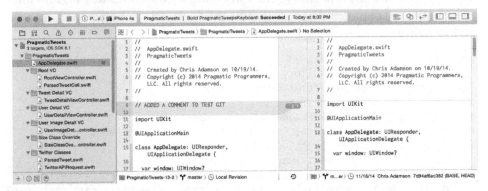

In this mode we see our locally modified version of the file on the left and the most recently committed version from the repository on the right, with blue swooshes in the middle divider indicating where lines have been added or removed between the two revisions. The clock icon in the bottom center lets us bring up a pair of vertical sliders so we can switch either side to show as new or as old a revision as we like. This may be helpful in the future if we discover we've introduced a bug and we want to look at old versions of the code to figure out exactly which change introduced it.

Now that we've made a change, and assuming we want to keep it (or, in a team environment, assuming that we want our teammates to have it), we should commit the change. Right-click or control-click the file, and choose Source Control→Commit Selected Files from the pop-up menu. To commit many files at once, we could ⌘-click to select all the changed files, but we only have the one for now. Xcode slides out a sheet that shows all the files to commit with a comparison view like we saw in the project workspace. This sheet gives us one last chance to review the changes (the *diffs*)—and make further changes if we like—prior to committing. The sheet also has a comment area at the bottom to add a log message to send to the repository with the commit. Enter a comment and click the Commit button to make the commit. The sheet dismisses and the second version of the file is now in the repository.

The Version editor has two other modes that help us in long-term projects. The middle button is the Blame mode, which annotates each line or group of lines with the last revision of the file that edited those lines, shown next.

```
⊞  <  >  │ 📄 PragmaticTweets › 📁 PragmaticTweets › 📄 AppDelegate.swift › No Selection
 1  //
 2  //  AppDelegate.swift                                           Chris Adamson        Nov 16, 2014
 3  //  PragmaticTweets                                             Created new PragmaticTweets
 4  //                                                              Repository
 5  //  Created by Chris Adamson on 10/19/14.
 6  //  Copyright (c) 2014 Pragmatic Programmers, LLC. All rights reserved.
 7  //
 8
 9  // ADDED A COMMENT TO TEST GIT                                  Not Committed
10
11  import UIKit                                                    Chris Adamson        Nov 16, 2014
12                                                                  Created new PragmaticTweets
13  @UIApplicationMain                                              Repository
14
15  class AppDelegate: UIResponder, UIApplicationDelegate {
16
17    var window: UIWindow?
18
19
20    func application(application: UIApplication, didFinishLaunchingWithOptions
          launchOptions: [NSObject: AnyObject]?) -> Bool {
21      // Override point for customization after application launch.
22      return true
```
🔲 PragmaticTweets-13-2 › ⑂ master › 🕒 Local Revision

In this mode we can see the log comments and revision numbers are different for the comment line that we just added as the second revision of the file. A third choice for the Version editor, Log mode, lets us see a scrolling list of commit dates, revision numbers, and log comments for the file without corresponding to individual lines like Blame mode does.

> **Joe asks:**
> ## Does Anyone Really Use Xcode for Source Code Management?
>
> Although we're grateful for Xcode to have some Git and Subversion awareness—it's certainly handy to review changes right in Xcode—we need to come clean and say that very few developers we know consider Xcode a suitable tool for source code management, at least on its own. It omits many of the more advanced merging and history-management features of Git. It also can't actually delete a file from either system, since deleting a file from a project removes it from the Xcode UI, so there's no way to commit the delete.
>
> Most people use other SCM systems with iOS projects, particularly for Git. When using a project hosted on GitHub, it's reasonable to start with the official app for Mac OS X provided by GitHub. Other developers we know use apps like SourceTree, Tower, or just the git command line.

Taking care of our code over the lifetime of the app is an important habit for the professional developer. As our project grows and matures, having the code under source control gives us the ability to keep track of what changes we made, when, and why. To really work, it requires some discipline; we won't have a good log of changes if we're not committing regularly and writing useful log messages that we will understand months from now. In a team environment, where we also use source control to share code between team members, this becomes even more important. Everyone needs to commit their code when new features and fixes are working (and *not* commit broken code that doesn't work or even build) and to pull updates from teammates so our code will integrate as expected.

Running on the Device

The next step on our path to getting the app into users' hands is to move beyond the Simulator and get the app running on actual iOS hardware. Doing this is going to require a real device and the spending of real money, but if you're not in a position to do that yet, feel free to follow along.

Running an app on the device requires joining Apple's iOS Developer Program at a paid level. The Standard program allows individuals and companies to distribute apps on the App Store, whereas the Enterprise and Education programs are for developing and distributing apps through internal, non–App Store channels. For this book, we'll limit ourselves to the Standard program, which currently costs US$99 (and similar values in other currencies) for a one-year membership.

The two essential benefits of standard program membership are the ability, by cryptographically signing our code, to install apps onto test devices and to distribute through the App Store. Since the former is a prerequisite for the latter—we shouldn't try to sell an app on the store until we've ensured it works on a real device—we'll start there.

Overlooked Developer Program Benefits

Joining Apple's Developer Program isn't just about signing apps. You get several other benefits for your $99. For starters, membership in this program is a requirement if you want to attend Apple's World Wide Developer Conference (WWDC).

In our opinion, the most overlooked and valuable perk of membership is support incidents. With these, members can send questions and code to an Apple support engineer and get detailed, code-level support on their problems. Members get two of these per year as part of the program membership and can purchase more if they run out. For problems that can't be solved with a web search or a forum post, it can be a great way to get unblocked.

Provisioning the App

Members have access to the *iOS Provisioning Member Center*, the part of the http://developer.apple.com/ website where we manage test devices and identify the apps we will run on them. First, though, we have to set up our signing certificate, a document that will allow Xcode to cryptographically sign apps, authenticating them for installation on test devices and for submission to Apple.

There are two ways we can get a signing certificate. We can either go through a multistep process within the Member Center website, or we can let Xcode do it for us. Let's take the easy route and do the latter. Open Xcode Preferences, select the Accounts tab, and sign in with your Apple ID, as seen in the following figure. Since we don't have a development certificate, we're asked if we want to create one. We do, so click Submit Request. We'll also be asked about creating a distribution request. We'll need it later, so go ahead and send that request too.

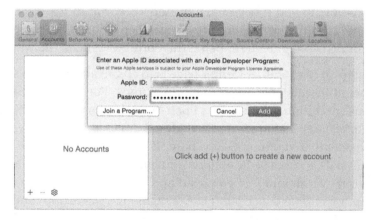

Once we have a certificate for app signing, we have several tasks to perform on the Member Center website. Go to http://developer.apple.com/ios, sign in with your Apple ID, and follow the link toCertificates, Identifiers & Profiles.

Now we can start registering test devices. These are the actual iPhones, iPod touches, and iPads we want to test our apps on. In the Member Center, under Certificates, Identifiers & Profiles, visit the Devices section. Click the plus button to add a device and enter a descriptive name (like "Chris' iPad Air 2") and the device ID. We can get the device ID by connecting the device via the dock cable and launching iTunes: click the device in the left column, and then click its serial number, which will then change to its identifier (UDID), as shown in the following figure (note that we have intentionally blurred a few digits of the ID and phone number in this screenshot). Once the UDID is showing, it can be copied to the clipboard with a ⌘C. Paste this value in the Device ID field on the Member Center page, and click Continue.

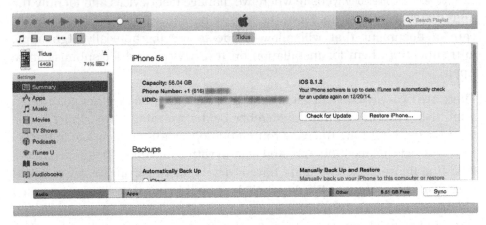

It's also possible to add a device via an Add To Portal in the Xcode Devices window (⇧⌘2), but that requires the developer to have access to the test devices. For distributed testers, using the Portal website is the way to go.

The next step on the Member Center page is to create an App ID, a string that uniquely identifies a single app or a group of apps. For a single app, the App ID allows use of certain APIs, such as Push Notifications and In-App Purchase. For a group of apps, a shared App ID allows them to share sensitive information with each other via the iOS Keychain. For apps that don't use these features, the App ID is supposedly optional, but enough app-signing steps require an App ID that we should just go ahead and create one. To create an App ID for one app, we enter a description like "Pragmatic Tweets app" and leave the Bundle Seed ID as Use Team ID. For the bundle identifier, we can either enter a reverse-domain name format string, like com.company.appname, to identify one app to sign. We can also use the wildcard character (*) to sign any app for testing. For now, let's use the wildcard.

Finally, we create a provisioning profile, which identifies a combination of certificate, App ID, and devices, and represents the certification for specific apps to run on specific devices. There are two kinds of profiles we can create; for the moment, we only care about development profiles, which are used for testing on devices that will be directly connected via Xcode. To create a new development profile in the Member Center, we click Provisioning Profiles: Development, and press the plus button. When asked what type of provisioning profile we need, we choose iOS App Development and click Continue. We then select an App ID and which certificate to sign with, and on the next page, select some or all of the devices we have configured. After a few seconds or minutes, the profile will be available to download as a .mobileprovision file. Once downloaded, drag it to Xcode to add it to the list of profiles. We can see this list by going to Settings→Accounts, selecting our Apple ID, and double-clicking our member name from the list on the right. The following figure shows an ADIOS2PRAGMATICTWEETSPROFILE1 profile that we created for signing the app locally:

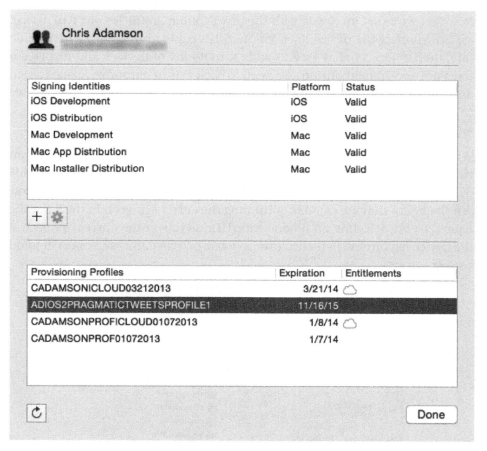

Creating a provisioning profile is also a task we can perform within Xcode—provided we have already set up the App ID and devices on the Member Center page. The Accounts preference pane also maintains an iOS Team Provisioning Profile, which is a wildcard signing profile that Xcode automatically keeps up-to-date and which can be used to sign most apps (those that don't require App ID-dependent features) for local testing.

Setting up app signing is a lot of steps, and it's nobody's favorite thing to do, but once we have the .mobileprovision, we're *this close* to running the app on our iOS device.

Signing and Running the App

Now that we've got a .mobileprovision file that identifies what we want to run, what devices we want to run on, and the fact that we're certified to do so, we're ready to run our app on an actual iOS device.

Now that we've set up Xcode with the provisioning profile for our iOS device, we can connect the device itself via the USB cable to the Mac. When we do this, the Devices window (⇧⌘2) adds it to its list of devices and displays a Use For Development button. We need to click this to authorize Xcode to sign and install development apps on the device. Once we've added a device, we will be able to use the Devices window to collect screenshots, console logs, and crash reports from the device.

With development enabled on the device, we should be able to build and run the app on the device. Back in the project workspace, pop up the right side of the scheme selector. In addition to the available simulators, we should now see all devices that are capable of running the current project. In the following figure, we are selecting an iPhone called Tidus to run the current project. If the device isn't in the list, check the sidebar on page 252, for some common causes.

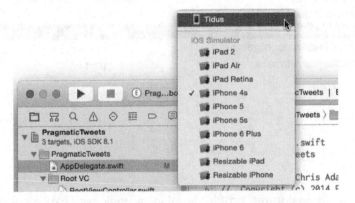

Prior to running, let's take a look at how all these app-signing pieces have come together. Click the project icon in the project window, select the PragmaticTweets target, and choose the Build Settings tab. Find the entry for Code Signing Identity (typing sign into the filter helps), and expand the spin-disclosure arrows to expose the Debug and Release settings. The pop-up menu, shown in the following figure, includes an automatically selected profile, selectable menu items for installed provisioning profiles, an option to not code-sign, and an Other option that takes a string for a profile name that will presumably become valid by build time (perhaps on a different machine). Whatever certificate was used to create the profile on the Portal site must be in the current keychain (as indicated by the Keychain Access application). This creates the chain of trust: the Portal and Xcode both know who we are from the certificate, and the provisioning profile associates that identity with the identifiers of devices in the profile, one of which is the one we want to install the app on.

With the device set in the scheme selector, click the Run button to build and run the app. The code builds, and after a brief pause, it starts running on the iPhone, iPod touch, or iPad. At this point, our testing experience is basically no different from running in the Simulator: we could set breakpoints and view log messages as in the last chapter, run logic tests with the Test command, or use the Profile command to have Instruments profile the app while it runs on the device.

So what do we test on the device? If we have features that don't work easily (or at all) in the Simulator, like motion sensing and location awareness, we can test those now. And even for less exotic features, we want to make sure that the app behaves well under real-world conditions. iOS devices have slower CPUs and less memory than desktop Macs, and cellular data connections have higher latency and lower throughput than wired Ethernet, so testing the app on real devices will let us see if it works well enough or if we need to make changes.

Joe asks:
How Come My App Won't Run on My Device?

You and everyone else, Joe...you *and everyone else.*

The challenges of app signing for iOS are notorious and are the cause of much pain among developers. Usually, there's some kind of coherent reason for the problem, although some of the cases are so aggravating!

If a device doesn't appear in the scheme selector, the causes are usually pretty sensible: the device hasn't been enabled for development; the device is running an older version of iOS than the target's iOS deployment target; the device is an iPhone and the project uses the iPad form-factor; and so on.

The really troublesome problems are errors when code signing occurs at the end of a build. These can come from a bad automatic choice of code-signing identity, an expired certificate or provisioning profile, or Keychain Access being set to a different keychain than the one the signing certificate was imported into. Sometimes, Xcode will just do stupid things, like copying expired certificates from a device into Keychain Access and announcing that there are two copies of the signing certificate when there can be only one. Xcode will also import expired profiles from the Portal into the Xcode's Settings→Accounts window, so it's wise to delete expired profiles via the Developer Program website.

Fighting through this stuff takes a combination of perseverance, logic, and more than a few trips to Apple's developer forums or other online resources. Apple Tech Note TN2407, "iOS Code Signing Troubleshooting," has a cursory selection of common problems, offering solutions to some of them. Beyond that, it's probably a trip to Stack Overflow for an answer.

It can still be a hassle for longtime iOS developers, but in time, it's at least possible to anticipate and avoid a lot of the common problems and understand what might be causing the more esoteric errors.

Icons and Launch Images

All this time, we have been focused on our app's code and worried about its appearance only to the degree that it mattered within our views. Although Pragmatic Tweets is only a sample app, we do want to take the time to consider what it will look like alongside other system apps.

App Icons

By default, our app has no icon, and it has the name we gave it when we created the project. It looks like the figure...and it's not pretty.

Let's get to work on that. We'll start with the name being cut off. Click on the project icon at the top of the File Navigator, select the Pragmatic Tweets target, and click the Info tab. We can set some of the app's metadata here, including the Bundle Name, which defaults to the internal PRODUCT_NAME. Instead, just change the bundle name to Prag Tweets.

Now about that generic icon. The first step here is to bring in a real designer. "Why?" you might ask. Why slow things down by bringing in someone else?

Deadlines are a fact of life. We have all been forced by one deadline or another to do something we didn't want to do. But when that happens, skip features; don't skip design. The biggest mistake developers make is not having a designer in the loop from the beginning. The design of your app is the way that users will perceive it. After spending countless hours thinking about the internal workings of your app, you don't want to leave the users' interaction left to chance. Just as classes need to be designed, user experiences need to be designed.

Interfaces designed by programmers tend to look like programming languages: specific and detailed but tedious. Users don't want tedious; they want it to *just work*. If you expose the switch to toggle the 20 percent feature, that leaves 80 percent to wonder at the complexity of the app.

Programmers fight for control; designers fight for the user. Make sure your app has someone fighting for the users. Don't ship an app that has not been designed from start to finish. If the idea is worth your time and energy, then it's worth getting a designer involved.

So, eating our own dogfood, we had Scott Ruth of BraveBit App Studio (http://bravebit.com) design a proper icon for Pragmatic Tweets.

One advantage of bringing in a designer who is specifically experienced with iOS design is the dizzying number of app icon sizes that are now required for app store submission. In previous editions of this book, we've tried to list all of these, but between iPhones at single, double, and triple resolution, different app icons for iPhone and iPad, additional icons for the settings app and Spotlight…it is now far too much for us to cover. Take a look at Icon and Image Sizes in the iOS Human Interface Guidelines if you're interested. But we're very much of the opinion that it can and should be your designer's problem.

Scott delivered our icons in the form of an Images.xcassets file, as seen in the following figure. This file has been present, albeit empty, since we started our app. By default, it has a single entry called AppIcon, with blank spots for all the known image sizes and pixel depths. Aside from providing app icons, this file can also be used for any images shown by the app (such as those used in UIImageViews). Simply add a file at 1x and 2x resolutions to the collection, and they become available to use for image views in storyboards. They can also be read by code by using the initializer UIImage (named:), passing in the filename without an extension.

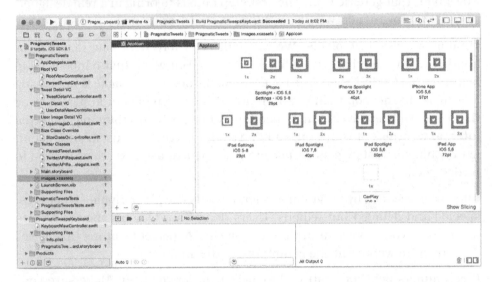

With a proper name and icon, our app looks a lot more polished on the home screen, ready for our users to open it.

Launch Images

Another bit of visual polish we can attend to is what the user sees at the instant the app is launched. When they tap the app icon, iOS presents a *launch image* until the app is fully initialized and showing its first view.

Prior to iOS 8, the launch image was a static .png file. Initially, Apple's guidance was that the launch image should look exactly like the app's first screen so that the user wouldn't notice the time it took to create and populate the first view. In practice, though, many apps used the static image as a "splash screen," displaying a logo for the app or perhaps its developer or publisher.

The problem with this scheme is that designers had to create static launch images for every combination of screen size and portrait-versus-landscape orientation, meaning they potentially needed a dozen or more different, yet related, launch screen designs. And that was *before* the iPhone 6 and iPhone 6 Plus.

iOS 8 tries to mitigate this crush of work with a new approach. The Launch-Screen.xib offers a launch image that will work at any combination of size, resolution, and orientation. The trick is that this file is a genuine iOS view, just like a scene from a storyboard (in fact, .xib files were used for single views of iOS apps before Xcode added storyboards).

By default, LaunchScreen.xib has only a title and a copyright statement on a white background. But these labels are set with autolayout constraints, so they will work at any combination of device shape, orientation, and pixel depth. All we need to do to have a fancy launch image is to customize this view with colors, images, fonts and styling, and so on.

We'll leave that as an exercise...for your designer.

Submitting Apps for Review

Once we've rigorously tested our app, we're ready to submit it to the App Store to send it out to the public. Or are we?

It turns out there are a bunch more steps to get our app up on the store. First off, we need to answer two questions: "What are we offering?" and "How do we communicate that?"

App Metadata

Submitting to the App Store requires a lot more than just a rigorously tested code base and an attractive visual design (thanks to our professional designer). We will be submitting an extensive collection of metadata, including but not limited to the following:

- A 1024×1024 icon for the App Store, which should match the icon in the Xcode project. Since Apple may come back and ask for art at varying sizes to promote the app in the store, it's useful to have graphic designers create icons and other art for the app at very high resolutions (or with vector graphics tools) so they can turn out new graphic assets at arbitrary sizes.

- At least one (and up to five) screenshots showing the app in action. These need to be in the Retina Display resolutions, for the various currently available iPhone and iPad screen sizes. Screenshots can be generated from the iOS Simulator's Save Screen Shot (⌘S) command or by using the Devices window, which offers a New Screenshot button when a device is connected.

- A description of the app and keywords to help find it. The description needs to be translated into every language for which we have localized the app.

- A decision about what price to charge for the app. For non-free apps, we also have to agree to an online sales contract with Apple and provide banking information to receive payments. These steps can take days or even weeks to complete, so they should be worked out well before we need to launch the app.

- An SKU number, meaning an arbitrary string by which we will track sales of the app.

- A support URL and support email address.

We also need to have an Explicit App ID, which is like the wildcard App ID we created before but uses a unique string, typically a reverse-DNS string like com.pragprog.yourhandle.PragmaticTweets. Create this in the Member Center before we continue.

Once all this metadata is ready, we can create an entry for the app on iTunes Connect, the website for the commercial aspects of our app. This is where we prepare the app's sales information for the store and where we'll track it after it goes on sale. Log in at http://itunesconnect.apple.com/.

From the iTunes Connect front page, click My Apps, and then click the plus button. This shows a pop-up asking if we're submitting an iOS or Mac app, and then shows the following panel in which enter the app's name, default language, the unique SKU number, and bundle ID (which is the reverse-domain name part of the App ID we set up on the Portal). If the name is already in use, we'll be returned to this screen and asked to pick another.

New iOS App

Name ?

Pragmatic Tweets

Version ?

1.0

Primary Language ?

English

SKU ?

com.pragprog.yourhandle.PragmaticTweets

Bundle ID ?

ADIOS2PRAGMATICTWEETSPROFILE - corr

Register a new bundle ID on the Developer Portal.

Cancel   Create

The page after this asks for most of the metadata we collected earlier: app description and keywords; support URL and email; screenshots and 1024×1024 icon; and so on. We also have to provide a version number and copyright holder and click radio buttons in a "content descriptions" grid to indicate the prevalence of factors like violence, nudity, and profanity, which are combined to set an age rating for the app. We can also decide to automatically release this version when it clears app review, or manually do so at a time of our choosing once it has been approved.

There is a section of this page called Build that just says "Submit your builds using Xcode 5.1.1 or later, or Application Loader 3.0 or later." That's what we'll do next: we'll submit from Xcode, and we'll come back to iTunes Connect to touch up any needed pre-release metadata later.

Uploading an App Binary

Once the metadata on iTunes Connect is ready, we need to use the deployment tools we already know about to prepare a distribution build for the App Store.

First, we go back to the Member Center to create a new distribution profile. This is a lot like the developer profile we created earlier, except that it doesn't need a list of devices since it's meant to verify our identity to Apple rather than clearing it to just run on one device. Also, this certificate will be specific to this app.

Go to Provisioning Profiles: Distribution to get started, and for the type of profile, choose App Store. We have to choose the App ID we created before, and at this point, it's crucial that the identifier string used for that App ID matches the bundle identifier shown in the target's summary in Xcode. Download the distribution profile and drag it to Xcode to add it to the Accounts window's list of profiles.

Now we can build the application archive that we will submit to the App Store. In the target settings, change the value for Code Signing Identity→Release to iOS Distribution. Next, create a new archive with Product→Archive. This automatically brings up the Organizer window, with its Archives tab, as seen in the following figure:

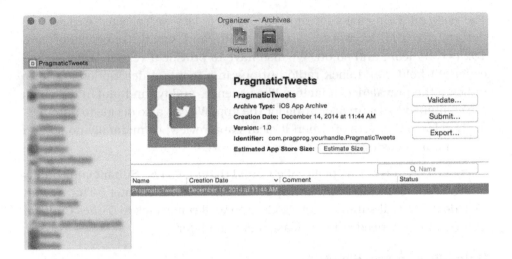

To submit to the App Store, we click the Submit button. This asks for our Apple ID and then checks with iTunes Connect to see if we have any applications set up and ready to receive a build. This test may fail if we haven't created a basic entry on iTunes Connect or if there's a mismatched version number or bundle identifier between iTunes Connect and the archive we just built. The version and bundle identifier are set in the target's summary; check there if the test indicates an error.

Assuming the organizer finds at least one app record on iTunes Connect waiting for an upload, we see a panel asking which app (on iTunes Connect) we're uploading and which distribution identity should be used to sign the app for submission to Apple. Choose the distribution identity we created earlier and click Next.

At this point, Xcode will run a series of validations on the app archive to ensure it meets certain minimum criteria, like whether the version number and bundle identifier are what iTunes Connect is expecting. If this validation and the upload to Apple succeed, we get a success message telling us that the app is now in line for review.

And now we wait.

If we check the app on iTunes Connect at this point, the status will say Waiting for Review. After some time (usually days, sometimes longer), the status will change to In Review, meaning that it has reached the front of the review queue and is being reviewed by Apple's testers.

At this point, two outcomes are likely: either the app will be approved or it will be rejected for some reason. If it's rejected, we'll get an email detailing the cause for the rejection, which is usually a crash in testing but is sometimes a violation of an Apple policy. At this point, it's back to the beginning: we need to fix the bug or resolve whatever issue Apple has brought up, tell iTunes Connect we're ready to submit a new binary, build a new app archive, and resubmit via Xcode.

On the other hand, if the app is approved, then it will appear in App Stores around the world in a few hours (or on our release date, if we told iTunes Connect to hold it). Either way, we dance the happy dance of actually getting our app through the App Store process and get ready for the users.

After the Gold Rush

There are a lot of ways to make a living on the App Store. Many people are surprised that lots of them don't involve selling apps directly to users. Many apps, perhaps most now, exist to enhance some existing service, and pay for themselves indirectly. These are apps like the airline app that has your boarding pass, the app that lets you stream video from a subscription service, the app from your favorite social network, and so on.

Most of the apps your authors have done for iOS (and Mac) have been like this: public apps to support some service, or in-house apps to make a company or organization more efficient. But we have tried to make a go of indie apps now and then. Here's a story of how that went.

Back in 2009, Chris realized that trying to find a favorite restaurant or hotel chain while driving on a freeway was nearly impossible to do safely. Maps apps weren't well suited to the problem, because aside from their fussy user interfaces, they just did a radius search, finding points of interest way off the freeway or even behind you.

After three months of coding, the answer to the problem was Road Tip, which used the MapQuest API to figure out what freeway you were on, where it went for the next 30–50 miles, where the exits were along that path, and what businesses were located within one to two miles of those exits. The UI was all table views with oversized text in large custom cells, easy to glance at and flick through with a single thumb. You could start from either a list of upcoming exits and drill down to see what was at each, or get an alphabetical list of businesses by type (gas, food, lodging) and see how far you'd have to hold out for your preferred business.

Million-dollar idea, right? Yeah, not so much. MapQuest got a 50 percent cut, since they provided the data that was essential for the app to work at all. After Apple's 30 percent cut, there wasn't much left to cover expenses. And people have been less and less willing to pay for apps. When MapQuest changed their API in 2014 and dropped the features the app needed to work, it was pulled from the store, having made barely $1,000 in net profit since its 2010 release.

This story is not meant to be discouraging. Road Tip had virtually no marketing, and a more sustained push to get the word out about it may have made it a hit. App development is risky and doesn't always work out. The upside is, there's always something new and cool to move on to.

After We Ship

So, we've shipped our app, and users around the country or around the world are using and enjoying it. Now what?

With iTunes Connect, we can use the Sales and Trends page to see how many people are downloading the app—whether the trend is positive or negative. Payments and Financial Reports will let us check Apple's transfers to our bank account with our cut of the app's sales if it's a paid app.

But are our users actually happy? We can check the reviews in the App Store, and hopefully users with a problem will send an email to the support address we provided, although it's also possible they left a one-star review in lieu of a bug report or just quit using the app altogether. It definitely helps to have feedback channels other than the App Store, like a Twitter account, Facebook page, or website, so it's easy for users to contact us if they need to.

What if—heaven forbid—the app is actually *crashing* out in the field? Actually, Apple gives us big help with that. In iTunes Connect, select the app and then click the button for its current version. In the version summary page, there's a link for Crash Reports. If we click this button, we'll get a summary of crash reports that have been collected from devices in the field and returned to Apple, a feature that users have to explicitly enable when they set up their devices. The following figure shows the Crash Reports page for an old game Chris put on the App Store and didn't keep up to date (he's since pulled it from sale because of this neglect). There are two common crashes identified by the names of the methods that crash. Reading further down the page, we see that the app has not been killed by the system for being too slow to start up, for becoming unresponsive (by blocking the main thread), or by running out of memory. So at least the problems are limited only to a few specific bad calls.

The crash entries have a Download button. If we click this, we get a folder containing one or more .crash files. We can double-click the .crash file to open it in the Console application (/Applications/Utilities/Console.app), but it's potentially more useful to open the file with Xcode.

We say "potentially" because of what Xcode may or may not be able to do with the crash log. By default, the crash log will start with some general identifier information, like the time and date of the crash, the version of iOS running at the time, and the thread that crashed. If we look at that thread later in the crash log, we get a *stack trace*, a listing of the function and method calls that led to the crash, like this (word-wrapped to fit book formatting):

```
Thread 4 name:  Dispatch queue: com.apple.root.default-priority
Thread 4 Crashed:
0    libsystem_kernel.dylib    0x3112f32c __pthread_kill + 8
1    libsystem_c.dylib         0x33c12f54 pthread_kill
2    libsystem_c.dylib         0x33c0bfe4 abort
3    libc++abi.dylib           0x30fdcf64 0x30fd6000 + 28516
4    libc++abi.dylib           0x30fda346 0x30fd6000 + 17222
5    libobjc.A.dylib           0x31acb2dc _objc_terminate
6    libc++abi.dylib           0x30fda3be 0x30fd6000 + 17342
7    libc++abi.dylib           0x30fda44a 0x30fd6000 + 17482
8    libc++abi.dylib           0x30fdb81e 0x30fd6000 + 22558
9    libobjc.A.dylib           0x31acb22e objc_exception_rethrow
10   MediaPlayer               0x319a33e8 -[MPMediaLibraryDataProviderML3
                                    performBackgroundTaskWithBlock:]
11   MediaPlayer               0x319a191a -[MPMediaLibraryDataProviderML3
                                    loadItemsUsingFetchRequest:]
12   MediaPlayer               0x3199f350 __56-[MPMediaEntityStreamArray
                                    _onQueueStartLoadingEntities]_block_invoke_0
13   libdispatch.dylib         0x324a3d4e _dispatch_call_block_and_release
```

```
14   libdispatch.dylib            0x324af79c _dispatch_worker_thread2
15   libsystem_c.dylib            0x33bcf1c8 _pthread_wqthread
16   libsystem_c.dylib            0x33bcf09c start_wqthread
```

The hexadecimal values are the memory addresses. Where we see two values added together is an entry point into a library or our code and a memory offset. Unfortunately, this does almost no good whatsoever, because we don't know which of them refer to our code or what methods in our code are involved.

However, *if* this build is still archived in Xcode—meaning it is still listed in the Organizer window's Archives tab—then the crash log can be *symbolicated*, meaning that Xcode can correlate what it knows about the binary submitted to Apple with the memory offsets in the crash log and change the address references to method calls with line numbers. This means that we won't see a line like this:

```
1    Recipes                      0x0009513c 0x93000 + 8508
```

We will instead see a much more useful stack entry:

```
1    Recipes                      0x0009513c -[PRPAppDelegate
                                  applicationDidFinishLaunching:withOptions:]
                                  (AppDelegate.m:32)
```

Just knowing the line number may not be enough for us to fix the error, but knowing that the app is crashing in some specific way on that particular line should at least give us some good hypotheses to try out. And it's certainly far better than where we stood with just a memory offset.

Onward!

With an app up on the App Store, we've achieved what we set out to do: we've written an app, fine-tuned its performance and appearance, found and fixed its bugs, and made it available to users around the world.

Now what do we do?

For every app we ship, we watch the sales and downloads, check the reviews, collect crash logs, and put out new versions with new features and bug fixes.

And then we decide what we want to do next. In this book, we've limited ourselves to the essential frameworks of iOS and the best practices of iOS development. We left out some really interesting stuff, and that material offers a sensible place to seek the next challenge. We can dig further into UIKit by developing custom UIViews and adding gesture recognizers to allow interaction with them. Or maybe we can try out the various media frameworks—Media Player, AV Foundation, Core Audio, and the like—that let our apps use the cameras, microphones, and music library. Or maybe we want to write a productivity app that will need to store the user's data in a relational database, something that Core Data could help with. Or make use of the accelerometer and gyroscope via Core Motion. Or...

There's too much neat stuff in iOS to fit in one introductory book anymore. What we've done in this book is to establish a core base of knowledge and a set of strong practices. We now know how to build apps well, test them, release them, and manage them throughout their life cycle. From here, it's a matter of choosing our path for the next app.

What shall we try to do next?

Index

Sound and Graphics

Add live sound to your apps and sprites to iOS.

Programming Sound with Pure Data

Sound gives your native, web, or mobile apps that extra dimension, and it's essential for games. Rather than using canned samples from a sample library, learn how to build sounds from the ground up and produce them for web projects using the Pure Data programming language. Even better, you'll be able to integrate dynamic sound environments into your native apps or games—sound that reacts to the app, instead of sounding the same every time. Start your journey as a sound designer, and get the power to craft the sound you put into your digital experiences.

Tony Hillerson
(196 pages) ISBN: 9781937785666. $36
https://pragprog.com/book/thsound

Build iOS Games with Sprite Kit

Take your game ideas from paper to pixels using Sprite Kit, Apple's 2D game development engine. Build two exciting games using Sprite Kit and learn real-world, workshop-tested insights about game design, including cognitive complexity, paper prototyping, and levels of fun. You'll learn how to implement sophisticated game features such as obstacles and weapons, power-ups and variable difficulty, physics, sound, special effects, and both single- and two-finger control. In no time, you'll be building your own thrilling iOS games.

Jonathan Penn and Josh Smith
(216 pages) ISBN: 9781941222102. $34
https://pragprog.com/book/pssprite

Seven in Seven

From Web Frameworks to Concurrency Models, see what the rest of the world is doing with this introduction to seven different approaches.

Seven Web Frameworks in Seven Weeks

Whether you need a new tool or just inspiration, *Seven Web Frameworks in Seven Weeks* explores modern options, giving you a taste of each with ideas that will help you create better apps. You'll see frameworks that leverage modern programming languages, employ unique architectures, live client-side instead of server-side, or embrace type systems. You'll see everything from familiar Ruby and JavaScript to the more exotic Erlang, Haskell, and Clojure.

Jack Moffitt, Fred Daoud
(302 pages) ISBN: 9781937785635. $38
https://pragprog.com/book/7web

Seven Concurrency Models in Seven Weeks

Your software needs to leverage multiple cores, handle thousands of users and terabytes of data, and continue working in the face of both hardware and software failure. Concurrency and parallelism are the keys, and *Seven Concurrency Models in Seven Weeks* equips you for this new world. See how emerging technologies such as actors and functional programming address issues with traditional threads and locks development. Learn how to exploit the parallelism in your computer's GPU and leverage clusters of machines with MapReduce and Stream Processing. And do it all with the confidence that comes from using tools that help you write crystal clear, high-quality code.

Paul Butcher
(296 pages) ISBN: 9781937785659. $38
https://pragprog.com/book/pb7con

Past and Present

To see where we're going, remember how we got here, and learn how to take a healthier approach to programming.

Fire in the Valley

In the 1970s, while their contemporaries were protesting the computer as a tool of dehumanization and oppression, a motley collection of college dropouts, hippies, and electronics fanatics were engaged in something much more subversive. Obsessed with the idea of getting computer power into their own hands, they launched from their garages a hobbyist movement that grew into an industry, and ultimately a social and technological revolution. What they did was invent the personal computer: not just a new device, but a watershed in the relationship between man and machine. This is their story.

Michael Swaine and Paul Freiberger
(424 pages) ISBN: 9781937785765. $34
https://pragprog.com/book/fsfire

The Healthy Programmer

To keep doing what you love, you need to maintain your own systems, not just the ones you write code for. Regular exercise and proper nutrition help you learn, remember, concentrate, and be creative—skills critical to doing your job well. Learn how to change your work habits, master exercises that make working at a computer more comfortable, and develop a plan to keep fit, healthy, and sharp for years to come.

This book is intended only as an informative guide for those wishing to know more about health issues. In no way is this book intended to replace, countermand, or conflict with the advice given to you by your own healthcare provider including Physician, Nurse Practitioner, Physician Assistant, Registered Dietician, and other licensed professionals.

Joe Kutner
(254 pages) ISBN: 9781937785314. $36
https://pragprog.com/book/jkthp

The Pragmatic Bookshelf

The Pragmatic Bookshelf features books written by developers for developers. The titles continue the well-known Pragmatic Programmer style and continue to garner awards and rave reviews. As development gets more and more difficult, the Pragmatic Programmers will be there with more titles and products to help you stay on top of your game.

Visit Us Online

This Book's Home Page
https://pragprog.com/book/adios2
Source code from this book, errata, and other resources. Come give us feedback, too!

Register for Updates
https://pragprog.com/updates
Be notified when updates and new books become available.

Join the Community
https://pragprog.com/community
Read our weblogs, join our online discussions, participate in our mailing list, interact with our wiki, and benefit from the experience of other Pragmatic Programmers.

New and Noteworthy
https://pragprog.com/news
Check out the latest pragmatic developments, new titles and other offerings.

Save on the eBook

Save on the eBook versions of this title. Owning the paper version of this book entitles you to purchase the electronic versions at a terrific discount.

PDFs are great for carrying around on your laptop—they are hyperlinked, have color, and are fully searchable. Most titles are also available for the iPhone and iPod touch, Amazon Kindle, and other popular e-book readers.

Buy now at *https://pragprog.com/coupon*

Contact Us

Online Orders:	*https://pragprog.com/catalog*
Customer Service:	*support@pragprog.com*
International Rights:	*translations@pragprog.com*
Academic Use:	*academic@pragprog.com*
Write for Us:	*http://write-for-us.pragprog.com*
Or Call:	+1 800-699-7764

CPSIA information can be obtained at www.ICGtesting.com
Printed in the USA
LVOW03s2222310315

432745LV00003B/5/P